Law and Autonomous Machines

ELGAR LAW, TECHNOLOGY AND SOCIETY

Series Editor: Peter K. Yu, *Drake University Law School, USA*

The information revolution and the advent of digital technologies have ushered in new social practices, business models, legal solutions, regulatory policies, governance structures, consumer preferences and global concerns. This unique book series provides an interdisciplinary forum for studying the complex interactions that arise from this environment. It examines the broader and deeper theoretical questions concerning information law and policy, explores its latest developments and social implications, and provides new ways of thinking about changing technology.

Titles in the series include:

Law and Autonomous Machines

The Co-evolution of Legal Responsibility and Technology

Mark Chinen

Seattle University School of Law, USA

Edward Elgar PUBLISHING

Cheltenham, UK • Northampton, MA, USA

Published by
Edward Elgar Publishing Limited
The Lypiatts
15 Lansdown Road
Cheltenham
Glos GL50 2JA
UK

Edward Elgar Publishing, Inc.
William Pratt House
9 Dewey Court
Northampton
Massachusetts 01060
USA

A catalogue record for this book
is available from the British Library

Library of Congress Control Number: 2019930684

This book is available electronically in the **Elgar**online
Law subject collection
DOI 10.4337/9781786436597

ISBN 978 1 78643 658 0 (cased)
ISBN 978 1 78643 659 7 (eBook)

Printed by CPI Group (UK) Ltd, Croydon CR0 4YY

Contents

Preface and acknowledgements

The idea for this book emerged from the intersection of three areas of interest. The first is of course the rise of artificial intelligence, its powering of machines and systems, and the effects it might have on our lives. The second is the legal responsibility of groups, including states, military organizations, and multinational corporations. The third has to do with complexity theory and the relationship between autonomous agents, human and artificial, and complex systems. As artificial intelligence, autonomous machines and systems, and intelligence enhancement have become more widely used, several of the issues that emerge with the legal responsibility of groups are arising in debates about how society in general and the legal system in particular should respond to these emerging, increasingly sophisticated technologies, particularly if they cause harm, and whether and how the law itself might change in relation to those machines and systems.

It was useful to frame this exploration in terms of a possible trajectory for the coevolution of autonomous technologies and legal responsibility, that is, to examine how emerging technologies are interacting with existing systems of responsibility, to identify particular trends, and to consider where those trends might lead. As such, this study is not intended to be a complete review of the existing legal doctrine as it might apply to autonomous technologies; excellent works of that kind already exist. Of course, this book must describe recent developments in the technology and the legal landscape to some extent, but its purpose is to be more thematic and speculative in nature. At the same time, over the course of writing the book, the project became more than tracing a possible trajectory: it also became a chance for reassessment. The emergence of artificial intelligence requires us to reconsider how we already address harms and to ask whether the justifications for our existing systems of responsibility are likely to remain persuasive as intelligent technologies become a greater, perhaps ubiquitous part of our daily experience.

Thanks are due to many people. This book stems from an article published originally in the *Virginia Journal of Law and Technology*.[1] The article benefited from the editorial work of the journal. Joshua Fensterbush, Kasie

---

[1] Mark A. Chinen, *The Co-Evolution of Autonomous Machines and Legal Responsibility*, 20 VA. J. L. & TECH. 338 (2016).

Kashimoto, and Maria Luisa Juarez y Hernandez provided valuable research assistance. My faculty colleagues at the Seattle University School of Law gave helpful comments at a presentation of an early version of the article at a faculty colloquium. Much of the material that makes up Chapter 4: Complexity Theory and its Meaning for Group and Individual Responsibility first appeared as a book chapter in *International Economic Law and African Development* (Laurence Boulle, Emmanuel Laryea, and Franzika Sucker, eds., Siber Ink, 2014). My thanks to the publisher for permission for use of the materials. The book also has been improved by comments and conversations with Ben Robbins and Stephen Wu, and by the suggestions given by the anonymous peer reviewers who reviewed the initial proposal for this project. My administrative assistant, Laurie Wells, helped with the preparation of the manuscript. All errors and omissions, however, remain my own.

My in-laws, Carl and Katherine Takushi, kindly allowed me the use of their home where I wrote the bulk of the manuscript. Finally, I wish to thank my wife, Ruby Takushi, and daughters, Maya and Grace Chinen, for their support as this book was being written.

A note on citations: citations follow the Bluebook Uniform System of Citation, with modifications to conform to the house style.

Introduction

The inevitable occurred on March 18, 2018, when an autonomous vehicle owned and operated by Uber Technologies, Inc. struck and killed Elaine Herzberg as she crossed a street with her bicycle. Her friends describe her as just emerging from homelessness. A human driver was in the sports utility vehicle, but the SUV was in autonomous mode when it struck Herzberg.[1] Video footage indicates it was night and Herzberg was not in a crosswalk. The footage also suggests the car did not apply brakes or otherwise attempt to avoid hitting Herzberg. A preliminary report of the National Transportation Safety Board revealed that the vehicle's self-driving system first detected Herzberg about six seconds before impact. As the car and Herzberg converged, the autonomous system classified Herzberg as an unknown object, next as a vehicle and then as a bicycle. Just 1.3 seconds before impact, the system concluded that an emergency braking maneuver was required; however, such maneuvers were not enabled while the vehicle was under computer control. This was to prevent "erratic vehicle behavior." The system was not designed to alert the human operator.[2]

Others had died in accidents involving self-driving cars before this incident,[3] but this was the first time someone with no voluntary connection to an autonomous vehicle had been killed by one. Immediately, discussions arose in the comments sections of news reports and via Twitter posts about who should be held responsible for Herzberg's death. Was it the car? Uber? Herzberg herself? The human driver who was there to override the SUV's systems in an emergency? (An accident report by the Tempe Police Department indicated that

---

[1]   Daisuke Wakabayashi, *Self-Driving Uber Car Kills Pedestrian in Arizona, Where Robots Roam*, N.Y. TIMES, Mar. 19, 2018, at A1.

[2]   U.S. Nat'l Transp. Safety Bd., Preliminary Report: Highway, HWY18MH010 (2018), at 2 [hereinafter NTSB Preliminary Report].

[3]   A recent article from the popular press is Adrienne LaFrance, *Can Google's Driverless Car Project Survive a Fatal Accident?* ATLANTIC, Mar. 1, 2016, http://www.theatlantic.com/technology/archive/2016/03/google-self-driving-car-crash/471678/. The first death in a self-driving vehicle occurred on May 7, 2016. See Bill Vlasic & Neal E. Boudette, *As U.S. Investigates Fatal Tesla Crash, Company Defends Autopilot System*, N.Y. TIMES, Jun. 16, 2016, http://www.nytimes.com/2016/07/13/business/tesla-autopilot-fatal-crash-investigation.html?_r=0.

the driver had been streaming a video program while in the car.[4]) The state of Arizona for failing to adequately regulate autonomous vehicles? (I will return to these facts and questions in Chapter 2.)

As that event was making headlines, another, perhaps more far-reaching development was coming to light. This was the news that information from millions of Facebook users had been acquired, without permission, by Cambridge Analytica, which had in turn used that information to construct behavioral models as it advised clients who wanted to frame and direct public opinion.[5] It was possible that as many as 87 million users had been affected.[6] There was debate about whether such efforts to sway the public succeeded, but at least some claimed that they had influenced important public decisions, including Brexit and the 2016 US election. Again, questions were raised about who should be blamed for the invasion of privacy, and again, there were likely culprits: Cambridge Analytica and its principals, of course, but also Facebook for collecting private data in the first place and then failing to protect it.

If nothing else, the loss of Herzberg's life and the Cambridge Analytica scandal announced that autonomous machines and systems and the harms they can cause are no longer a distant prospect. The issue of how law can be used to prevent them from harming others and how to assign responsibility if they do is fast becoming ripe. Policymakers, industry leaders, and legal scholars have seen this day coming for some time and there is a growing literature on the role law can and should play as artificial intelligence and the technologies it powers become a greater part of everyday experience.

This book contributes to that discussion by plotting a possible trajectory for the relationship between the law and autonomous machines and systems. That trajectory begins where it often does when something new appears on the scene: communities use already existing legal doctrines and principles to comprehend and respond to it. This in turn leads to debate about how well suited these doctrines and principles are to new developments and whether there will be a need for significant changes in them.

---

[4]   Associated Press, *Police: Backup Driver in Fatal Uber Crash was Distracted*, N.Y. Times, June 22, 2018, https://www.nytimes.com/aponline/2018/06/22/us/ap-us-uber-autonomous-vehicle.html.

[5]   Matthew Rosenberg, Nicholas Confessore & Carole Cadwallader, *How Trump Consultants Exploited the Facebook Data of Millions*, N.Y. Times, Mar. 17, 2018,   https://www.nytimes.com/2018/03/17/us/politics/cambridge-analytica-trump-campaign.html.

[6]   Cecilia Kang & Sheera Frenkel, *Facebook Now Says Improper Data Use Affected 87 Million*, N.Y. Times, Apr. 4, 2018, https://www.nytimes.com/2018/04/04/technology/mark-zuckerberg-testify-congress.html?hp&action=click&pgtype=Homepage&clickSource=story-heading&module=first-column-region&region=top-news&WT.nav=top-news.

My thesis is that the growing sophistication of machines and systems creates impulses for legal norms and machines to coevolve. In a sense, this coevolution is already happening in scholarship and within the industry along two parameters and lines of development. One is the nexus between the machine and human activity. At present, the legal system is trying as much as possible to associate the actions of artificial agents and their consequences to individuals or groups of human beings, and at this point the technology is still limited enough for this approach to remain viable. At this point it is human beings who use technology as tools, and it is those human beings who are ultimately responsible for any harms caused by those tools. The doctrines being used include individual tort liability, product liability, agency, joint criminal enterprise, aiding and abetting, conspiracy, and command responsibility. With modifications, such doctrines seem to work relatively well for less sophisticated machines and more or less so in cases where sophisticated machines are clearly carrying out the will of humans.

However, this is where the second parameter, the degree of autonomy of the machine or system as decision maker, makes itself felt. Although some commentators argue that autonomous technologies will always remain a tool used by human beings, others believe that the more autonomy machines and systems achieve, the more tenuous becomes the strategy of attributing and distributing legal responsibility for their behavior to human beings. Strict liability is of course always available, but the law tends to be more comfortable with assigning legal liability to someone when he is personally culpable for a harm and far less so with liability or guilt by association. In this sense, the law corresponds to prevailing views of individual moral responsibility.

Thus, as machines and systems reach higher levels of autonomy, the effectiveness of specific proposals such as "use product liability and other tort doctrines if a patient is harmed by the use of nanotechnology" or "apply the doctrine of command responsibility if an autonomous weapon 'commits' an act that would constitute a war crime if a human committed it," will depend in part on our comfort with solutions to the problem of associational responsibility. Even in cases where autonomous technologies are clearly being used or supervised by human beings, some of the incentives created by legal rules, such as the incentive to take due care, weaken because humans will have less control over truly independent technologies. Further, since a machine or system cannot at this point feel legal sanctions, other purposes of the law, particularly those that motivate criminal law, are thwarted. As a result, we may be forced to become more comfortable with group legal responsibility or responsibility by association, or face the prospect of manufacturers, owners, or users of such machines and systems becoming insulated from legal responsibility.

For these reasons, one would expect two things to occur. First, a growing awareness of how permeable the concept of responsibility is, in part because technology itself has the potential to affect the way we understand ourselves and our own agency, could make legal doctrines based on associational responsibility more acceptable to us, and alternative forms of redress or compensation for harm, such as insurance, might gain greater importance. I argue, however, that although we might be open to some changes to the rules of responsibility, the idea of personal responsibility and the legal doctrines informed by it will likely persist. Second, our understandings of responsibility will likely join with other incentives to design even more sophisticated artificial agents. We would expect to see designers try to instill a sense of legal responsibility within the machine itself. Of course, as just discussed, machines and systems are not cognizant of the law, far less do they subjectively appreciate or value it. For now, all we can do is program the machines to act as much as possible in conformity to the law, for example, by instructing autonomous cars to obey traffic laws or autonomous weapons to obey the law of war. But this raises a question whether law can always be reduced to rules of decision in the settings in which we expect autonomous machines and systems to operate. In addition, many of the legal issues involving autonomous machines will be retrospective in nature: we will need to determine *ex post* whether an artificial agent's action has legal significance. As we will see, however, these questions are not keeping designers from trying to create autonomous technologies that conform to law.

The need to instill machines and systems with a sense of law will vary according to their level of sophistication, but over the long term, technologies at the highest levels of autonomy will need to be programmed so they are "motivated" to engage in the kinds of pro-social behaviors the law is designed to promote. The case of HAL in *2001: A Space Odyssey* and critiques of Asimov's laws of robotics suggest this can succeed only to some extent, but as autonomous technologies gain those kinds of prosocial capacities, this will strengthen calls already being sounded to grant autonomous machines and systems legal and moral rights. Some are already urging that autonomous technologies be given legal personhood to satisfy third parties who have been harmed by them while at the same time avoiding some of the problems raised by associative responsibility. If this happens, the world will of course be a very different place, and the law will have gained another subject.

This book is divided into three parts. Part I, comprising Chapters 1 and 2, surveys briefly the issue of autonomous machines and the existing legal approaches that frame and address the problem. Developments are occurring at almost bewildering speed, so Chapter 1 identifies only basic trends. Those trends point to a future in which artificial intelligence will be ubiquitous, not only with respect to our forms of transportation, but more importantly behind the scenes as significant aspects of everyday life are impacted by artificial intelligence. In this context, law will need to address large and complex systems of humans and machines who work together. Chapter 2 discusses how commentators are using existing legal concepts taken from torts, contracts, and international law to respond to the issue of harm and reviews the debate about the extent to which such doctrines in their current forms can address the situations that will arise when autonomous machines become more prevalent.

Part II turns to the relationship between law and ethics. To the extent that the legal doctrines discussed in Chapter 2 do not adequately address harms caused by autonomous machines, it is in large part because of the law's discomfort with associative responsibility, a discomfort shared and informed by most of the literature on moral responsibility. Chapter 3 observes that the legal approaches currently used to frame and address harms caused by autonomous machines focus primarily on individual legal responsibility. Even applications of the law to groups still tend to frame their analyses in individualistic terms. This dovetails with generally accepted understandings of moral responsibility, which can be traced from Aristotle to the present day. This raises the question whether approaches designed with the individual in mind are well suited to address large systems which will produce and employ autonomous machines.

Chapter 4 turns to the problem of group responsibility. Within ethics, the literature on the moral responsibility of groups is most relevant to the problems of associative responsibility. That literature provides some guidance on whether it is coherent to ascribe responsibility to groups; if so, which types of groups might be subject to responsibility; how the responsibility of the group can be distributed to its members; and the "pragmatics" of ascribing responsibility to groups. At the same time, in part because of differences between law and ethics, and because of the nature of the problem, the literature does not provide completely satisfactory answers. Concepts from complexity theory suggest that the problem might be intractable. This is because the "behaviors" of groups might be the nonlinear, emergent phenomena that arise from the complex interactions of individuals and subgroups. This creates an argument that it is hard, if not impossible, to trace causal lines between the actions of individuals and what happens at the group level. In such situations, any responsibility we attribute to an individual for what happens at the group level would necessarily be a fiction. The chapter will conclude by discussing the relevance of group responsibility and complexity theory to the problem of autonomous machines and systems.

Part III explores further how one could reexamine our current understandings of responsibility in light of autonomous machines and systems. The concern there might be that gaps between harms caused by autonomous technologies and existing legal and moral concepts of responsibility lead to two interweaving "strategies" to narrow those gaps. Chapter 5 discusses the first: to refine or alter the concept of responsibility. Such attempts come from a number of perspectives. One is to rely more on concepts that underlie strict liability. Another is to focus on the distinction made by some contemporary ethical theorists between responsibility as identifying an agent as contributing to a particular harm on the one hand and having the agent suffer consequences because of that contribution on the other. This is amenable to another approach that centers more on the victim of harm than on the perpetrator. An approach that centers more on compensating the victim provides a natural segue to compensation systems like commercial and social insurance. It is almost certain that insurance will be used to compensate injured parties and will play an important role in responding to harm caused by autonomous machines. At the same time, insurance has its limitations because of the problem of moral hazard, it does not perform the more punitive or retributive functions of holding someone responsible for a harm, and there are some limits to insurance as a means of pooling risk. The chapter will discuss these approaches and assess the strengths and weaknesses of insurance schemes as they apply to autonomous machines.

Chapter 6 turns to the second strategy to narrow gaps in responsibility, this time from the human perspective. One way to alter concepts of responsibility is to extend the boundaries of agency to include humans and artificial agents together, thus raising again the issues posed by group responsibility. However, those modifications require the expansion of ethical and legal subjects capable of bearing responsibility that many individual human beings will find hard to accept, although some change might be possible at the margins. The chapter will discuss those approaches and support my argument that they are ultimately unworkable on a large scale.

Part IV moves from a focus on the human being as the locus of responsibility to autonomous machines and systems. The impasses discussed at the conclusions of Chapters 5 and 6 (as well as the simple desire to avoid liability) motivate in part the second strategy to close possible gaps between machines and harms caused by them: to reduce harm by designing autonomous machines and systems that "obey" the law. This is the topic of Chapter 7. As discussed above, at this point of course, autonomous technologies are not cognizant of the law, far less do they appreciate or value it in the subjective sense; all we can do is program machines and systems to operate in ways that conform to the law. The chapter will discuss ways in which machines and systems are being designed to comply with the law and assess the debate about the extent to which this strategy can be successful. It will also point out that if this effort succeeds, it will not be surprising if autonomous technologies, not human beings, set appropriate standards of care.

Chapter 8 projects further into the future. It discusses ways in which autonomous technologies might be designed to exhibit prosocial behaviors and to have systems of ethics. This leads to Chapter 9, which will discuss efforts to give autonomous machines and systems legal personality and explore whether they should be given legal rights and moral consideration.

Part IV puts the discussion into perspective. Chapter 10 concludes the book by arguing that to some extent, the trajectory of the coevolution of legal responsibility and autonomous machines laid out in Chapters 5 through 9 needs to be cabined. As will be seen in Chapters 2 and 3, the law already applies to complex systems, albeit with concepts borrowed heavily from individual legal and moral responsibility. It is only if society feels it is necessary to become finer grained in assigning responsibility, to move from largescale entities that design and manufacture autonomous machines and systems to individual designers and engineers who could be said to have contributed to the defects that led to harms and to individuals in the chain of command who use autonomous machines, that the problems of associational responsibility discussed in this article become more salient. Autonomous technologies would then set us along that trajectory, if by that time their decision-making capacity is so sophisticated it is hard to attribute responsibility for harms they cause to their human coworkers, supervisors, or those who designed them, but they are not autonomous enough to merit legal, let alone moral agency, so that they can be meaningfully blamed and punished for what they have done. It ends by identifying points along the trajectory that will merit careful attention by jurists and policymakers.

PART I

The rise of autonomous technologies and
current law

1. The emerging challenge

By the time this book goes to press, the death of Elaine Herzberg and the massive data breach involving Facebook and Cambridge Analytica will likely have been overtaken by other events. But both will remain emblematic of harms caused or assisted by increased computing power—power that will over time increase to almost unimaginable levels—as well as the growing presence of sophisticated technology that draws on that power, and improvements to technology that allow devices to sense their environments and to respond to them. The Herzberg incident concerns death caused at least in part by an autonomous machine. Car accidents resulting in fatalities are on one side of the range of physical threats that autonomous machines and systems could pose to human beings and property; harms inflicted by autonomous weapons programmed to seek out potential targets and to destroy them are on the other. The Facebook/Cambridge Analytica debacle represents something more insidious, perhaps far more impactful than anything short of war. This is using information gleaned from large data sets to predict and potentially influence human behavior, at the cost of individual privacy—perhaps, as discussed in a later chapter, at the cost of liberty and identity. In the most dire scenarios, autonomous machines and systems more intelligent than human beings begin to act for themselves. By then, machines and systems will have control over large swaths of the infrastructure and processes that enable human social life. The potential for a dystopia at that point would be great.

Yet the attraction of developing greater machine and system autonomy is powerful precisely because autonomous technologies have potential to benefit human life. Immediately after Herzberg's death was reported, a reader of one report expressed regret at her loss, but also pointed out that hundreds more people would die in automobile accidents caused by human error that very day. Since driver error is by far the most common cause of car accidents, once perfected, autonomous vehicles could reduce fatalities by several orders of magnitude. (In the United States, there were an estimated 6,000 pedestrian deaths in 2016.) In health care, autonomous medical technology might be one of the few ways in which nation states will be able to meet their international human rights obligations to provide medical care to their growing populations. Then of course there are powerful market incentives, at work well before the advent of autonomous systems, to increase efficiencies in manufacturing and services through automation. One estimate is that artificial intelligence will add $15.7 trillion to world GDP by 2030.[1]

At the outset, it is worth discussing what this book means when it uses terms such as "artificial intelligence," "autonomous machines," and "autonomous systems." There are no universally agreed definitions, and the terms are often used interchangeably. "Autonomy" has been defined as "the quality or state of being self-governing" or "self-directing freedom and especially moral independence."[2] Obviously, such definitions have human beings in mind, and, as will be discussed later in this book, the issue arises whether such a definition is faulty because of its anthropocentrism. Some have argued that any self-executing system that can sense and respond to external stimuli can be considered autonomous. On this view, a mousetrap qualifies. The components of the trap are the hardware. Arming the trap by pulling the hammer (the U-shaped piece of thick metal wire that dispatches the mouse) back against the spring and keeping it in place with the hold-down bar comprise instructions. The hold-down bar itself, which when jostled triggers the hammer, acts as a sensor. Once armed, the mousetrap needs no further human intervention; it has become self-executing.[3]

Most researchers, however, require more of machines and systems for them to be considered autonomous. Not only must a device or system be capable of sensing its environment and responding as instructed; to be fully autonomous or intelligent it must also be capable of retaining the experiences of its interactions with the environment and then adapting its responses to better perform vis-à-vis its surroundings along some criteria or set goal: it is capable of learning. Others set a still higher standard: that the machine or system be able to determine its own goals and means of achieving them. Murray Shanahan

---

[1] Nicolas Rapp and Brian O'Keefe, *These 100 Companies are Leading the Way in A.I.*, FORTUNE, Jan. 8, 2018, http://fortune.com/2018/01/08/artificial-intelligence -ai-companies-invest-startups/. A review of various forecasts is provided in Daniel Fagella, *Valuing the Artificial Intelligence Market, Graphs and Predictions*, TECHEMER-GENCE, Mar. 1, 2018, www.techemergence.com/valuing-the-artificial-intelligence -market-graphs-and-predictions/.

[2] Merriam-Webster Dictionary, *Autonomy*, www.merriam-webster.com/dictionary /autonomy.

[3] Patrick Chisan Hew, *Artificial Moral Agents Are Infeasible with Foreseeable Technologies*, 16 ETHICS & INFO. TECH. 197, 198 (2014). In this regard, Merel Noorman and Deborah Johnson argue that machine autonomy does not equate to freedom to make choices. In their view, human actors exert influence on machines by framing the problem they are intended to solve and thus delimit their behavior. Humans will set the norms and rules by which machines act, and machines will not be used until humans have confidence that machines can operate predictably and reliably. Merel Noorman and Deborah G. Johnson, *Negotiating Autonomy and Responsibility in Military Robots*, 16 ETHICS & INFO. TECH. 51, 58–9 (2014).

associates general intelligence with having a commonsense view of one's surroundings and a measure of creativity in responding to new situations.[4] There is of course the famous Turing test in which the human being becomes the measure of intelligence: a computer will have achieved intelligence when we are unable to tell if we are interacting with a human being or a computer. Others require that machines have some form of self-awareness or con-sciousness—the debates surrounding John Searle's Chinese room argument go to what we mean by cognition and understanding, and whether it is possible to devise machines that can achieve them.

When we arrive at more stringent definitions of intelligence and autonomy we brush up against philosophical debates about what it means to be human, since in the western tradition so much of what constitutes the person turns on our cognitive abilities. This book will address some of those issues in later chapters as it reviews the work of certain scholars, particularly when it dis-cusses possible rights for autonomous machines and systems, but for the most part it will take a somewhat pragmatic approach to what constitutes autonomy and intelligence and focus on capabilities instead of comprehension. This book opts for an understanding of autonomy that leans more in the direction of the mousetrap than toward a machine or system with a sense of self and having free will. For this book's purposes, machines and systems are autonomous when they can perform relatively sophisticated tasks without human super-vision. This would include a self-driving vehicle. Obviously, those tasks are more complex than trapping mice (although it can be conceded that catching mice is difficult, and a task for which the mousetrap is brilliantly well suited). I will also use the terms "artificial agents" and "autonomous technologies" as synonyms for autonomous machines and systems, even though some would argue that autonomous machines and systems will never constitute true agents and that technology has its own specific meaning. Finally, I will often refer to artificial intelligence alone, since it is artificial intelligence that will power increasingly autonomous machines and systems.

Shanahan thinks it likely that artificial intelligence will make itself felt in two major waves. In the first wave, machines and systems that fall short of achieving what he terms general intelligence will begin to be introduced.

---

[4]   Murray Shanahan, THE TECHNOLOGICAL SINGULARITY 6 (2015). *See also* Ben Goertzel, The Embodied Communication Prior: A Characterization of General Intelligence in the Context of Embodied Social Interaction, 2009 8th IEEE Int'l Conf. on Cognitive Informatics, June 15–17, 2009, at 38 (proposing a model for intelli-gence and cognition); Shane Legg and Marcus Hutter, A Collection of Definitions of Intelligence, in ADVANCES IN ARTIFICIAL GENERAL INTELLIGENCE: CONCEPTS, ARCHITECTURES AND ALGORITHMS 17 (Ben Goertzel and Pei Wang eds., 2007) (dis-cussing 70 definitions of intelligence).

We are experiencing the first wave now.[5] Then at some point in the future, improvements in technology and in computing will allow machines or systems to achieve general intelligence, perhaps through replication of the human brain or through straight programming. Shanahan thinks it likely that once this happens, machines that surpass humans in intelligence and capabilities will soon follow.[6] This would usher in the second wave of artificial intelligence. In Shanahan's view, the second wave will result in profound challenges to the way we think about ourselves and the world. The existential risks that such intelligence could pose are discussed by Nick Bostrom.[7] This book will explore aspects of this second wave, particularly in Chapters 7–9, but the challenges the law will face with the advent of sophisticated technology will likely arise before machines are completely autonomous in the sense of being cognizant and capable of forming and pursuing their own goals. The machines and systems that represent Shanahan's first wave of artificial intelligence pose problems of their own even if they do not have general intelligence. At the same time, general intelligence serves as a helpful benchmark for the purposes of this book. I will often use phrases such as "machines and systems of increasing sophistication" or "increasing autonomy" to refer to technologies that draw closer to general intelligence.

A WORLD WITH ARTIFICIAL INTELLIGENCE: UBIQUITY IN SCOPE

That the law stands to be challenged arises from the fact that the world could look quite different when artificial intelligence and the machines and systems it drives, even those representing Shanahan's first wave, become more prevalent. There are several ways to envision this first wave. One is to identify areas of contemporary human life in which we would expect artificial intelligence to be used. A study panel reports that applications and devices using artificial intelligence are being developed in eight domains: transportation, home and service robots, health care, education, services to underserved communities, public safety (that is, law enforcement), employment and the workplace, and

---

[5]   For a discussion of some of the advances that are making the first wave possible, *see* Yann Lecun, Yoshua Bengio, and Geoffrey Hinton, *Deep Learning*, 521 NATURE 436 (2015) (reviewing deep learning techniques that are used for image, video, speech, and audio processing and for text and speech processing).

[6]   Shanahan, *supra* note 4, at 85–109.

[7]   Nick Bostrom, SUPERINTELLIGENCE: PATHS, DANGERS, STRATEGIES (2014, with new afterword 2016).

entertainment.[8] According to that report, progress has been uneven between
these areas and there will be continued demand for enormous resources to
further them; the next decade or so is likely to see incremental developments
continuing in those areas. The report does not see artificial intelligence in
itself capable of threatening humanity, and thus rejects the potentiality for an
AI-dominated dystopia: despite Watson's ability to compete in Jeopardy! or
the intellectual prowess of DeepMind's AlphaGo, the authors find it unlikely
that within the next decade artificial intelligence will have developed to the
point of strong autonomy, let alone decide to harm human beings.

Killer robots therefore might not yet pose an immediate threat to humanity,
but artificial intelligence stands to have a profound impact on society nonetheless. Taken together, the eight domains identified in the report encompass
almost every area of human experience. In each domain, one would expect
researchers and businesses to push the boundaries of a machine's ability to
assist and enhance human activities in these areas and perhaps to replace them.
More specific examples will be used in later chapters; what follows is a discussion of a smattering of developments and trends to give a sense of artificial
intelligence's possible scope.

In transportation, autonomous vehicles are of course already being tested in
some locations, with optimistic forecasts seeing vehicles in operation within
three or four years. Artificial intelligence is in the home via devices such as
Alexa and Google Home (the robot vacuum cleaner has been in place for some
time). Developers are exploring how artificial intelligence can be used in
medical treatment and in diagnoses, and there is a burgeoning use of artificial
intelligence in smart devices to monitor health and disease.[9] In education, at
least one review has found that tutoring programs that use artificial intelligence
perform better than computer assisted models and human teachers in large
classes, albeit slightly worse than one on one human tutors.[10] Advances in

---

[8]   2015 Study Panel, Artificial Intelligence and Life in 2030. One Hundred Year
Study on Artificial Intelligence. Sept. 2016, https://ai100.stanford.edu/2016-report.
The panel restricted its scope to the likely impact of artificial intelligence on North
American cities. Another overview of the scope of the industry is found in Daniel
Fagella, *Artificial Intelligence—An Overview by Segment*, TECHEMERGENCE, Mar.
29,   2018,   www.techemergence.com/artificial-intelligence-industry-an-overview-by
-segment/.
[9]   JASON, Artificial Intelligence for Health and Health Care, Dec. 2017, www
.healthit.gov/sites/default/files/jsr-17-task-002_aiforhealthandhealthcare12122017
.pdf. The report states that two early challenges are, first, obtaining access to large
health databases so that artificial intelligence can be trained, and second, meeting rigor-
ous regulatory standards for medical treatment. *Id.*
[10]   Benedict du Boulay, *Artificial Intelligence as an Effective Classroom Assistant*,
IEEE INTELLIGENT SYSTEMS, Nov./Dec. 2016, at 77, 80.

transportation, education, and health care, among other areas, could benefit underserved communities who would not otherwise receive social services.[11] In the area of law enforcement, artificial intelligence is being used to locate missing children and to detect online child exploitation and insurance fraud.[12] Facial recognition technology enhanced by artificial intelligence is being used to recognize suspects in crowds.[13] Algorithms are being used to predict recidivism, raising concerns about bias.[14]

Another domain is business and finance. Here too, artificial intelligence is being employed to enhance human activity, and perhaps in time will replace humans. Artificial intelligence is driving some automatic contracting for goods and services. In financial services, technology is being developed to assist in the loan application process and to assess credit risk.[15] Some of these activities reach systemic levels. High volume trading and algorithmic trading already have an impact on markets.[16] Although it is different from AI, block chain, discussed in more detail in the next chapter, might make possible self-executing contracts, as well as rudimentary business entities in which people and smart contracts themselves can participate. In the entertainment industry, work is being done to use artificial intelligence for marketing and advertising, to personalize user experiences, and to aid in the production process, at this point

---

[11] Shannon Farley, *Nonprofits, Not Silicon Valley Startups, Are Creating SAC AI Apps for the Greater Good*, RECODE, June 22, 2017, www.recode.net/2017/6/22/ 15855492/ai-artificial-intelligence-nonprofit-good-human-chatbots-machine-learning.

[12] Intel, *The Future of AI in Law Enforcement: Intel-powered AI Helps Find Missing Children*, www.intel.com/content/www/us/en/analytics/artificial-intelligence/ article/ai-helps-find-kids.html; Intel, *The Future of AI in Finance, Intel-Powered AI Helps Fight Fraud*, www.intel.com/content/www/us/en/financial-services-it/article/ insurance-fraud-revealed.html.

[13] Rob Thubron, *Chinese Police Use Facial Recognition Tech to Identify Suspect from Crowd of 50,000*, TECHSPOT, Apr. 13, 2018, www.techspot.com/news/74150 -chinese-police-use-facial-recognition-tech-identify-suspect.html.

[14] Julia Dressel and Hany Farid, *The Accuracy, Fairness, and Limits of Predicting Recidivism*, SCIENCE ADVANCES 4, eaao5580 (2018) (evaluating algorithms that predict recidivism); Julia Angwin et al., *Machine Bias*, PRO PUBLICA, May 23, 2016, www. propublica.org/article/machine-bias-risk-assessments-in-criminal-sentencing.

[15] Allen Taylor, *AI Credit Scoring: Fad or the Future?*, LENDING TIMES, July 19, 2017, https://lending-times.com/2017/07/19/ai-credit-scoring-fad-or-the-future/; Tatjana Kulkarni, *The Rise of Alternative Data in the Lending Market*, BANK INNOVA-TION, Sept. 21, 2017, https://bankinnovation.net/2017/09/the-rise-of-alternative-data-in -the-lending-market/.

[16] UK Government Office for Science, *The Future of Computer Trading in Financial Markets: Final Project Report (2010)*, www.cftc.gov/sites/default/files/idc/ groups/public/@aboutcftc/documents/file/tacfuturecomputertrading1012.pdf.

largely through image recognition.[17] In turn, the gaming industry is responsible for many of the advances in computing, as gamers seek more realism in their online experiences.[18]

Since the workplace is such an important part of human life, it is worth discussing developments in this area in more detail. An early study estimated that 47 percent of US employment is at risk of automation.[19] Other studies, however, predict less impact.[20] Advanced computation stands to transform the workplace environment and alter employment itself. Large technology companies such as Amazon, Google, Microsoft, and IBM are making artificial intelligence technology available to a wider range of business customers.[21] Since full autonomy is unlikely to be achieved in the near to medium term, most artificial intelligence applications will likely be more in the nature of intelligence augmentation, in which human capacities are increased through the use of artificial intelligence.[22] This is already occurring in several fields, such as law and medicine, with impacts on the way firms are structured. Ravin Jesuthasan and John Boudreau believe the increased use of automation working with human beings will lead to a much more diffuse type of business organization in which the organization will serve as a source of capital and coordination, but will use a combination of employees, computer-based enhancement systems, third parties, and so on.[23]

Finally, the coming decade may not see the advent of killer robots, but research and development will continue in the use of artificial intelligence and autonomous systems in warfare. The ultimate goal for using artificial intelligence in warfare is that it become "a true assistant that aids in understanding

---

[17]   Kumba Sennaar, *AI in Movies, Entertainment, and Visual Media—5 Current Use-Cases*, TECHEMERGENCE, Nov. 20, 2017, www.techemergence.com/ai-in-movies-entertainment-visual-media/.

[18]   Shanahan, *supra* note 4, at 31.

[19]   Carl Benedikt Frey and Michael A. Osborne, *The Future of Employment: How Susceptible Are Jobs to Computerization?* Sept. 12, 2013, www.oxfordmartin.ox.ac.uk/downloads/academic/The_Future_of_Employment.pdf.

[20]   John Boudreau, *Will Automation "Terminate" Occupations?* CLARITY, July 21, 2016, www.visier.com/clarity/will-automation-terminate-occupations-deconstructing-work-reveals-the-answer/.

[21]   Cade Metz, *Google Sells A.I. for Building A.I. (Novices Welcome)*, N.Y. TIMES, Jan. 17, 2018, at B1; Cade Metz, *Google Makes its Special A.I. Chips Available to Others*, N.Y. TIMES, Feb. 12, 2018, at B3.

[22]   David Lavenda, *Artificial Intelligence vs. Intelligence Augmentation*, NETWORK WORLD, Aug. 5, 2016, www.networkworld.com/article/3104909/software/artificial-intelligence-vs-intelligence-augmentation.html.

[23]   Ravin Jesuthasan and John Boudreau, *Thinking Through how Automation Will Affect Your Workforce*, HARV. BUS. REV., Apr. 20, 2017, https://hbr.org/2017/04/thinking-through-how-automation-will-affect-your-workforce.

the operational environment while supporting the operations process."[24] This would involve the use of autonomous and semiautonomous systems with learning capability, as well as applications for "indications and warnings, counter-messaging and cyber defense, among other uses."[25] Present applications are steps toward that goal. Such applications include computer visioning systems to help analysts recognize potential targets, the use of artificial intelligence to project equipment maintenance needs, and deep learning to detect heretofore unseen threats.[26] Finally, one cannot ignore that many working in artificial intelligence have grave concerns about the advent of autonomous weapons. They worry that autonomous weapons will usher in a revolution in warfare that will allow war to be waged faster and at a greater scale. They could be used as weapons of terror and thus make asymmetric warfare more deadly and a ready option for substate and nonstate actors.[27]

A WORLD WITH ARTIFICIAL INTELLIGENCE: UBIQUITY IN EXPERIENCE

Artificial intelligence will thus likely make itself felt in almost every area of human life. Another way to consider what challenges it might pose is to imagine what everyday life will be like where autonomous systems are operating. Writing in 2004, Howard Schrobe discussed four aspects of the emerging technology that set it apart from previous developments. He observed that computation is embedded in many everyday devices, thus creating the possibility that each device can detect others and act in concert. Computation is increasingly mobile. Systems are constantly on, always available for software updates, which means that devices are constantly developing. Finally, many computational "nodes" are equipped with sensors and effectors that mean

---

[24] James J. Mingus and David Dilly, *On Warfare and Watson: Invest Now to Win with Artificial Intelligence*, ARMY, Sept. 2017, at 32.

[25] *Id.*, at 33.

[26] *Id.*, at 32. For a discussion of artificial intelligence in cyber warfare, *see* Alessandro Guarino, *Autonomous Intelligent Agents in Cyber Offence*, 2013 5ᵀᴴ INT'L CONF. ON CYBER CONFLICT (K. Podins, J. Stinissen, and M. Maybaum eds., 2013), https://ieeexplore.ieee.org/xpl/mostRecentIssue.jsp?punumber=6560495#.

[27] *See, e.g.*, Markus Wagner, *The Dehumanization of International Humanitarian Law: Legal, Ethical, and Political Implications of Autonomous Weapons Systems*, 47 VAND. J. TRANSNAT'L L. 1371 (2014) (discussing the negative impacts of autonomous weapons on existing law, ethics, and politics); Human Rights Watch, *Losing Humanity: The Case against Killer Robots* (2012), www.hrw.org/report/2012/11/19/losing-humanity/case-against-killer-robots (arguing for a ban on autonomous weapons); Open Letter to Professor Sung-Chul Shin, President of KAIST, March 2018, www.cse.unsw.edu.au/~tw/ciair//kaist.html.

they interact with and can affect the physical world.[28] The result is a blended world in which people move seamlessly and almost subconsciously between the online and real worlds, between interactions with humans and interactions with sophisticated technology.

In a recent book, Mireille Hildebrandt draws a vivid picture of how this world will be experienced.[29] Hildebrandt follows a woman in the not too far distant future as she goes through her day. As she awakes, her mobile device will have already monitored how well she slept and what mood she is in. The device will have instructed other devices in the home to play music, adjust lighting, and suggest food that responds to that mood. The woman is transported to work via an autonomous vehicle. Throughout the work day, she is helped in her tasks by devices designed to recognize items that need particular attention and assist her as she works on individual and team projects. When she receives a call from her child's school telling her that the child is ill, technology helps her as she arranges childcare and pickups with her former spouse. It also helps her reschedule appointments.[30]

This is a world in which technology not only addresses but also anticipates human wants and needs. In one sense, it is a deeply personalized world. One could go into even more detail on the life of the woman in Hildebrandt's snapshot. During her lunch break, her portable device (which could be in the form of a wearable device) might remind her that it is time to think about making plans for the summer holidays. It will have access to the woman's previous travel history and itineraries, her interests, and her reading and shopping patterns. The woman might ask the device to suggest some destinations in Latin America. The device will do so, providing details about particular hotels, plane bookings, and so on. The woman might instruct the personal assistant to bring up the topic a week from now. The device will keep track of price changes, reservations, and so on that might affect the options it previously presented to the woman.[31] All of this would be made possible by the personal device's ability to act autonomously and to interact with other autonomous systems that assist with reservations, weather forecasts, and so on. The result is a form of service that is highly individualized, but in another sense impersonal, because all of the woman's interactions will be with various autonomous systems, not human beings.

---

[28]   Howard E. Schrobe, *Foreword*, in SMART ENVIRONMENTS xi (Diane J. Cook and Sjal K. Das eds., 2005).

[29]   Mireille Hildebrandt, SMART TECHNOLOGIES AND THE END(S) OF LAW 68–75 (2015).

[30]   *Id.*

[31]   *Id.*

THE CREATORS OF ARTIFICIAL INTELLIGENCE AND AUTONOMOUS MACHINES AND SYSTEMS

The two previous sections suggest that artificial intelligence and the machines and systems it drives are likely to be present in almost every domain of life, and that our personal experience of artificial intelligence will be one in which we move fluidly through real and virtual worlds. The ubiquity of artificial intelligence and autonomous technologies and machines, in terms of their scope and in our daily experience, will of course not come to pass on its own. Individuals and entities ranging from individual app designers to startup companies to major corporations, suppliers and contractors, governments to some extent, and all their employees are involved in the design and production of the software, firmware, and hardware that will make autonomous machines and systems possible. They form the web of persons and entities who contribute to these machines and systems and thus are possible candidates for responsibility for what those technologies do.

It goes without saying that the design and production process of technology is already complex. The iPhone is a good example, particularly since it has some learning functionality. It is designed in California, as is its software. Its components are purchased from more than 200 suppliers from all over the world.[32] Those components are shipped to production facilities for assembly, packaging, and distribution. The web of suppliers is broader because many of the iPhone's suppliers are major companies in their own right, each with their own subsidiaries, inhouse designers, and supply chains. Any major manufacturer of autonomous devices and systems would likely have similar organizational characteristics: some centralized control, but design and manufacturing processes spread over a number of divisions within the firm, and with outside suppliers.[33] Each business entity within that chain or web of subsidiaries can be broken down into its own departments and working groups.

---

[32] Christopher Minasians, *Where are Apple Products Made?* MACWORLD, Sept. 18, 2017, www.macworld.co.uk/feature/apple/where-are-apple-products-made-3633832/. *See also* David Barboza, *An iPhone's Journey, From the Factory Floor to the Retail Store*, N.Y. TIMES, Dec. 29, 2016, www.nytimes.com/2016/12/29/technology/iphone-china-apple-stores.html; *Apple's Product Development Process—Inside the World's Greatest Design Organization*, INTERACTION DESIGN FOUND., Mar. 2018, www.interaction-design.org/literature/article/apple-s-product-development-process-inside-the-world-s-greatest-design-organization.

[33] For example, Adnan Shaout, Monika Arora, and Selim Awad discuss the complexities of designing software for automobiles in *Automotive Software Development and Management*, 2010 INT'L COMP. ENG'G CONF. (ICENCO) 9 (2010).

In addition to the complexity of manufacturing technology, there is the complexity of software design. Artificial intelligence and autonomous machines and systems are of course enabled by computer programs. Much of software development is project based and can be seen as having a life cycle of planning, assessing requirements (including consulting stakeholders in the project), and design build (logically structuring and coding the software, testing, and implementation).[34] It should be pointed out that these approaches to development are not limited to software. For example, systems engineering is understood as a multidisciplinary approach that has stages analogous to the life cycle approach to software development.[35]

Software development projects are designed and implemented by large multidisciplinary project teams, who are responsible for producing complex systems involving highly interactive hardware and software. Frequently project requirements may change during project development to take account of both emerging technologies and new techniques. Given the multiplicity and variety of interfaces which exist between the various phases, across the numerous disciplines, and along the different levels of management audience, it is not surprising that many projects fail to be completed or to deliver the expected benefits.[36]

John McManus points out there are strong pressures to bring products to market, and so little if any time is given to testing. "Today's computer programs," he writes, "are huge and complex and it is harder to test software with millions of lines of code. Too often the testing falls to the unfortunate user who decides to use a new program or IT system."[37]

Because of these challenges, it is not surprising that there are different schools of thought on how to develop software. One approach is the lifecycle model described above. Others follow principles set out in the Agile Manifesto, a statement made by software developers in the early 2000s, meant to address the risk of software programs that do not meet user needs. Those principles are: "Individuals and interactions over processes and tools"; "Working software over comprehensive documentation"; "Customer collaboration over contract negotiation"; and "Responding to change over following a plan."[38] One offshoot from those principles is scrum methodology, a software development approach used for complex projects in which the project is broken into several pieces which are completed in very short time frames. The end

---

[34] John McManus, RISK MANAGEMENT IN SOFTWARE DEVELOPMENT PROJECTS 2.3 (2004).

[35] Shaout et al., *supra* note 33, at 10.

[36] *Id.*

[37] *Id.*, at 1.8.3.

[38] Agile Manifesto (2001), agilemanifesto.org.

product is then viewed by development teams and stakeholders together.[39] This approach appears to be somewhat more organic than the life cycle approach, although in theory nothing precludes the latter from responding to feedback from stakeholders throughout the life cycle. These approaches to design and manufacturing and software development leave one with the impression of complex products that require the input of many people and entities, each of whom is likely responsible for a very small part of the overall resulting technology. Autonomous systems and devices are being designed, developed, and manufactured in the same way.

RESPONSIBILITY FOR HARMS CAUSED BY AUTONOMOUS MACHINES

The foregoing discussion of artificial intelligence's growing ubiquity and of the complex processes by which artificial intelligence and the systems and devices driven by it are developed provides the context for the inquiry of this book. Autonomous systems and machines that "malfunction" have the potential to make themselves felt at individual and systemic levels in almost every aspect of human life. When that happens, who will be responsible?

Peter Asaro sets out the challenges that autonomous machines and systems pose to moral theory, which also serve as challenges to law:

> [T]he crucial things we need are theories of punishment, agency and responsibility that apply to ... complicated systems, systems of humans and machines working together[.] ... Theories in which responsibility and agency can be meaningfully designed and shared, so that large organizations of people and machines can produce desirable results and be held accountable and reformed when they fail to do so.[40]

Asaro's requirements are interesting in several respects. First, it is a given for Asaro that autonomous machines and systems will be part of everyday life; hence the need for theories of punishment, agency, and responsibility that will ensure desirable results from the interaction of humans and machines, and reform when needed. Second, his challenges imply that what will eventually have to be addressed is not individuals primarily, but large, complicated systems or organizations instead. This reflects the reality just discussed, in which autonomous technologies are designed and manufactured by large organizations or through long supply chains in which sophisticated technolo-

---

[39] Emily Bonnie, Fundamentals of the Scrum Methodology, 12 June 2014, WRIKE, www.wrike.com/blog/fundamentals-of-the-scrum-methodology/.

[40] Peter M. Asaro, *Determinism, Machine Agency, and Responsibility*, 2 POLITICA & SOCIETÀ 265, 291–2 (2014).

gies are already being used, and in which such new technologies will operate in systems or organizations of which people are also a part. Finally, Asaro implies that artificial agents will reach levels of autonomy at which it is as appropriate, or perhaps more so, to refer to "humans and machines working together" and "large organizations of people and machines" as it is to refer to "humans using machines in their work" or "large organizations of people who use machines." Asaro is speaking to the field of ethics, but his challenges help assess how well law meets analogous concerns, and if not, how law might be changed to do so.

It is helpful in this regard to consider in a very preliminary way law as a form of responsibility. To be subject to civil or criminal liability is of course to be answerable to the law, and while it is not the purpose of this book to go into foundations, it must be conceded that there is no consensus on what those foundations are. I agree with Anthony Duff that one could try to frame questions of legal responsibility through the various schools of jurisprudence: legal formalism, positivism, realism, legal process, critical legal studies, and law and economics, and to some extent these schools of thought must be reckoned with.[41] Further, it is possible to narrow these questions into pure legal analysis: it might be sufficient to understand the problem via a closed system such as the Hohfeldian analysis of duties and rights; it is not required that legal liability and constraint perform some function to further an instrumental goal; rather, they can be viewed as simply following legal principles as they apply to a set of facts. It might be enough to ask whether a person owes a duty to another. If that person breaches that duty, the other has the right to be placed in the position they would have been in had that duty not been breached. One might say the same of legal responsibility in a positivist conception of law such as Kelsen's, or even in Luhman's view of law as an autonomous system in itself that should be treated as separate and apart from its larger social environment.

For this study, however, it seems more helpful to justify and evaluate possible changes to law by treating the law in its instrumental and expressive aspects. Law, and legal responsibility in particular, might be explained and evaluated by what it can accomplish, or as an expression of prior political and moral decisions and attitudes of a society about various aspects of life. Although this book will focus primarily on civil law, Anthony Duff uses the instrumentalist and expressive framework to tackle the vast literature on criminal law, the law we most associate with punishment. An instrumentalist account of the criminal law would ask about its purposes: perhaps to protect

---

[41]   Antony Duff, *Theories of Criminal Law*, *in* THE STANFORD ENCYCLOPEDIA OF PHILOSOPHY (Edward N. Zalta ed., Summer 2013 edn.), https://plato.stanford.edu/archives/sum2013/entries/criminal-law/.

the community from unwanted acts, to deter people from committing them through the threat of punishment, and to incarcerate people who pose a threat to society. Or we might understand it as reflecting prior decisions that certain behaviors merit the highest condemnation of a society, and retribution.[42] From either perspective, because criminal liability leads to the most severe of societal sanctions, the methods by which criminal liability is defined and imposed become crucial.

In the area of tort law, Jules Coleman, Scott Hershovitz, and Gabriel Mendlow write that there are two major strands of tort theory prevalent in the United States.[43] The most prominent theory comes from law and economics. From that perspective, tort law should be understood as "aiming to minimize the sum of costs of accidents and the costs of avoiding them." For these scholars, the economic analysis of tort law works best when it serves a normative function, asking questions such as "what substantive liability rules have the greatest impact on reducing the incidence of accidents at the lowest cost?" or "what substantive and procedural rules will lead to optimal investments in safety?"[44] For the authors, the most influential alternative theory is one of corrective justice. Under this view, tort comprises first order and second order duties. First order duties prohibit certain behaviors, such as assault or battery, or injuring someone. Second order duties stem from the principle of corrective justice: "an individual has a duty to repair the wrongful losses that his conduct causes."[45] Such wrongfulness need not be morally wrong. To return to Hohfeld, every duty creates a right in the person to whom the duty is owned. If a person suffers loss because of a breach of duty, this triggers the second order duty of repair.[46] To be sure, this might seem like a return to an insular analysis separate and apart from society, but such isolation is never really possible. A statement like "an individual has a duty to repair the wrongful losses that his conduct causes" seems meaningless unless it resonates with a broader reality.

Finally, one might also think of contract in instrumental and expressive terms. Contract law can be thought of as the legal rules and principles that enable people to enter into mutually beneficial economic relationships. This includes doctrines that help determine when a contractual obligation exists,

---

[42] *Id.*

[43] Jules Coleman, Scott Hershovitz, and Gabriel Mendlow, *Theories of the Common Law of Torts, in* THE STANFORD ENCYCLOPEDIA OF PHILOSOPHY (Edward N. Zalta ed., winter 2015 edn.), https://plato.stanford.edu/archives/win2015/entries/tort-theories/.

[44] *Id.*

[45] *Id.*

[46] Proponents of civil recourse theory would say that there are no second order duties; rather, the breach of a first order duty gives the injured party the power to bring an action. *Id.*

when there has been a breach of that obligation, and what remedies are available to the injured party. Ideally, these rules would be crafted to facilitate people's bargaining and to prevent unfair surprise. At the same time, contract law might be said to have its expressive elements too. As is true with corrective justice theories of tort law, contract law can be articulated as the creation, this time with the consent of the parties, of legal duties with associated rights, the breach of which triggers a duty, this time to put the injured party in the same position had there been performance. Sometimes it is grounded in our belief that promises should be kept. Sometimes it is grounded in our belief that a person who relies on a promise to his or her detriment should be compensated.

How then might the instrumental and expressive aspects of the law respond to the call for systems of responsibility to address the growing reality and ubiquity of autonomous machines and systems? Does the law present "[t]heories in which responsibility and agency can be meaningfully designed and shared, so that large organizations of people and machines can produce desirable results and be held accountable and reformed when they fail to do so"? The instrumental question is what law, including theories of liability and responsibility, might do to help accomplish the goals we as a society might have regarding artificial intelligence. But there is also the expressive aspect as well. When Elaine Herzberg lost her life, others owed her a duty not to harm her, but she obviously was harmed. The inquiry is whether the software designers, engineers, and manufacturers, as well as the company that authorized the testing of the autonomous car and the human driver behind the wheel, owed duties to her, and whether they breached that duty, thereby triggering the second order duty to repair what of course is irreparable. Similarly, when people working with large data sets used personal information to predict how others would behave and then tried to influence them, what duties in tort or in contract did they owe to the individuals whose information was used and to those who were targeted to be persuaded? At this relatively early stage in the development of autonomous machines and systems, these inquiries remain focused on the human subjects involved, but even without full autonomy the link between all the people who contributed to a harm and legal liability can be tenuous. As a consequence, scholars and policymakers are asking: when vehicles and systems achieve even higher levels of autonomy, will these connections become even more strained?

"CULTURAL SOFTWARE"

In 1907, the Georgia Court of Appeals affirmed the dismissal of suit brought by R.M. Lewis, whose son had been killed when, according to the complaint, a car speeding through the streets of Atlanta ran into a crowd of children who had been playing on the sidewalk and in the street.[47] According to the complaint, the owner of the car, Martin Amorous, had allowed his son Clinton to drive the car, and Clinton in turn had permitted a certain young man named Pybus to take over the wheel. Pybus was driving during the accident. At the time of the dismissal of suit, Pybus had already been convicted and imprisoned for involuntary manslaughter in connection with the death of Ms Lewis's son.

The complaint against the owner relied on two theories. One was based on agency: the plaintiffs argued Pybus had committed the tort while within the scope of an agency that existed between him and the owners (as well as the owners of the garage where the automobile was kept). This theory, the trial court had found, was unsatisfactory because the connection between Pybus and the owners was too tenuous. The second theory was based on strict liability: "automobiles are to be classed with ferocious animals, and ... the law relating to the duty of the owners of such animals is to apply."[48] The trial court rejected that claim, and the appeals court agreed, reflecting with a bit of wistfulness on its members' own experience with cars:

> It is not the ferocity of automobiles that is to be feared, but the ferocity of those who drive them. Until human agency intervenes, they are usually harmless. While by reason of the rate of pay allotted to judges in this state few, if any, of them have ever owned one of these machines, yet some of them have occasionally ridden in them, thereby acquiring some knowledge of them; and we have, therefore, found out that there are times when these machines, not only lack ferocity, but assume such an indisposition to go that it taxes the limits of human ingenuity to make them move at all. They are not to be classed with bad dogs, vicious bulls, evil disposed mules, and the like.[49]

Early cases seem to follow this pattern, although there were some exceptions. The car itself, although qualitatively different from all other carriages on public highways at the time, was not in itself so dangerous as to make its owners liable for all harms involving it. Rather, the focus was on Pybus, the driver, and how he had operated the car.[50] The Georgia court noted that the Georgia legislature had not yet enacted regulations "which the introduction of this new mode of conveyance would seem to make salutary."[51] For the time being, though, the common law would do. "Until some change is made," the court wrote, "the responsibility of persons owning, keeping, and operating

---

[47]   *Lewis v. Amorous*, 3 Ga. App. 50 (1907).

[48]   *Id.*, at 340.

[49]   *Id.*

[50]   Xenophon P. Huddy and Howard C. Joyce, THE LAW OF AUTOMOBILES 35–9 (4th edn. 1916).

[51]   *Id.*, at 341.

motor cars will be determined according to the precedents of the common law and the general law upon cognate subjects."[52]

The possible trajectory for law and autonomous machines and systems that this book plots out will likely follow a pattern that seems to emerge whenever we use cultural tools such as law to apply to potentially new situations. It is the pattern one sees with the introduction of new technology such as the automobile early in the twentieth century. J.M. Balkin argues that human understanding and human institutions such as law are made possible through conceptual tools which he refers to as "cultural software."[53] Such tools are "the abilities, associations, heuristics, metaphors, narratives, and capacities that we employ in understanding and evaluating the social world."[54] Balkin, writing at the height of the critical legal studies movement, tries to respond to arguments that language and law are at best indeterminate. In Balkin's view, a deeper understanding of how these conceptual tools operate, are transmitted, and evolve helps explain how "cultural understandings can be shared while still accounting for the considerable differentiation and disagreement in belief among members of the same culture or interpretive community."[55]

One of the most important themes that emerges from Balkin's work is that all cultural tools, be they tools of understanding, technology, or social institutions, are subject to "bricolage," a term Balkin borrows from Claude Levi-Strauss. Such tools are subject to bricolage in that they are themselves the cumulative result of earlier tools. "The history of thought," he writes, "is the history of the cumulative marshaling of existing capacities to form new ones, the use of older cultural software to create new 'idea-programs.'"[56] Balkin argues that this has four implications: "Cultural bricolage (1) is cumulative, (2) involves unintended uses, (3) is economical or recursive, and (4) has unintended consequences."[57]

That cultural tools are cumulative implies "[t]he tools … one can create at a particular time depend largely on the available materials that lie to hand." Further, "[t]he complexity and performance of a tool are necessarily limited by

---

[52] *Id.* For a discussion of Detroit's experience with automobiles, *see* Bill Loomis, *1900–1930: The Years of Living Dangerously*, Detroit News, Apr. 26, 2015, www .detroitnews.com/story/news/local/michigan-history/2015/04/26/auto-traffic-history -detroit/26312107/.

[53] J.M. Balkin, Cultural Software (1998) (*see* in particular ch. 2).

[54] *Id.*, at 6.

[55] *Id.*, at 7.

[56] *Id.*, at 31. Mark Tushnet also uses the concept of bricolage in comparative constitutional studies in Mark Tushnet, *The Possibilities of Comparative Constitutional Law*, 108 Yale L. J. 1225, 1285–301 (1999).

[57] Balkin, *supra* note 53, at 32.

the nature of the tools available to construct it."[58] It is not surprising, then, that in the Georgia automobile case, the lawyers and judges used the existing law of animals, agency, and strict liability to grapple with an accident involving what was then new technology. For the appeals court, a car was not like a ferocious or dangerous animal, thus strict liability would not apply. If Balkin is right, it is not surprising that more than 100 years later, we use already existing legal doctrines to address the rise of artificial intelligence and autonomous systems and machines with tools very similar to those used by the Georgia appeals court. These doctrines, these ways of framing the legal issues, with their strengths and limitations, will affect the capacity of legal doctrine to address new technologies. For example, robots are being compared to animals, but we can ask whether the analogy to animals is apt. What is lost and what is gained in our being able to respond to autonomous machines and systems when we use the concept of animals to make decisions about liability?

Cultural bricolage also means tools can be put to uses for which they were not originally intended. The multipurpose nature of these tools is reflected in institutions. Balkin writes that "human institutions solve problems of organization, reproduction, and stabilization by adopting and adapting features of other social structures that their members are familiar with. In this way new forms of human sociability are constructed out of older ones."[59] For him, kinship is a good example of this kind of institutional tool; it is an obvious means by which a society organizes itself, and extensions of this concept have been used by many cultures to encourage cooperation beyond blood relatives. In the area of autonomous machines and systems, we are seeing people employ the ancient law of Roman slavery and the law related to children and to the owners of animals, in part because these are relationships with which we are familiar and for which law already exists. But, to return to the earlier point about the cumulative nature of tools and about their enabling and disabling nature, these doctrines stand to frame how we will understand our relationship with autonomous technologies, particularly the most sophisticated of them. As will be discussed later, it might be problematic to use old analogies to slavery when we use law to shape how autonomous systems and systems will be treated, not so much because artificial agents might not have the kind of autonomy that applies to humans and animals, but because using long discarded systems of law would signal a return to attitudes that made slavery possible.

By "economical and recursive," Balkin means that a relatively small set of cultural tools can be used in a large number of ways, thereby creating new conceptual or institutional tools that in turn are applied to older tools. Balkin uses

---

[58]   *Id.*
[59]   *Id.*, at 33.

gender to illustrate this point: gender is not only used to distinguish between male and female, but also in a number of other contexts, including stereotypes; objects, such as ships and hurricanes; and simply for conceptual purposes, such as languages that divide nouns into gender categories that have nothing to do with biological gender; yet the use of gender in these other ways can affect the way male and female are understood.[60] (Gender is also constraining when it fails to account for people who do not identify with one of the two traditional categories.) For our purposes, the economy and the recursive nature of tools create the possibility that whatever solutions the law might reach as applied to autonomous systems could in turn affect the legal doctrines themselves. Further, as will be discussed in Chapter 9, the concepts we use to consider whether autonomous machines themselves should enjoy legal rights, such as cognition, sentience, and identity, will likely be affected by that very inquiry.

Finally, according to Balkin, "[t]he bricoleur's economical and cumulative use of tools in unintended ways can and often does lead to unexpected and unintended consequences both for good and for ill."[61] This result is closely related to another important theme of Balkin's work. Tools are transmitted and evolve over time.[62] As with any product of an evolutionary process, a social tool results from historical developments that foreclose certain avenues of development and open up other possibilities, thus leading to two crucial aspects of social tools. First, the path dependent nature of such social tools re-iterates the need to look closely at how legal concepts work within a particular context. The second aspect is, as Balkin puts it, that

> [c]ultural tools produced by bricolage never work perfectly: when they do work it is usually only well enough for the purpose at hand[.] ... There was never a time when the products of cultural bricolage lack a certain jerry-built character, when they do not have unexpected side effects or the potential for such side effects. The history of the development of culture is always the history of muddling through.[63]

---

[60] Balkin, *supra* note 53, at 34.

[61] *Id.*

[62] Balkin relies on the memetic transmission of cultural information, introduced by Richard Dawkins and developed by scholars such as Susan Blackmore and Robert Aunger. *See* Richard Dawkins, THE SELFISH GENE (1989 edn.); Susan Blackmore, THE MEME MACHINE (1999); DARWINIZING CULTURE (Robert Aunger ed., 2000); Robert Aunger, THE ELECTRIC MEME (2002). Memes, to use Balkin's language, are pieces of cultural software or, as Dawkins describes them, replicators, that are the basic units of cultural information. DAWKINS, *id.*, at 192. These pieces of cultural software are subject to high levels of variability and become units of selection, and the "environment" in which such memes "compete" is the human mind and various media, such as books and sound recordings, that preserve memes outside of the body.

[63] Balkin, *supra* note 53, at 39. The idea that cultural tools work only well enough for the purpose at hand is put forward by Jody Kraus in her discussion of the transmis-

We should expect, then, that attempts to use currently existing law to govern artificial agents will have the jerry-rigged feel, at least to some extent, and that they will have unexpected consequences. Further, it should not be surprising that these developments will be incremental and inconsistent. Indeed, there may come a time when we ascribe personhood and rights to the most sophisticated machines, which will have resulted by muddling through the problems that come to light.

We thus find ourselves at the cusp of a world in which artificial intelligence is everywhere, used or involved in almost every important aspect of our lives and in the way we experience the day to day. The means of developing the hardware, software, and infrastructure that will make this possible are already in place: complex webs of individuals and entities involved in the development and manufacture of sophisticated technology. People have already been harmed, even in these early days of autonomous machines and systems. Law in its instrumental and expressive aspects is being called upon to anticipate and respond to these developments. This is part of the broader question of who should be held responsible for harms caused at least in part by artificial intelligence.

If Balkin's framework accurately depicts the development of cultural tools, we would expect societies to approach problems raised by autonomous machines and systems by using preexisting legal and moral concepts and doctrines, but we would also expect the application of those tools to lead to unintended consequences that will in turn result in changes in those concepts. The interaction between cultural tools does not happen in a linear fashion, but even now, before the most sophisticated machines and systems have been manufactured and deployed, the literature is mapping out lines of development that fit into Balkin's framework. The development of autonomous machines and that of current systems of liability are already interacting at a conceptual level. Some observers have argued that technology is running ahead of the law in this area, creating new facts on the ground to which law must respond.[64] It is more accurate, however, to say that designers, programmers, policymakers, and jurists use the current systems of liability and the assumptions that underlie them to frame and address potential legal issues raised by autonomous machines. In a sense, existing law is permitting and guiding their development. At the same time, observers are debating the extent to which this law is sufficient to address foreseeable issues. This is leading to speculation about how

---

sion of business norms: Jody S. Kraus, *Legal Design and the Evolution of Cultural Norms*, 26 J. Legal Stud. 377 (1997).

[64] Ugo Pagallo, The Laws of Robots 19–20 (2013).

the law will need to change and about how future machines will need to be designed. These are topics for the next few chapters.

2. Existing law and other forms of governance

At the end of Chapter 1, this book argued it is natural when faced with something like the advent of new technology to address it with preexisting conceptual tools, thus setting in motion dynamics for change that have the potential to have a recursive impact on the tools themselves. This of course means we must have some understanding of how scholars and policymakers believe currently existing law, both its doctrines and underlying principles, will or should apply to autonomous machines and systems. Over the past several years, legal scholars have engaged in detailed applications of current legal doctrines to problems that are expected to arise when autonomous technology is evaluated under legal doctrines of torts, contract, and the law of war.[1] The growing literature also includes proposals on how such machines and systems should be regulated. This chapter does not attempt to repeat those studies, but instead sketches the landscape filled in by those more thorough works to support one of the arguments of this book: that the tool-like nature of these doctrines and other means of governance like regulation makes it likely that the relationship between law and autonomous machines and systems will be complex and dynamic.

The situations being considered fall into three broad categories. The first has already been discussed: a self-driving vehicle collides with a person, and perhaps the passenger-operator-driver is injured as well. Other scenarios fall into this category: for example, nanodevices used for therapeutic purposes do not work as intended and worsen a patient's condition. The Facebook/Cambridge Analytica affair falls into several categories, but it fits here insofar as an individual's privacy has been violated. The second category involves autonomous contracting. This includes scenarios in which a computer program operated by an online business enters into a contract with a human being or another entity when the online business did not authorize the contract. The

---

[1] Several commentators have outlined the contours of a law of autonomous machines in the areas of product liability, crime, contracting, and the law of war. In particular, *see* Samir Chopra and Laurence F. White, A LEGAL THEORY FOR AUTONOMOUS ARTIFICIAL AGENTS chs 2, 4 (2011); UGO PAGALLO, THE LAWS OF ROBOTS chs 3–5 (2013).

third category is autonomous weapons systems. Examples include situations in which an autonomous weapons system capable of selecting and attaching its own targets fails to distinguish between civilians and military personnel. To this we could add a fourth category: systemic harms that harm the public, the economy, or the environment. Facebook/Cambridge Analytica would also fall into this category, as would computer-driven high volume trading that goes awry on a stock exchange.

The main part of this chapter is organized primarily along the first three categories of harms. Legal assessments of harms caused by self-driving vehicles and other autonomous devices gravitate toward product liability as the likely basis for assigning legal responsibility, with some discussion of agency law. Agency law is also the lens through which electronic contracting is assessed. The existing doctrines of command responsibility, and sometimes state responsibility, are applied to harm to civilians caused by autonomous weapons and systems. This chapter will spend less time on large systemic harms. Such global events are difficult to grapple with whether or not caused by autonomous technologies, and are often better addressed prospectively through legislation. At the same time, when there are systemic harms, such as financial crises, the doctrines this chapter examines certainly play a role, albeit usually on an individual basis. With respect to regulation, this chapter will show that one is already seeing a familiar spectrum of potential regulatory responses to any phenomenon with systemic impact, ranging from private ordering via contract and private industry codes to direct regulation by government agencies.

TORT LAW

As discussed in Chapter 1, the death of Elaine Herzberg, brought about by an autonomous vehicle being tested by Uber, represents the complexity of issues likely to arise when an accident involves an autonomous machine or system. Recall the US National Transportation Safety Board's preliminary report on the incident. It concluded tentatively that at the time of the collision, the sensors and other hardware in the car appeared to be operating. The vehicle, manufactured by Volvo Cars, had its own anticollision system; however, as already related, the car had been modified so that the anticollision features would be turned off when the car was being operated by the computer. The NTSB reported that according to data recorded by the self-driving system itself, the system first detected Herzberg about six seconds before impact:

> As the vehicle and pedestrian paths converged, the self-driving system software classified the pedestrian as an unknown object, as a vehicle, and then as a bicycle with varying expectations of future travel path. At 1.3 seconds before impact, the self-driving system determined that a braking maneuver was necessary to mitigate

a collision[.] … [E]mergency braking maneuvers are not enabled while the vehicle is under computer control, to reduce the potential for erratic vehicle behavior. The vehicle operator is relied on to intervene and take action. The system is not designed to alert the operator.[2]

According to news reports, that the software did not recognize the bicycle as such immediately was due to an intentional decision to make the software detect fewer false positives in order to make the overall ride smoother. A vehicle that is programmed to be overly cautious would be too jerky in its operation. Recall finally that the Tempe police department accident report suggests that the human operator was watching streaming video on her smartphone at the time of the accident.

As of this writing, the legal implications of Herzberg's death are still being worked out and a full account of the facts has not yet been established. (Criminal charges are not being brought against Uber, but charges against the human operator are still possible.) Yet, based on what information is available, the situation is not unlike the one discussed in Chapter 1 when the courts in Georgia were confronted with the legal implications of automobiles as they were first introduced to the streets of Atlanta. The Herzberg incident occurred in the early days of autonomous vehicles, when, particularly in the testing stage, human operators can still take control of the wheel. As expected, the existing laws of negligence and product liability are being applied here, with criminal liability perhaps being considered as well. There is a strong argument that the human operator was negligent, if indeed it was the case that she was watching streaming video on her smartphone at the time of the accident, while the vehicle was in autonomous mode. Was it also negligent for those involved in the testing program to disable the vehicle's collision avoidance features while the vehicle was in autonomous mode or to adjust the obstacle recognition system to be less sensitive to objects to prevent the SUV from overreacting to too many false positives?

Negligence and Product Liability

The generic prima facie case for any legal liability under tort, contract, or property requires a showing that "(1) The defendant owed the plaintiff some legal duty; (2) The defendant breached that duty; (3) The breach caused harm to the plaintiff; and (4) The plaintiff is entitled to a remedy requiring the defendant

---

[2]   U.S. Nat'l Transp. Safety Bd., Preliminary Report: Highway, HWY18MH010 (2018), at 2.

to compensate the plaintiff for the harm."[3] Under negligence, everyone has a duty to avoid injuring others and is responsible for foreseeable harms caused by a breach of that duty. Liability under negligence is unavailable if any of the elements for recovery is not met: a duty of care, breach of that duty, and a causal link between the breach and the injury to the victim. People who do breach the duty of care can therefore be relieved of that responsibility if there is a break in the causal chain or if the victim contributed to the injury or assumed the risk. It is not surprising, then, that early attention is being paid to whether Herzberg was in a crosswalk or whether the human operator was indeed watching streaming video just before the accident. The answers to those questions will bear on any negligence that might exist because of the decision—again, if proven—on the part of the testers to override the vehicle's automatic braking system and to lower the self-driving system's sensitivity to obstacles in the road.

Irrespective of the final outcome of any legal proceedings that will arise from the incident, the law of negligence seems sufficient to respond to the events in Arizona. In all likelihood it will lead to outcomes that are consistent with our expectations regarding how tort law involving automobile accidents functions. However, as Gary Marchant and Rachel Lindor, among many others, point out, driver error—the major cause of vehicle accidents—will be largely factored out when autonomous vehicles are fully developed and perfected. As that happens, liability will focus more and more on the manufacturer and those who designed the vehicle, or on those responsible for the infrastructure needed for autonomous vehicles.[4] Of course, it is standard practice in virtually all automotive cases to consider whether possible defects in design and manufacture, or a failure to warn, contributed to the harm. The NTSB's primary mission is public safety, not dispute resolution, but in the Herzberg incident it is relevant that its preliminary report indicates that at the time of the accident, all of the system's sensors appear to have been operating normally, and that the vehicle's automatic braking system, which had been installed by the manufacturer, had been disabled during autonomous mode. Among other things, it confirms that we use well-accepted procedures, concepts, and casts of

---

[3] Sidney W. DeLong, AN INTRODUCTION TO CONTRACTS: THE LAW OF TRANSACTIONS 17 (2017).

[4] Gary E. Marchant and Rachel A. Lindor, *The Coming Collision between Autonomous Vehicles and the Liability System*, 52 SANTA CLARA L. REV. 1321, 1327 (2012). For a recent discussion of the impact this will have on the automobile insurance industry, *see* Leslie Scism, *Driverless Cars Threaten to Crash Insurers' Earnings*, WALL ST. J., July 26, 2016, www.wsj.com/articles/driverless-cars-threaten-to-crash -insurers-earnings-1469542958.

characters to make sense of the incident. It is also an indication of the kind of inquiry that will occur when a human operator is no longer present in the car.

As is well known by those in the field, product liability law falls into the categories of design and manufacturing defects and the failure to provide adequate warning of any foreseeable harms. In the United States there are in general two tests for design defect. The first is the consumer expectations test: "The article sold must be dangerous to an extent beyond that which would be contemplated by the ordinary consumer who purchases it, with the ordinary knowledge to the community as to its characteristics."[5] Under a cost-benefit approach articulated by the Third Restatement of Torts, a design is defective "when the foreseeable risks of harm posed by the product could have been reduced or avoided by the adoption of a reasonable alternative design ... and the omission of the alternative design renders the product not reasonably safe."[6]

There is a debate among scholars and policymakers as to whether existing product liability law will adequately address harms caused by autonomous vehicles. Some, such as Andrea Bertolini, argue it will.[7] For example, with regard to the cost-benefit approach to defect, that the technology involved is sophisticated does not render the test itself unintelligible in her view. In a recent article, Mark Geistfeld examines how a combination of existing state tort law and federal regulation can be used to address a number of scenarios involving autonomous vehicles.[8] Others, however, are less confident that current law will be sufficient. Jeffrey Gurney is concerned about the fit of product liability law in general: in his view such law is ill equipped to handle the kinds of cases to which negligence law is adapted.[9] For this reason, he advocates retaining existing negligence law, but putting the manufacturer in

---

[5] RESTATEMENT (SECOND) OF TORTS § 402A cmt. i (AM. LAW INST. 1965).

[6] RESTATEMENT (THIRD) OF TORTS: PROD. LIAB. § 2(b) (AM. LAW INST. 1998). For a recent discussion of the development of strict product liability and alternative histor- ies of the doctrine, *see* Kyle Graham, *Strict Products Liability at 50: Four Histories*, 98 MARQUETTE L. REV. 555 (2014).

[7] Andrea Bertolini, *Robots as Products: The Case for Realistic Analysis of Robotic Applications and Liability Rules*, 5 LAW INNOVATION & TECH. 214, 222–3 (2007).

[8] Mark A. Geistfeld, *A Roadmap for Autonomous Vehicles: State Tort Liability, Automobile Insurance, and Federal Safety Regulation*, 105 CAL. L. REV. 1611 (2017). *See also* James M. Anderson et al., RAND CORP., AUTONOMOUS VEHICLE TECHNOLOGY: A GUIDE FOR POLICYMAKERS 118–27 (2014) (applying existing product liability rules to autonomous vehicles); David C. Vladek, *Machines without Principals: Liability Rules and Artificial Intelligence*, 89 WASH. L. REV. 117, 132–40 (AM. LAW INST. 2014) (same); U.S. Chamber Institute for Legal Reform, Torts of the Future II: Addressing the Liability and Regulatory Implications of Emerging Technologies, Apr. 2018 (same).

[9] Jeffrey K. Gurney, *Imputing Driverhood: Applying a Reasonable Driver Standard to Accidents Caused by Autonomous Vehicles, in* ROBOT ETHICS 2.0: FROM

the place of the human driver.[10] He argues in this regard that shifting liability to car manufacturers is plausible because human drivers will have less and less control over the vehicle: "When an autonomous vehicle manufacturer's marketing campaign indicates that users no longer have to pay attention to the road, that manufacturer can hardly complain when it is ultimately liable for the accidents caused by its vehicles."[11] One might respond that as human beings cede more control over devices such as automobiles, negligence on the part of the driver will become less and less important, taking with it a large part of what constitutes contemporary negligence law. At the same time, Gurney's point is well taken with regard to doctrines such as contributory negligence and assumption of risk, particularly with respect to the victims of harms caused by autonomous machines. The irony, however, is that those doctrines will be used defensively to shield otherwise liable parties from responsibility under tort.

Asaro agrees many of the legal issues raised by such machines will be covered by product liability rules,[12] but, unlike Bertolini, fears it will be hard to tell whether a manufacturer has taken proper care in the design of the machine.[13] Samir Chopra and Laurence White are even less optimistic, particularly with regard to autonomous systems that are primarily software driven. In their view, catastrophic damage caused by systems embedded in a tangible medium is most likely to lead to recovery under standard product liability rules.[14] Otherwise, they agree with Asaro that it will be hard for a plaintiff to meet the burden of showing that an artificial agent was defective, in part because it will be hard to show that there was a reasonable alternative design.[15] Further, since some machines and systems must be configured by the user, there will be arguments that the user has broken the chain of causation that would lead to liability of the manufacturer or designer.[16]

AUTONOMOUS CARS TO ARTIFICIAL INTELLIGENCE 51, 55 (Patrick Lin, Ryan Jenkins, and Keith Abney eds., 2017) [hereinafter ROBOT ETHICS 2.0].

[10]   *Id.*, at 55–6.

[11]   *Id.*, at 53.

[12]   Peter M. Asaro, *A Body to Kick, but Still No Soul to Damn: Legal Perspectives on Robotics, in* ROBOT ETHICS: THE ETHICAL AND SOCIAL IMPLICATIONS OF ROBOTICS 169, 170 (Patrick Lin et al. eds., 2012) [hereinafter *Body to Kick*].

[13]   *Id.*, at 171.

[14]   Chopra and White, *supra* note 1, at 144.

[15]   *Id.*

[16]   *Id.*, at 137, 144. On the other hand, Marchant and Lindor worry that under current law, manufacturers will be deterred from designing such cars and thus call for legislative protection or federal preemption to allow their development. *See* Marchant and Lindor, *supra* note 4, at 1330–35, 1337–9. In the area of medical robots, Edoardo Datteri suggests that existing legal and ethical frameworks will be able to respond adequately for retrospective harms. Edoardo Datteri, *Predicting the Long-Term Effects of*

Such problems will be exacerbated as machines and systems become more sophisticated. On this subject, Curtis Karnow argues traditional tort theories will not be able to address harms caused by truly autonomous machines.[17] For him, true autonomy involves "self-learning ... programs that generate their own heuristic."[18] That kind of autonomy weakens existing tort law because in his view, negligence and product liability law (as well as strict liability, discussed below) are predicated on foreseeability. In the law, foreseeability "refers to the sort of future events that we think it is reasonable to have people guard against."[19] The justification for foreseeability construed in this way has moral grounds. "The law is prophylactic," Karnow writes. "It is moral for this reason (among other things): it punishes only transgressions that (it presumes) people are actually capable of avoiding."[20] Karnow's point is cogent. In tort law and in contract law as well, a person is liable only for damage that is reasonably foreseeable as a consequence of his or her breach of duty. A person might reasonably be expected to take due care in light of things that he or she can foresee—it makes no sense, and might well be impossible, to take precautions for something that is beyond one's contemplation. This idea is also linked to personal culpability, which legal responsibility and its consequences almost always require. (Such culpability will be discussed in Chapter 4.) A person who understands that his or her action could result in a particular harm to someone but who acts anyway can be said to be culpable to some extent, even though he or she might not have intended that result.

Even putting aside for the moment the problem of foreseeability, Karnow assumes plausibly that manufacturers and designers have strong incentives to design machines that either meet consumer expectations or represent a reasonable weighing of costs and benefits. "[I]t would be entirely illogical to apply manufacturing defect liability to autonomous robots that, as they come off the assembly line ... are all exactly the same and ... conform to design—at least they are when delivered into the hands of the consumer."[21] Once such machines

---

Human-Robot Interaction: A Reflection on Responsibility in Medical Robotics, 19 Sci. Eng. Ethics 139 (2013).

[17] Curtis E.A. Karnow, *The Application of Traditional Tort Theory to Embodied Machine Intelligence*, in Robot Law 51 (Ryan Calo, A. Michael Froomkin, and Ian Kerr eds., 2016).

[18] *Id.*, at 55.

[19] *Id.*, at 72.

[20] *Id.*

[21] *Id.*, at 69. With regard to computer software, Lewis Bass and Thomas Redick argue that software designers and developers might already be subject to liability for negligence. For them, "negligent software *design* generally encompasses failures related to software design approach and software logic choices which prove harmful to the user during intended and foreseeable system uses. A programmer must anticipate

leave the factory, under current law the manufacturer is not responsible for any changes that are made to the products thereafter. This problem is compounded exponentially once machines are truly autonomous because in the end, their behavior will be unpredictable. Karnow argues that "[w]ith autonomous robots that are complex machines, ever more complex as they interact seamless[ly], porously, with the larger environment, linear causation gives way to complex, nonlinear interactions."[22] Here, Karnow appears to be using concepts from complexity theory, a topic I set out in more detail in Chapter 4. Under that theory the complex interactions of agents can give rise to emergent phenomena that cannot be predicted. If this is true, then by definition the requirement of foreseeability implicit in tort doctrines cannot be satisfied, because fully autonomous robots engaged in complex interactions with themselves and with their environments could have causal effects that are impossible to foresee, as the law understands that term. The theory has even broader implications for common understandings of responsibility that will be discussed later.

With regard to product liability and failure to warn, Karnow feels those doctrines will not have much traction against machines that match his criteria for autonomy, because for him these doctrines are rooted in foreseeability. The failure to warn fails because the doctrine depends on the manufacturer or seller's ability to anticipate "the harm that the instructions would have avoided."[23] The same holds for reasonable alternative design. To repeat the standard established by the Third Restatement, a design is defective "when the foreseeable risks of harm posed by the product could have been reduced or avoided by the adoption of a reasonable alternative design ... and the omission of the alternative design renders the product not reasonably safe." As will be discussed in Chapter 4, complexity theory suggests that prediction is possible only in the short term. Thus a manufacturer would be unable to determine whether there was a reasonable alternative design.[24]

It should go without saying that for Karnow, the more general doctrine of negligence will fail for the same reasons that will cause product liability and failure to warn to fall short. In his view, as long as autonomous machines lack the ability to form their own heuristics about their environments, an argument can be made that they remain "tethered" to human beings who employ them,

---

that some users may subject the software-controlled equipment to unanticipated uses or environments. Negligent software *development,* on the other hand, generally involves an error in the coding process."
Lewis Bass and Thomas Parker Redick, Products Liability: Design and Manufacturing Defects § 2:18 (2nd (2017–2018) edn.).

[22] *Karnow, supra* note 17, at 73.
[23] *Id.,* at 69.
[24] *Id.,* at 71.

and thus in theory those human beings should be able to have some sense of the harms those machines could cause. That changes once machines are able to make decisions on their own.[25]

Strict Liability

In the Georgia automobile case discussed in Chapter 1, the plaintiff argued that even though someone else had been driving, the owners of the car should be held responsible for the death on a theory of strict liability. Persons can be held liable without regard to negligence if they engage in extraordinarily hazardous activities. The automobile, argued the plaintiffs, posed an inherent risk to others because of its speed and power. Recall that the Georgia appeals court rejected that argument; it was the driver, not the automobile itself, who was a danger. What happens, though, if a machine is both driver and vehicle?

To the extent that ordinary negligence and product liability fall short in responding to damage caused by sophisticated autonomous machines, some scholars and policymakers propose strict liability be used to hold responsible manufacturers, computer programmers, and engineers involved in their design and manufacture.[26] In its favor, strict liability avoids some of the conceptual issues surrounding negligence and product liability as applied to autonomous machines. It is unnecessary, for example, to ask whether designers engaged in a cost-benefit analysis in selecting a particular design; under strict liability the designer would be responsible for harms by fiat. At the same time, as is true with all legal doctrines, strict liability has its limitations.

One issue as applied to autonomous machines and systems is that as currently formulated, the common law of strict liability is associated with hazardous activities, such as blasting for construction purposes, or possessions, such as certain breeds of dogs. Karnow's argument is apt in this regard: it may be that early versions of robots and the like will cause unexpected harms, but in virtually all instances one of the primary justifications for robots is that they are expected to perform tasks more efficiently than human beings, and more

---

[25] On this subject, Sabine Gless, Emily Silverman, and Thomas Wiegen argue that under current German and U.S. law, *operators* of self-driving cars are subject to liability for negligent injury or homicide in part because they can foresee that such cars can malfunction. However, "foreseeing and controlling the conduct of self-teaching robots may become so difficult for human operators that we may need to raise the requirements for criminal negligence liability, lest the risk of punishment inhibit the further development and use of robots." Sabine Gless, Emily Silverman, and Thomas Wiegen, *If Robots Cause Harm, Who Is to Blame: Self-Driving Cars and Criminal Liability*, 19 New Crim. L. Rev. 412, 438 (2016).

[26] Vladek, *supra* note 8, at 146.

safely in the case of autonomous vehicles. They will be designed that way and, short of defects in manufacturing (which manufacturing defect law is able to resolve), it is hard to argue such machines are inherently dangerous. A later section of this chapter will consider the development of a superintelligence contemplated by Bostrom, which, if theoretically and technologically achievable, could pose an existential threat to humankind. Once we reach that level of threat, however, it is hard to imagine any form of responsibility would be adequate to address it, let alone strict liability.

Short of a superintelligence, then, in the main, strict liability in the traditional sense as addressing extreme hazards would not apply to well-designed machines. In this regard, Karnow argues that even strict liability is based on foreseeability. This is because whether something constitutes an unreasonable danger requires one to predict how much danger there might be. A person can foresee that explosives are hard to control and are hazardous. To repeat Karnow's view, one cannot predict what a truly autonomous machine, as he understands that term, can do because nonlinear phenomena will emerge from the complex interactions between the machines and their environments. Strict liability would have to be stretched to create liability beyond predictability to reach people in other ways, such as status. I will examine strict liability and these issues in more detail in Chapter 5.

Intrusions on Privacy

The harms discussed so far involve fairly concrete forms of injury or damage to people or property caused by autonomous machines or systems. Autonomous devices and systems in the home also could present risks to safety and property, but here the focus is on intangible but nevertheless significant harms. The danger to privacy is the main concern and comes from two sources: intelligent devices for daily use and large data sets comprising personal information. As to devices, Margo Kaminski and her coauthors identify the potential risks posed by those used in the home.[27] These include data privacy, boundary management, and social relations. Privacy becomes an issue because robots and other devices in the home will be able to observe and store private information such as medical prescriptions, bank account numbers, and so on.[28] This will allow the collection of large amounts of information about households' daily routines, which can be used to make predictions and inferences about those

---

[27] Margot E. Kaminski et al., *Averting Robot Eyes*, 76 MARYLAND L. REV. 983 (2017).

[28] *Id.*, at 994.

who live there.[29] Boundary management problems will arise because people might underestimate how much robots will be able to detect and infer from what they observe and might not appreciate their enhanced power. Thermal imaging and enhanced listening devices will render useless commonsense ways people seek privacy, such as closing doors, moving to other parts of the house, and so on.[30] Other issues with social boundaries may emerge because some humans will develop relationships with robots that are designed to display social intelligence. Robots currently do not yet recognize the full range of social norms and cues, such as not entering bedrooms or opening closed doors and so on, which could constrain how someone behaves in her own home. Finally, to improve function, home robots will be linked to third parties, who, because they are "observing" the home from afar, are less susceptible to the same social cues that would make them respect a person's privacy were they physically present in the home.[31]

It is questionable whether we would welcome a sophisticated device into our lives that has the power to observe us in our most private moments, record those moments for all time, and in certain aspects know us better than we know ourselves. Yet, our concerns might not be so great but for the fact that all of that information can be shared. The collection of personal data and its linkage to third parties, and the storage of that information in large data bases, is thus the second major threat to privacy. The nongovernmental organizations Privacy International and Article 19 catalog those risks:

> AI-driven consumer products and autonomous systems are frequently equipped with sensors that generate and collect vast amounts of data without the knowledge or consent of those in its proximity;
> AI methods are being used to identify people who wish to remain anonymous;
> AI methods are being used to infer and generate sensitive information about people from their non-sensitive data;
> AI methods are being used to profile people based upon population-scale data; and
> AI methods are being used to make consequential decisions using this data some of which profoundly affect people's lives.[32]

Their list identifies ways in which artificial intelligence is already being used, in ways that go beyond one's sense of integrity in the home to one's participa-

---

[29]   *Id.*, at 994–5.

[30]   *Id.*, at 996.

[31]   *Id.*, at 997–8.

[32]   Privacy International & Article 19, Privacy and Freedom of Expression in the Age of Artificial Intelligence, April 2018, at 17 (bullet points omitted), https://privacyinternational.org/sites/default/files/2018-04/Privacy%20and %20Freedom%20of%20Expression%20%20In%20the%20Age%20of%20Artificial %20Intelligence.pdf.

tion in broader society, where intersecting "statuses" attached to one's gender, race, sexual orientation, income, physical and mental health, religion, age, marital status, and the like help determine the prospects of one's success in the world. Artificial intelligence can be used to inform other people where an individual falls within one or more of those categories.

Those who collect that data and use it are held responsible for those uses, primarily through the right to privacy. In the European context, the General Data Protection Regulation (GDPR), which came into effect in May 2018, applies to the collection and use of data about natural persons. The regulation is based on six principles: personal information must be processed "lawfully, fairly, and transparently in relation to the data subject"; collected for "specified, explicit and legitimate purposes"; limited to what is necessary to achieve the purpose of processing; be accurate; when in a form that can identify a data subject; be stored in that way for no longer than is necessary; and be processed in a way that maintains the security of personal data. Persons or firms who control such data are responsible for complying with those principles.[33]

In the United States, privacy law as it relates to personal information is far less robust. In Kaminski and her coauthors' judgment, US privacy law is not equipped to address the kinds of privacy issues which intelligent devices pose, including the dissemination and use of personal information to third parties. There is no federal US counterpart to the GDPR (as of this writing a privacy protection regime has just been enacted in California); what data protection law exists is industry specific. The Health Insurance Portability and Accountability Act, which protects medical information, is perhaps the best example of this kind of law; the Family Educational Rights and Privacy Act, which protects information about a person's academic performance, is another. According to Kaminski and coauthors, administrative law also is involved because the Federal Trade Commission has become a de facto privacy regulator.[34] Each of these regimes hinges on a relationship between an individual and those who are obligated to protect information, either as a patient health care provider, student teacher, or consumer manufacturer or supplier. Those not in such relationships are not protected. The authors note that state attorneys general have also acted to protect privacy, but they have tended to focus also on consumer relationships. There is also state tort law on such matters as intrusion upon seclusion and public disclosure of private facts. However, such torts depend on whether a person has a privacy interest or is in complete seclusion.

---

[33]   Parliament & Council Regulation, 2016/679, art. 5, 2016 O.J (L266) (EU), on the Protection of Natural Persons with regard to the Processing of Personal Data and on the Free Movement of such Data, and Repealing Directive 95/46/EC (General Data Protection Regulation).

[34]   Kaminski et al., *supra* note 27, at 1000.

The issue when autonomous technologies are involved, particularly home devices, is whether a person has such an interest or is in seclusion when he or she voluntarily allows a robot in the home.[35] Fourth Amendment jurisprudence is evolving in this area but struggles with the third party doctrine, that information shared with third parties does not require a warrant.[36] Finally, the authors argue, the law tends to focus on "one-time notice and consent."[37] Thus, users may not have an opportunity to retract consent once given.

Irrespective of the regime, as discussed earlier, it is the controller of the data (to use the GDPR's term) that is the focus for responsibility. Such controllers are normally business firms composed of people who in turn make business decisions on how personal data will be used. Thus far, human beings are the final deciders. Foreseeable advances in technology raise the question whether, in the future, the increasing use of artificial intelligence to maintain databases and formulate and perform queries in order to recognize patterns in the data will make it harder to say that people have adequate control over collecting and processing personal data. For example, in a 2013 paper, Matthew Malensek, Sangmi Pallickara, and Shrideep Pallickara proposed an algorithm for autonomously optimizing the many queries that are made over large data sets.[38] Algorithms such as that one are likely to be developed, thus making the process of data analysis more autonomous. More will be said about strict liability in Chapter 7, but unless privacy protection regimes like the GDPR and HIPAA can be turned into strict liability regimes, they are premised on data collection and processing being subject to human control.

AUTONOMOUS CONTRACTING AND ELECTRONIC AGENTS

Automation has been taking place since long before the advent of the computer, but autonomous machines and systems have only been made possible because of advances in computational power, as well as the development of more sophisticated sensors and activators. It is not surprising, then, that nascent forms of autonomous contracting and the literature addressing it appear somewhat earlier, since the contracting process does not require advanced hardware. In addition to contract formation, the financial services

---

[35] *Id.*

[36] *Id.*, at 1000–1001.

[37] *Id.*, at 1001.

[38] Matthew Malensek, Sangmi Pallickara, and Shrideep Pallickara, Autonomously Improving Query Evaluations over Multdimensional Data in Distributed Hash Tables, Aug. 2013, www.cs.colostate.edu/~malensek/publications/malensek2013autonomously .pdf.

industry in particular has begun to use computers to assess compliance with
and to perform contractual obligations.

Harry Surden describes a progression in autonomous contracting in which,
first, written contracts were simply stored on computers in plain language
form.[39] Computers were used for easy access to plain language contracts, and
even now technology is not yet at the point where it can process such language.
The next stage for particular classes of contracts, such as financial contracts,
was to memorialize certain contractual terms and conditions in the form of
highly structured data that can be read and "understood" by computers, rather
than in plain language. This reduces transaction costs by permitting computers
to verify, accurately and cheaply, when certain contractual conditions have
been met, and then perform in turn. Contracts made via the Electric Data
Interchange have been in place since the 1970s. These, however, were subject
to umbrella data exchange agreements between private parties that directed
how electronic contracts between the two would be formed.[40] Surden observes
that at present it is not possible to structure more sophisticated contracts in
this way; nevertheless, contracts whose terms can be memorialized in machine
readable form are significant in terms of their volume.[41] Researchers are now
exploring ways in which computer-based systems can assist or replace humans
in the contracting process, at least with respect to certain kinds of contracts.
These activities include autonomous computer agents that assist in forming
supply chains by locating and linking potential suppliers and then forming the
contractual linkages that lead to assembly and on to distribution.[42]

The legal question raised by autonomous contracting is whether transactions
between autonomous systems and humans or other systems can create contractual obligations, and who is responsible if those obligations are breached.
Before the advent of computer contracting, it was a given that only people
and legal entities for whom people acted on their behalf could be parties to
contracts. The classic form of contract formation via offer and acceptance and
consideration presumes a world in which humans acting in their individual
capacity or as agents for entities bargain with each other and eventually reach
agreement. But even prior to computers, the requirements that stemmed from
the traditional view of bargaining were being relaxed to take into account

---

[39]   Harry Surden, *Computable Contracts*, 46 U.C. Davis L. Rev. 629 (2012).

[40]   Adrian McCullagh, The Validity and Limitations of Electronic Agents in
Contract Formation: A Brief Discussion under the Electronic Transactions Act in
Australia (undated), at 1, https://law.uq.edu.au/files/18238/A-McCullagh_The-Validity
-and-Limitations-of-Software-Agents-in-Contract-Formation.pdf.

[41]   Surden, *supra* note 39, at 683–5.

[42]   Farhad Ameri and Chrisitan McArthur, *A Multi-Agent System for Autonomous
Supply Chain Configuration*, 66 Int'l J. Adv. Mfg. Tech. 1097 (2013).

actual business behavior. For example, under Uniform Commercial Code §
2-204(a), "[a] contract for the sale of goods may be made in any manner sufficient to show agreement, including conduct by both parties which recognizes
the existence of such a contract." Under this approach the classic bargain
followed by a handshake was no longer necessary; assent to contractual obligation could be evidenced in many ways.

Despite the relaxation in the rules of formation, there nevertheless must
be some indication of assent to be bound to the contract, because contractual
duties are understood to be voluntarily assumed. This becomes the issue for
autonomous contracting: suppose a contract is formed between two computer
programs, both of which are sophisticated enough not only to enter into a contract, but also to effectuate most of the performance. Perhaps this is a contract
for the purchase and sale of foreign exchange, with payment and delivery to
be made via electronic transfer on a specific date. What if, just before the date
of performance, there is a hardware malfunction in one of the computers so
that payment is made, but no delivery? Who is responsible in such a situation?

The standard answer is to use concepts from agency law to find that there
is a contract and that some human or legal entity is contractually bound. The
computers are electronic agents, instructed by humans or business entities to
contract on their behalf. Under standard agency law, a principal is bound by
the contracts made by her agent. Chopra and White use shopping websites as
an example. The seller as principal "cannot be said to have a preexisting 'intention' in respect of a particular contract that is 'communicated' to the user."[43]
Instead, "in the case of a human principal, the principal has knowledge only of
the rules the artificial agent applies."[44] Chopra and White suggest that apparent
authority can be used to determine whether a principal is liable for contracts
that have been entered into by the autonomous system.[45] Apparent authority is
"the power held by an agent or other actor to affect a principal's legal relations
with third parties when a third party reasonably believes the actor has authority
to act on behalf of the principal and that belief is traceable to the principal's
manifestation."[46] The authors argue that apparent authority correctly allocates
costs among the operator, agent, and user.[47] In the case of the website and
web-based checkout, the principal holds out the website as the vehicle through
which the user is able to contract. These manifestations give the purchaser
reason to believe that using the checkout procedures will bind the seller. The
seller as principal would be bound by the actions of the electronic agent even

[43]   Chopra and White, *supra* note 1, at 36.
[44]   *Id.*
[45]   *Id.*, at 44.
[46]   RESTATEMENT (THIRD) OF AGENCY § 2.03 (AM. LAW INST., 2006).
[47]   Chopra and White, *supra* note 1, at 47–8.

though it is unaware of the precise details of the particular contract involved. At the same time, costs would shift to the user if it is unreasonable for the user to believe such power exists, for example, when a computer error causes the program to offer a product at an unrealistically low price.[48]

The concept of the electronic agent presents an opportunity to consider more generally how agency might apply to autonomous systems and machines. A number of commentators have joined Chopra and White in proposing agency law as a way to determine when humans are responsible for torts "committed" by robots in addition to contracts, since principals are liable for the torts committed by agents while acting within the scope of agency. This rule of agency appears to jibe well with our understandings of individual culpability. As discussed in Chapter 1, current law fits best when the "actions" of machines can be closely associated with humans, either because the machine is so unsophisticated that it can be understood as merely a tool or, in the case of sophisticated machines, because it is understood as acting on behalf of a human principal. It is unproblematic to say "he damaged his neighbor's bushes with the pruning shears," thus attributing responsibility for the damage to the person who wielded the tool.

For more sophisticated technologies, agency law seems an appropriate fit because autonomous machines and systems are being developed for the use of human beings. If a completely autonomous machine is designed for and used or directed by humans to achieve a particular end, it seems relatively straightforward to use "agential" concepts to distribute liability for harms caused by that machine to the human or collection of humans who used it. A self-driving car is not dissimilar to a human chauffeur. If the autonomous vehicle causes harm while it is transporting its owner, as principal the owner of the car would be responsible since the car would have caused the damage while within the scope of its agency.[49] To the extent that a frolic and detour would relieve an owner/passenger from liability, it would be possible to turn again to the manufacturer as designing a car capable of acting outside of the scope of its agency authority. The analysis of the shopping website discussed above and the robot chauffeur indicates that agency law seems to be a valid way to determine when a human is responsible for acts of an autonomous system.

At the same time, as Chopra and White indicate, certain changes would need to be made to existing agency law for it to have wider application. As an initial matter, it is unclear whether a computer program can be an agent

---

[48]   *Id.*

[49]   Chopra and White take this approach, although this is supplemented by arguing that autonomous machines should be given some form of legal agency. *See id.*, at 127–35.

under common law.[50] For contracts, the question has been largely answered in the affirmative or implied through legislation such the Uniform Electronic Transactions Act.[51] However, under other articulations of agency law, such as the Third Restatement of Agency, there is a strong argument that computer programs do not qualify. Under the Restatement, an agent is a "person." In turn, a person is defined as "(a) an individual; (b) an organization or association that has legal capacity to possess rights and incur obligations; (c) a government, political subdivision, or instrumentality or entity created by a government; or (d) any other entity that has legal capacity to possess rights and incur obligations."[52] Thus, if agency law is applied to autonomous machines or systems, the question arises as to whether those machines or systems should be given legal capacity to possess rights and incur obligations as persons.

Whether autonomous machines should be given legal capacity is a broader question that will be explored in Chapter 9. To return to contracts, although the question of the enforceability of contracts via electronic agents has largely been settled, Anthony Belia questions whether it is appropriate to frame electronic agents as a specific application of general agency law.[53] He argues that agency principles qua agency do not apply to the relationship between a human and a software program. Belia points out that actual authority granted by a principal to an agent requires the agent's consent to enter into the relationship. This consent is accompanied by a set of fiduciary duties the agent owes

---

[50] *Id.*, at 50.

[51] The Uniform Electronic Transactions Act, adopted in 47 states, defines an electronic agent as "a computer program or an electronic or other automated means used independently to initiate an action or respond to electronic records or performances in whole and in part, without review or action by an individual." UNIF. ELEC. TRANSACTIONS. ACT § 2(6) (UNIF. LAW COMM'N 1999). Section 14 provides that "A contract may be formed by the interaction of electronic agents of the parties, even if no individual was aware of or reviewed the electronic agent's actions or the resulting terms and agreements." *Id.*, § 14(a). The same is true with contracts entered into by individuals who transact with an electronic agent. *Id. See, e.g., Traynum v. Scavens*, 416 S.C. 197, 207 (2016) (finding that an insurance company's website acted as an electronic agent such that an insurance contract formed online was binding on the policyholder). The act contemplates that an autonomous computer could qualify as an electronic agent. *Id.*, § 2(6).
The UNCITRAL Model Law on Electronic Commerce uses the concept of a data message as opposed to an electronic agent. It is defined as "information generated, sent, received or stored by electronic, optical or similar means." UNCITRAL MODEL LAW ON ELECTRONIC COMMERCE (UNCITRAL 1996), art. 2(a). Article 11 provides that a contract formed via a data message "shall not be denied validity or enforceability on the sole ground that a data message was used for that purpose." *Id.*, art. 11(1).

[52] RESTATEMENT (THIRD) OF AGENCY §§ 1.01, 1.04(5) (AM. LAW INST., 2006).

[53] Anthony J. Belia, *Contracting with Electronic Agents*, 50 EMORY L. J. 1047 (2001).

to the principal. A computer program cannot give such assent, nor does it owe such duties. For Belia, it is of course possible to hold the human responsible for anything the computer program does, but this would no longer be agency law, at least under the framework of actual authority. In his view it is also questionable to apply apparent authority to the "actions" of the computer program because apparent authority presupposes underlying actual authority.[54] Agency authority, either actual or apparent, is not needed to hold humans responsible for computer contracting. "[E]lectronic agents present simply another mode by which natural persons can conduct their business."[55]

Belia's broader point is that certain aspects of agency law are lost when applied to autonomous systems. These include protections to principals and to third parties. As discussed, Belia observes that agents owe principals duties of loyalty, obedience, and full disclosure for which the agents are liable if breached. Further, although an agent is always liable for torts she commits, a principal is not if the torts were committed outside of the scope of agency; the case is similar for torts committed by independent contractors as opposed to employees. The doctrine balances the rights of an injured third party with those of the principal. Since an agent is always liable for its torts, the third party has a source of compensation for damage while the principal is protected from activities that go beyond the scope of agency or that were beyond the principal's control.

The same is true with contract. In May 2018 Google demonstrated Google Duplex, a chat bot that employs computer learning to engage in simple conversations in a limited number of situations. In the demonstration, Google Duplex calls a hair salon to make an appointment. When an employee answers the phone, Google Duplex states in a natural voice that it would like to make an appointment on behalf of a client. Google Duplex and the employee engage in a conversation about available slots and the kind of service the client wants. The employee asks for the name of the client and the interaction ends. There is no indication the employee is aware that she is interacting with a computer system.

Suppose agency law applies. There is a strong argument that Google Duplex has entered into a service contract on behalf of its principal. The principal has been fully disclosed in that Google Duplex stated it was working for a client (and thus as an agent) and eventually identified her when it gave the salon the client's name. If Google was a human agent, it would not be liable for the contract because the principal has been fully disclosed. But what if Google Duplex had not disclosed its principal? An agent is liable for contracts she enters into

---

[54]   *Id.*, at 1062–3.
[55]   *Id.*, at 1067.

for her principal if the agent does not disclose that she is acting for another and identify that person. The doctrine protects third parties since the only person with whom they are negotiating is the agent. Unless the chat bot is given some endowment and some autonomy over that endowment (this possibility is discussed further in Chapters 7 and 9), the effect of autonomous contractors is to remove one level of protection from third parties who enter into contracts with persons or entities that are acting on someone else's behalf.

If agency law does not map well onto the behavior of autonomous machines and systems, then we must fall back to a regime in which the human is always liable for what a robot in her employ does. This, however, might not be appropriate in some contexts. Chapter 1 discussed how largescale securities trading takes place via algorithms. Ugo Pagallo argues that in that situation, treating a robot trader as the tool of human beings, and thus attributing responsibility only to humans, is problematic for three reasons. First, in his view it seems inapt to describe sophisticated robots needed for largescale trading as simply tools. Second, Pagallo argues that just because a human has delegated some authority to a robot, it does not follow necessarily that the human is responsible for the robot's actions (note that this is the same issue addressed in agency law such as frolic and detour and the scope of agency). Third, the "robots as tools" approach does not help in the distribution of responsibility between human beings.[56] Pagallo further argues that humans have a claim not to be financially ruined by the decisions of their robots.[57] It is partly for these reasons that he agrees with scholars such as Chopra and White that agency concepts should govern electronic contract, but probably not when massive losses occur.[58]

THE LAW OF WAR AND AUTONOMOUS WEAPONS

As discussed in Chapter 1, strategists foresee using artificial intelligence in several aspects of military operations, but the applications that have garnered the most attention are those intended to be used in battle—autonomous weapons in particular, and to some extent autonomous advisers designed to assist commanders at higher levels of command. During armed conflict, the law of war requires that those engaged in hostilities distinguish between combatants and civilians and use force proportionally: force only to the extent necessary to respond to armed attack or to achieve a military objective.[59] Current

---

[56] Pagallo, *supra* note 1, at 99.
[57] *Id.*, at 102.
[58] *Id.*, at 99.
[59] For a discussion of the principles of the law of war, including the principles of distinction, proportionality, and military necessity, *see* OFF. OF GEN. COUNSEL, U.S. DEP'T OF DEFENSE, DEPARTMENT OF DEFENSE WAR MANUAL 50–69 (June 2015).

law places the responsibility to comply with that law on the individual soldier, those in command in the field, and their superiors.

As is true with the application of tort, contract, and agency principles, commentators debate whether the current law of war is adequate to address the deployment of autonomous weapons. At present, the weapon itself could not be found liable for breaches of the law of war, so by default joint criminality and command responsibility would be used in cases where autonomous weapons were involved in suspected war crimes. Here I focus on command responsibility. As articulated by the International Committee of the Red Cross:

> Commanders and other superiors are criminally responsible for war crimes committed by their subordinates if they knew, or had reason to know, that the subordinates were about to commit or were committing such crimes and did not take all necessary and reasonable measures in their power to prevent their commission, or if such crimes had been committed, to punish the persons responsible.[60]

Jack Beard argues that it is unclear whether an officer in the field, let alone her superior commanding officer, would have the *mens rea* required to cause her to be liable for a war crime "committed" by an autonomous weapon.[61] Christopher Toscano, however, believes the existing law of command responsibility is adequate to address crimes caused by autonomous weapons.[62] Much would depend on the circumstances. Obviously, someone in command who instructs a machine to commit a war crime would be personally liable for that crime. Further, if a commander knows or should know that an autonomous weapon cannot distinguish between civilians and combatants, there is a strong argument that the commander would be liable if he ordered the weapon to be deployed in an area where there are many civilians. The issue of *mens rea* could arise, however, when a weapons system has a high degree of autonomy. At that point its behavior is unpredictable, so the commander would not know that the weapon is about to commit a war crime, or she would have to become aware of a series of crimes before she herself becomes responsible for them.

---

[60]   International Committee for the Red Cross, Customary IHL Database, Rule 153, https://ihl-databases.icrc.org/customary-ihl/eng/docs/v1_rul_rule153. The database uses material taken from Jean Marie Henckaerts and Louise Doswold-Beck, CUSTOMARY INTERNATIONAL HUMANITARIAN LAW: RULES 1 (reprinted with corrections 2009).

[61]   Jack M. Beard, *Autonomous Weapons and Human Responsibilities*, 45 GEO. J. INT'L L. 617, 651–7 (2015); HUMAN RIGHTS WATCH, LOSING HUMANITY: THE CASE AGAINST KILLER ROBOTS 41–2 (2012), www.hrw.org/report/2012/11/19/losing-humanity/case-against-killer-robots (arguing that it will be difficult to hold military commanders liable for war crimes committed by robots).

[62]   Christopher P. Toscano, *"Friend of Humans": An Argument for Developing Autonomous Weapon Systems*, 8 J. NAT'L' SEC. L. & POL'Y 189, 235–7 (2015).

If there were good reasons why the commander would not know about such crimes, then there would be a gap in responsibility, because the autonomous weapon itself would be largely immune. Because of this potential gap, scholars such as Robert Sparrow argue that autonomous weapons should be banned.[63] At the same time, just as some commentators contend strict liability should be applied to cases involving self-driving cars, some argue that if a superior or commanding officer is not found liable, the state itself could be found responsible under the international law of state responsibility. The weapon's actions would be attributed to the state, since it was deployed to serve a state function.[64]

This brief review of tort, contract, and the law of war as applied to autonomous machines and systems leads to several preliminary conclusions. How well current law is poised to address harms caused by autonomous machines and systems falls along a range that depends in part on the sophistication of machines, the degree of human control over them, and the kind of harm involved. In this regard, Trevor White and Keith Blum set out a rough framework of the ability of law to address harms.[65] They distinguish between three cases. The first is when humans, such as a human user of autonomous devices or a manufacturer, are clearly liable. For them, this kind of case does not pose any new challenges to existing law. In the second case, the robot is partly responsible for the harm. Here, the law will require some change to determine when the robot is liable and how to allocate responsibility between the robot and humans. The third case involves catastrophic harms caused by machines. Under their matrix, liability law becomes less effective the more serious a harm is, to the point of not working at all when a harm is catastrophic. As robots become more sophisticated, their potential liability becomes greater, reaching the level of human liability when they reach human intelligence and even greater liability as they surpass humans.[66] Ugo Pagallo describes a similar range but in terms of the literature in the field: from those who argue autonomous machines will raise no novel issues of legal responsibility, to those who argue there will be new forms of responsibility but humans will remain respon-

---

[63] Robert Sparrow, *Killer Robots*, 24 J. APPLIED PHIL. 62, 70–71 (2007).

[64] *See* Marco Sassoli, *Autonomous Weapons and International Humanitarian Law: Advantages, Open Technical Questions and Legal Issues to Be Clarified*, 90 INT'L L. STUD. 308, 315–16 (2014).

[65] Trevor N. White and Seth D. Blum, *Liability for Present and Future Robotics Technologies*, *in* ROBOT ETHICS 2.0, *supra* note 9, at 66.

[66] *Id.*, at 67.

sible, and finally to those who argue that new forms of legal responsibility will need to rest on the machines themselves.[67]

More can be said about White and Blum's second case, in which an autonomous machine is partly responsible for a harm. As autonomous technologies grow more sophisticated, a point is reached under our common views of explanation and blame at which it becomes at least as plausible to say that the machines and systems themselves are liable for any harms they cause as it is to say that human beings associated with them are. As discussed, for White and Blum it follows that some means must be devised to allocate responsibility between the machines and humans. (Hence resonating with Pagallo's second category of positions taken in the literature: that there will be new forms of responsibility, but humans will remain responsible for harms.) It also motivates Asaro's call for systems of responsibility that account for groups composed of humans and robots. This turn to groups will be explored in more detail in Chapters 3 and 4. But the question is whether we presently have adequate legal means to address situations when autonomous machines can be said to share liability. At this point, we approach the issues of culpability that Karnow identifies for negligence, product liability, and strict liability—as does Beard with regard to command responsibility—and which are implicit in Belia's criticisms of using agency law as an alternative method to sort out the lines of responsibility. Before examining these issues more thoroughly, however, it is appropriate to discuss two other ways to address responsibility for harms: private ordering and legislation.

OTHER FORMS OF GOVERNANCE: FROM PRIVATE ORDERING TO LEGISLATION

Dynamism in Legal Norms

It is helpful at this juncture to provide more context to the development and operation of law as a form of governance. I have found two perspectives on this matter useful in previous work. The first comes from Laurence Boulle as he describes how law operates in economic globalization. So far, this chapter has discussed "hard" forms of law, represented by the doctrines of tort, contract, agency, and the law of war. For Boulle, the "law" of globalization is an emergent phenomena "comprising international treaties, national laws

---

[67] Ugo Pagallo, *What Robots Want: Autonomous Machines, Codes and New Frontiers of Legal Responsibility, in* HUMAN LAW AND COMPUTER LAW: COMPARATIVE PERSPECTIVES, 25 IUS GENTIUM 47, 53 (Mireille Hildebrandt and Jeanne Gaakeer eds., 2013).

and court decisions; sub-national laws and regulations; standards of business groups and industry bodies, and the practices of private corporations."[68] As will be discussed in more detail below, this description of hard and soft forms of law applies equally well to the "law" that now governs or is proposed to govern autonomous technologies.

The second perspective on legal norms as a form of governance comes from Iris Chiu. Chiu describes the regulatory space of the finance industry,[69] but her description is apt for the potential regulation of autonomous technologies. The regulatory landscape she sees is "decentred," that is, "populated by resourceful, competent and powerful industry participants, and on the other hand consisting also of agencies of authority that have a public character."[70] Chiu identifies and assesses the strengths and weaknesses of various forms of governance that range from self-regulation by private actors to "regulator-led governance."[71] Toward one end of the spectrum, for example, is "transactional governance," in which parties set private rules through contract. Chiu believes that private ordering better reflects the preferences of the individual parties, but warns that contractual terms arising from particular transactions often become standardized. That is not wrong per se, but could lead to systemic risk if those standards are suboptimal under some criteria. This might be so because private contracts do not often address systemwide failures and do not absorb externalities.[72] On the other end of Chiu's spectrum is "metaregulation." This is the attempt to reconcile private ordering with public values through regulators. Metaregulation leaves room for parties to order their affairs privately, but ensures the parties are informed by and take into account public values. Chiu argues, however, that those values can be eclipsed easily by the technical demands of a particular system—what she terms "capture by technocracy." This in turn leads to a lack of accountability because it is difficult for nonexpert outsiders to monitor financial activities.[73]

---

[68] Laurence Boulle, THE LAW OF GLOBALIZATION 363 (2009).

[69] Iris H-Y Chiu, *Enhancing Responsibility in Financial Regulation—Critically Examining the Future of Public–Private Governance: Part I*, 4 LAW & FIN. MARKETS REV. 170 (2010) [hereinafter "Chiu part 1"]; Iris H-Y Chiu, *Enhancing Responsibility in Financial Regulation—Critically Examining the Future of Public–Private Governance: Part II*, 4 LAW & FIN. MARKETS REV. 286 (2010).

[70] Chiu part 1, *supra* note 69, at 171.

[71] *Id.*, at 173–81.

[72] *Id.*, at 174.

[73] *Id.*, at 179–80.

Transactional Governance in Autonomous Technology

The respective frameworks provided by Boulle and Chiu provide a helpful way to understand how private and public ordering governance is contemplated for autonomous machines and systems. Take, for example, Chiu's "transactional governance." Chapter 1 discussed how autonomous machines and systems are a combination of machinery and computer software and described how this technology and software is usually designed and manufactured through complex supply chains and processes. Here it is worth observing that the industry already has well-established ways of shielding itself from possible liability.[74] One, of course, is the use of subsidiaries and independent contractors and suppliers to cabin risk.[75] Further, robotics and other technology manufacturers allocate the risk of potential harms that could be caused by their systems via contract. Such protections include warranty limitations or disclaimers for both hardware and software. For example, a contract for one system that includes a combination of equipment and software provides:

> Except as otherwise expressly stated in the agreement: a. the hardware, software, deliverables, services, and maintenance & support are provided to customer as is; and b. [seller] excludes and disclaims all warranties, whether express or implied, regarding the hardware, software, services, deliverables and maintenance & support including, without limitation, any implied warranties of merchantability, fitness for a particular purpose, non-infringement of the intellectual property rights of others,

---

[74] Frances Zollers and colleagues review the history of litigation against software developers for defective software in *No More Soft Landings for Software: Liability for Defects in an Injury that Has Come of Age*, 21 SANTA CLARA HIGH TECH. L.J. (2005). Issues revolve around whether computer software is an intangible, a service, or a good. To the extent that courts consider software a good, litigation centers on the effectiveness of warranties, as well as claims of misrepresentation. *Id.*, at 757–8. *See also* Farhah Abdullah et al., *Strict versus Negligence Software Product Liability*, 2 COMP. & INFO. SCI. 81 (2009) (discussing conceptual issues posed by bringing claims for defective software). Some of these issues were purported to be resolved by the Uniform Computer Information Transactions Act, but only two states, Virginia and Maryland, have adopted it.

[75] This method of avoiding risk is also supported by legal doctrines such as the component parts doctrine, which shields a manufacturer or seller of a component from liability, unless the component itself was defective or the supplier participated in the integration of the component into the finished product, which in turn caused the product to be defective and caused the injury. *Webb v. Special Elec. Co.*, 63 Cal.4th 167, 183 (2016). It is arguable that the doctrine could apply to suppliers of computer programs. A copy of computer software is considered a component for purposes of patent infringement. *Microsoft v. AT&T*, 550 U.S. 437, 451–2 (2007). At the same time, I am not aware of a case in which the component parts doctrine has been used to protect a software designer in a tort action.

and any warranty that may arise by reason of custom, usage of trade, or course of dealing. Customer is responsible for the selection of any hardware, system, and software to achieve their intended results.

Note that under the contract, as between the vendor and the customer, the customer accepts responsibility for the "selection of any hardware, system, and software to achieve their intended results." Accompanying this disclaimer are limitations on liability for any damage caused by the hardware or software. An end-user license agreement associated with this contract contains similar provisions in which the customer accepts the software that is being licensed as is, thus foregoing any warranties for the software. The contract itself also requires the user to acknowledge that the software being licensed is not fault-tolerant and not intended for use in high risk environments, such as in "the operation of nuclear power plant facilities, aircraft navigation, air traffic control, life support machines, weapons systems or any other application where the failure or malfunction of any product can be reasonably expected to result in death, personal injury, severe property damage or environmental harm." This acknowledgment helps shield the company from any responsibility for use of the software in any such environment. Similarly, in another contract, the manufacturer of a robot used for a particular medical treatment provides that the customer is solely responsible for data protection.[76]

Assuming these contracts are representative of industry practice, they indicate that developers of autonomous systems are well aware of the potential risks that their technologies pose, and from their perspective it is rational to place on end users the responsibility for these risks. The justification for doing so, of course, is that the customer or end user knows best about its particular circumstances, circumstances of which the designer, manufacturer, or vendor cannot be aware and cannot anticipate. Since virtually all autonomous machines and systems will be distributed in commercial contexts, we would expect such contracts to be the starting point for allocations of responsibility. To the extent that such contractual disclaimers and limitations are standardized, it is at least a question whether those private norms are suboptimal in

---

[76] Courts have upheld these kinds of limitations on liability. For example, the Utah Supreme Court found that a clause limiting liability was enforceable when a software upgrade overwrote a dentist's existing files. *Blaisdell v. Dentrix Dental Systems, Inc.*, 286 P.2d 616, 621 (Utah 2012). On the other hand, a US district court found that a plaintiff had stated a valid claim of breach of warranty for defective software, despite having agreed to a warranty disclaimer. *Caudill Seed & Warehouse Co.*, 123 F. Supp. 2d 826, 829 (E.D. Pa 2000). In that case, however, the software company had agreed to repair or replace the software, and the court concluded that the warranty disclaimer defeated the essential purpose of what was the customer's sole remedy for breach of warranty. *Id.*

terms of that allocation, particularly if there is inequality in bargaining power between designers and manufacturers and customers. The counterargument to the industry position is that vis-à-vis the customer, the designers and manufacturers are in a better position to know about the capabilities and inherent risks of their products.

It should also be noted that the contractual provisions just discussed cover technology and software that can barely be said to employ artificial intelligence, if at all. One can imagine that software developers will argue they should be shielded even more from liability caused by software that has been designed to learn and to reprogram itself. The rejoinder that a designer or manufacturer should be responsible for a product that is self-evolving returns us to Karnow's concerns. The issues raised under the application of existing law related to liability under tort, contract, agency, and the law of war, therefore replay themselves in contracts between designers and manufacturers of autonomous technology and its users.

Regulation of Autonomous Machines and Systems

Regulation, as Chiu points out, is a way to ensure that public values are reflected in the activity of private business. It is beyond the scope of this book to describe all the types of legislation that exist or are being proposed for the governance of autonomous technology. This includes proposals to ban autonomous weapons by treaty and statute and others to shield manufacturers from liability arising from autonomous technology. Here it is possible to give one or two examples of some early legislation on autonomous vehicles.

Nevada is among a number of US states to have adopted statutes that permit the testing and operation of autonomous vehicles. As an illustration of Boulle's point that the "law" governing any given area is an amalgam of various types of hard and soft law, the Nevada statute adopts definitions and concepts from SAE International, a professional organization of engineers and other participants in the automotive, aerospace, and commercial vehicle industries. The statute also coordinates with US federal regulations. The statute contemplates autonomous vehicles with a human operator and those without a human in the vehicle.[77] When a human operator is present, the vehicle must be able to comply with all traffic laws and allow her to take control of the car, inform her when the vehicle is in autonomous mode, and alert the operator when she needs to take control. In autonomous vehicles in which a human operator is not present, the vehicle that does not have a human operator must be able to

---

[77]   Nev. Rev. Stat. § 482A 070(2) (2017).

minimize the chance of accident by going into a "minimal risk condition."[78] This is "a reasonable safe state" that includes coming to a complete stop.[79]

The Nevada legislation also addresses risk in at least two respects. First, the tester of an autonomous vehicle must submit proof of insurance and/or self-insurance of no less than $5 million and make a cash deposit or post security for that amount within the state.[80] Second, the statute shields manufacturers of motor vehicles or autonomous driving systems that have been converted or modified by third parties from liability for any defects in the conversion or modification, unless the defect was already present.[81] North Carolina goes somewhat further in addressing safety and liability issues. For example, if a vehicle is fully autonomous, the registered owner of the vehicle is responsible for any moving violations by the autonomous vehicle.[82] When there is a crash, the driver or drivers is/are required to stop, notify law enforcement, and provide vehicle registration and insurance information to those affected by the crash. When the crash results in bodily injury or death, the operator must remain present at the scene until permitted to leave by law enforcement.[83] An autonomous vehicle is deemed to meet those requirements if the vehicle itself or the operator of the vehicle notifies law enforcement, calls for medical assistance if appropriate, and remains present until released.[84]

Space and time do not permit a full analysis of whether Chiu's concern that more direct forms of regulation, such as Nevada and North Carolina's respective autonomous vehicle statutes, are vulnerable to capture by technocracy, to use her term. At the same time, a few things are worth noting. Both jurisdictions memorialize through statute norms and standards developed by professional organizations and experts in the field of engineering. This of course is natural, given the technical nature of autonomous machines and the software that drives them. It is quite likely that one would see legislatures turn to other professional bodies for specific uses of autonomous technology. This adoption of norms from professionals would not be unique to autonomous machines, as Boulle observes. It does mean, however, that the same issues that challenge technocratic governance and the administrative state are likely to accompany legislative "solutions" to the problem of liability for harms caused by autonomous machines—a concern that the technological reasons for a particular norm will be beyond the reach of the public. With regard to the two

---

78   *Id.*, § 080(2)(b).
79   *Id.*, § 2.7.
80   *Id.*, § 060.
81   *Id.*, § 090.
82   N.C. Gen. Stat. § 20-401(e) (2017).
83   *Id.*, §§ 20-166, 20-166.1.
84   *Id.*, § 20-401(g).

autonomous vehicle statutes, those were adopted by legislatures accountable in theory to the public through the electoral process. At the same time, the regulations that implement the statute will of course be drafted and implemented by administrative agencies, with related concerns about legitimacy.

From the perspective of this book, the primary challenge of legislation and regulation is not so much their limitations in addressing problems, but rather that, as tools for governance, they must still contend with the issues of responsibility wrestled with in the existing legal doctrines covered earlier in this chapter. As machines and systems become more autonomous, the link between the human and the harm becomes more and more tenuous. Recall that the North Carolina autonomous vehicle statute specifies that the registered owner of an autonomous vehicle will be responsible for any moving violations caused by it. This is an entirely plausible result. It is of course also a form of strict liability. It calls again to mind the Georgia automobile case, in which the Georgia appeals court refused to apply strict liability to reach the owners of what was then new technology. At the beginning of this chapter, I asked if the result would have been different had the vehicle been both vehicle and driver. The North Carolina legislature has answered that question and made its own allocation of responsibility, at least with regard to moving violations. Since the statute contemplates that if there is a crash, the autonomous vehicle will follow the standard procedures that apply to all crashes, including allowing for an investigation, it may be that conventional doctrines such as contributory negligence will play some role in the resolution of any disputes that arise from the accident. But if it is determined that the vehicle that has committed a moving violation was the cause of the crash, the registered owner of the vehicle will be hard pressed to raise a defense. One can respond of course that allocating responsibility through democratic forms of governance is better than leaving the issue to be resolved by judges, but responsibility by fiat begins to brush up against concerns about individual culpability—concerns that inform some of the antimajoritarian rights that are also part of democratic legal systems.

It is to this tension between the felt need to hold someone or something responsible when autonomous technology is involved in some harm, on the one hand, and possible strains in our current legal doctrines, on the other, that the next two chapters turn.

PART II

Individual and group responsibility

3. Individual responsibility

The previous chapter suggested that as autonomous machines and systems become less tethered to human control, there is a tendency to try to expand the number of persons who might be held responsible should autonomous technology be involved in a harm. This chapter examines this propensity in more detail, as well as the legal doctrines that apply to groups of people. One of my arguments in this chapter is that, to the extent that the doctrines discussed in Chapter 2 do not adequately address autonomous technologies, one reason is that the law tries to avoid responsibility by association. The legal doctrines used to frame and address harms are informed almost exclusively by the paradigm of the responsible human individual, so that even when the law purports to encompass groups of people, the analysis tends to be framed in individualistic terms. The chapter locates this emphasis on individual responsibility within moral responsibility. This stress on individual responsibility and the strong tie to ethics raises questions about how well legal responsibility based on personal culpability fares when it is applied to technology with high degrees of autonomy. The discussion here also motivates Chapter 4's closer focus on group moral responsibility.

EXPANDING THE RANGE OF RESPONSIBLE PEOPLE

As discussed in Chapter 2, White and Blum argue that at some point, legal liability for harms caused by autonomous machines will need to be allocated between the machine itself and human beings. The authors suggest that when this happens, designers will likely be subject to greater liability. If robot designers know that certain designs tend to yield harmful robots, a case can be made for holding the designers at least partially liable for harm caused by those robots, even if the robots merit legal personhood. Designers could also be similarly liable for building robots using opaque algorithms, such as neural networks and related deep learning methods, in which it is difficult to predict whether the robot will cause harm. Those parties that commission the robot's design could be similarly liable.[1]

---

[1]   Trevor N. White and Seth D. Blum, *Liability for Present and Future Robotics Technologies, in* ROBOT ETHICS 2.0: FROM AUTONOMOUS CARS TO ARTIFICIAL

I will explore the possibility of legal personhood for autonomous machines in Chapter 9. The point to be made here is that White and Blum are not alone in arguing that greater machine autonomy will require us to widen the range of candidates for responsibility. The belief is that responsibility will need to be shared.

Much of this discussion is happening in the development of design standards for the industry and in recommendations for public policy and legislation. In 2016, for example, the British Standards Institution issued design standards concerning responsibility for ethical harms caused by robots.[2] This was followed in 2017 by standards issued by the Institute of Electrical and Electronics Engineers (IEEE).[3] That same year, the European Parliament's Committee on Legal Affairs (EPCLA) issued recommendations to the European Commission regarding possible legislation to govern autonomous machines.[4] There seems to be a consensus among those groups that at a minimum, autonomous machines should be designed for traceability: it should be possible to trace robot-caused harms back to those who designed, manufactured, trained, or used the technology. BSI standard 5.1.1(c) states, for example, "it should be always be possible to find out who is responsible for any robot and its behavior."[5] Similarly, the IEEE provides that "[i]f an AI/AS causes harm it must always be possible to discover the root cause … for said harm."

Like the North Carolina statute discussed in Chapter 2, some of these organizations move beyond traceability to actually allocating responsibility, at this point to human beings. There is no sense yet of sharing responsibility between humans and autonomous machines. In 2010, for example, a working group of scholars issued a set of principles that expands the responsibility of the designers, manufacturers, and users of autonomous machines through two principles. Under the first principle, liability for harms is not diluted simply because many people participate in the design of the machines. Second, responsibility rests with the designer to the extent that a robot's behaviors and effects are reason-

---

INTELLIGENCE, 66, 72 (Patrick Lin, Ryan Jenkins, and Keith Abney eds., 2017) [hereinafter ROBOT ETHICS 2.0].

2   British Standards Institution, Robots and Robotic Devices: Guide to the Ethical Design and Application of Robots and Robotic Systems [hereinafter BSI Standards].

3   INST. ELECTRONIC & ELEC. ENG'RS, ETHCIALLY ALLIED DESIGN: A VISION FOR PRIORITIZING HUMAN WELL-BEING WITH ARTIFICIAL INTELLIGENCE AND AUTONOMOUS SYSTEMS: VERSION ONE (2016).

4   Report of the Committee on Legal Affairs with Recommendations to the Commission on Civil Law Rules on Robotics A8-0005/2017 (Jan. 27, 2017) [hereinafter EU Legal Affairs Report].

5   BSI Standards, *supra* note 2, standard 5.1.1(c).

ably foreseeable during the design phase.[6] Similarly, BSI standard 5.1.1(b) provides that "humans, not robots, are the responsible agents."[7] This approach coincides with that taken by the EPCLA. The Committee states: "at least at the present stage the responsibility must lie with a human and not a robot."[8] Such standards and policy recommendations thus foresee situations when responsibility for harms caused by autonomous technologies will need to be attributed to designers, manufacturers, and users (and possibly consumers), and among humans who work with those technologies.

Such allocations of responsibility, however, raise ethical and legal problems that have appeared intractable so far, thus raising questions whether spreading responsibility as recommended will be legitimate. These problems have to do with the legal and moral responsibility of groups: first, the responsibility of groups of people who design, manufacture, train, and use robots; second, the responsibility of groups of humans and robots who "work" together. Taken one way, standards that spread responsibility among designers, manufacturers, and users, or that allocate responsibility to humans in the case of human-robot activities, could require society to shift responsibility for harms that in every-day speech would be described as being caused by an individual robot, to individual human members in a design team or manufacturing chain, or to the human beings who have acted together with that robot. The concern is that this would amount to a form of responsibility by association.

LAW BEYOND INDIVIDUALS

Before addressing the previous point in more detail, it is a given that law has always had to do with groups, and a number of legal doctrines attempt to address groups of people as such. Product liability law deals with large enterprises. There are doctrines of aiding and abetting and joint tortfeasorship. Laws govern business entities as such, and also regulate the components of those entities; subsets of agency, partnership, corporate,

---

[6]   Keith W. Miller, *Moral Responsibility for Computing Artifacts: "The Rules"*, 13 IT PROFESSIONAL 57 (May/June 2011). Versions of the rules and commentary are available at https://edocs.uis.edu/kmill2/www/TheRules/.

[7]   BSI Standards, *supra* note 2, standard 5.1.1(b).

[8]   EU Legal Affairs Report, *supra* note 4, at 17, ¶ 56. In the area of self-driving cars, a commission appointed by the German Federal Minister of Transport and Digital Infrastructure reached a similar conclusion: "In the case of automated and connected driving systems, the accountability that was previously the sole preserve of the individual shifts from the motorist to the manufacturers and operators of the technological systems and to the bodies responsible for taking infrastructure, policy, and legal decisions." Ethics Commission, German Federal Ministry of Transport and Digital Infrastructure, Automated and Connected Driving 11 (2017).

and limited liability law set out rights and responsibilities of the owners and managers of the firm. In criminal law there is conspiracy in some domestic legal systems and joint criminality in others, and also at the international level. By definition, international law has to do with nation states. Finally, there is of course the whole of regulatory law, in which legislation and underlying regulations address almost every aspect of modern society, including large organizations.

Law therefore does treat large systems. At the same time, when theories of punishment, agency, and responsibility are involved, the law tends to become individualistic in nature. It tends to see legal responsibility emerging from a set of binary relations between individuals (inchoate offenses notwithstanding), even though those theories are justified in part by their impacts on the larger society. In product liability, for example, the manufacturer would of course be liable if it made errors in assembling an autonomous machine, but the manufacturer would itself be considered a unitary whole in the analysis. Indeed, the manufacturer is viewed as a legal person with certain legal rights concomitant with its legal powers. It is rare that individual designers and engineers employed by the manufacturer are found personally liable for harms, although there are exceptions. Similarly, in contract law, the focus is on two individual contract parties, with some doctrines that address the interests of third parties. Corporations and other business entities are treated as individuals in their relations with third party creditors. In criminal law, conspiracy is controversial in some legal systems precisely because it is believed that it strays too far from individual culpability. The same is true for joint criminal enterprise. In the law of war, the analysis of war crimes focuses on the actions of individual soldiers and commanders. On the level of state responsibility in international law, the state is viewed as a monolithic whole, with little attention paid to the components of the state. Even in the area of regulation, when enforcement is involved, the subjects of enforcement tend to focus on individual subjects or business or political subjects viewed as individuals.

The issue is whether this emphasis on individual responsibility poses problems for legal systems of responsibility, agency, and punishment that will need to reach large systems of humans and machines.

LESSONS FROM ETHICS

Because much of the rest of this book draws from the ethical literature, it is worthwhile at this point to discuss why it does so, particularly when there is a strong legal tradition that law and ethics are and should remain separate. It is not the purpose of this book to review that debate, but a few remarks are appropriate. There are at least three valid arguments for separation. The first is H.L.A. Hart's argument for such a barrier in *Positivism and the Separation of Law and Morals*, which engendered the famous debates between himself and Lon Fuller.[9] In that article, Hart argues that there have been no schools of jurisprudence which have refuted Austin and Bentham's arguments that "first, in the absence of an expressed constitutional or legal provision, it could not follow from the mere fact that a rule violated standards of morality that it was not a rule of law; and, conversely, it could not follow from the mere fact that a rule was morally desirable that it was a rule of law."[10] Law and ethics do not entail one another.

Hart does make some room for morals related to fitness for survival and administrative justice,[11] but I find persuasive Leslie Green's response that there are in fact much broader connections between law and morals that do not require the entailment Austin and Bentham find missing.[12] Green argues that law and morals are necessarily related in at least four important ways: first, "law regulates objects of morality"; second, "law makes moral claims on its subjects"; third, "law is justice-apt"; and fourth, "law is morally risky."[13] The first two relations do not require much explanation. With respect to the first, Green says, "Wherever there is law, there is morality, and they regulate the same subject matter—and do so by analogous techniques."[14] One implication is that they are coextensive in scope. Legal systems "regulate things that the society (or its elites) takes to be high-stakes matters of social morality."[15] Law makes moral claims on its subjects in that "[e]very legal system contains obligation-imposing norms and claims legitimate authority to impose them."[16]

By law being justice-apt, Green means that in contrast to other human activities, "[l]aw is the kind of thing that is *apt* for inspection and appraisal in light of justice."[17] Hart also sees morality as serving an appraisal function, but Green appears to argue that law's particular susceptibility to such an appraisal suggests there is something crucial about the relationship between the two—not that morality is prior to law, but that they must, as it were, be in constant dialogue. Finally, for Green, law is morally risky because by its nature it is

---

[9]   H.L.A. Hart, *Positivism and the Separation of Law and Morals*, 71 HARV. L. REV. 593 (1958). *See also* chapters 8 and 9 of H.L.A. Hart, THE CONCEPT OF LAW (2nd edn. 1994) [hereinafter THE CONCEPT OF LAW] for further discussion of the relationship between law and morals.

[10]   *Id.*, at 599.

[11]   THE CONCEPT OF LAW, *supra* note 9, at 193–9.

[12]   Leslie Green, *Positivism and the Inseparability of Law and Morals*, 83 N.Y.U. L. REV. 1035 (2008).

[13]   *Id.*, at 1047, 1048, 1050, and 1052. (Emphasis omitted.)

[14]   *Id.*, at 1047.

[15]   *Id.*

[16]   *Id.*, at 1048.

[17]   *Id.*, at 1050.

prone to legalism: "the overvaluation of legality at the expense of other virtues that a political system should have (including other virtues that law should have) and the alienation of law from life."[18] The fact that law has vices as well as virtues "marks a connection between law and morality of a reverse kind."[19]

At least two other arguments merit discussion. Martti Koskenniemi makes one in the context of international law and politics. If international law relies on ethics, he warns, such law risks being captured by powerful elites. "[T]he problem lies in the implied suggestion that the proper realm of the important lies in the personal, subjective, even emotional—and in particular in the conscience of those whom the dictates of power and history have put in decision-making positions." For him, the turn to ethics simply enables those with enough power to impose their moral convictions on others.[20] His "solution" is a return to a reformed type of formalism that limits the impulses of elites and implies accountability to a broader community, as well as the validity of the views of others.[21]

Koskenniemi's warning is well taken. At the same time, three remarks can be made. First, his criticism appears to center on the difference between subjective, situational forms of decision making and other forms of decision making that purport to be based on principles that are more rulelike and can apply in more than one situation. Ethicists would take issue with the claim that ethics or morals are a purely subjective, emotional matter. Certainly Kant's categorical imperative purports to apply universally and serves as the standard by which a person's moral decisions can be assessed by others. Second, Koskenniemi's fear that ethics can be reduced to a form of politics applies to all other approaches to law—a point on which Koskenniemi has written at length.[22] Third, in the context of international law, scholars writing from a Third World perspective argue that international law should be tied even more closely to matters of ethics, particularly matters of justice.[23] They argue that the postcolonial critique of law leads to the conclusion that "international law is not an alternative to other narratives of justice ... but is simply one more terrain on which contestation over the contours of justice take place."[24] If their

---

[18] *Id.*, at 1058.

[19] *Id.*, at 1054.

[20] Martti Koskenniemi, *"The Lady Doth Protest too Much"*: *Kosovo and the Turn to Ethics in International Law*, 65 MOD. L. REV. 159, 173 (2002).

[21] *Id.*, at 174.

[22] *See, e.g.*, Martti Koskenniemi, *The Politics of International Law—20 Years Later*, 20 EUR. J. INT'L L. 7 (2009) (discussing how international law has become a form of political discourse).

[23] Richard Falk et al., *Introduction, in* INTERNATIONAL LAW AND THE THIRD WORLD: RESHAPING JUSTICE 1, 5 (2008).

[24] *Id.*

thesis that international law has played a role in the current disparities in the distribution of global wealth and power is correct, it cannot be applied without raising justice issues, and thus calls for moral reflection.

A third argument for the separation of law and ethics is that moral reflection provides no real benefit to law. Along this vein, Richard Posner argues that moral theory (at least the kind as taught in modern universities) cannot help jurists decide hard cases.[25] For him, a jurist's or legislator's time would be better spent taking a pragmatic approach to legal issues and looking to the empirical sciences for guidance.[26] In this respect, I find Jeremy Waldron's assessment of Posner to be helpful. Waldron believes the real thrust of Posner's critique is not so much that there is a distinction between legal and moral questions, but rather that there is a distinction between tractable normative questions and intractable ones, and the methods of moral philosophy have not proven to be any better at helping resolve the latter.[27] Waldron therefore argues that a better way to articulate Posner's form of pragmatism is that both his approach and those taken by academic moralists try to answer the same domain of normative questions, but "some of them are tractable, and some are not; some involve irreconcilable disagreement and some do not."[28] In my assessment, Waldron's distinction between tractable and intractable normative questions is a good one and makes room for moral theory: if a question is intractable, it will be so whether it is legal or not, but if it is tractable, there seems to be no reason why one should not at least first see whether moral theory cannot contribute to its resolution before rejecting it, particularly given that, as Green observes, many of the techniques used in legal and moral analysis are similar.

I conclude that it is appropriate to draw lessons from the literature of moral responsibility in evaluating efforts to expand liability for harms caused by autonomous technology. At the same time, in contrast to scholars such as Michael Moore, whose work is discussed later in this chapter, I am not arguing that the only purpose of law is to achieve moral ends. This should certainly be one of its objects, and perhaps this should be the controlling purpose, but even if one does not accept this position, the fact that there are plausible arguments that there should be such a connection is enough to drive the dynamics this book is describing. Balkin's view of cultural tools as bricolage is helpful here. Law, like any other cultural tool, is capable of multiple uses, such as achieving other societal goals like efficiency, risk reduction, or giving expression to societal values. It is of course an open question whether society *should* use

---

[25] Richard A. Posner, THE PROBLEMATICS OF MORAL AND LEGAL THEORY (1999) (*see esp.* ch. 2).

[26] *Id.*, at 227–64.

[27] Jeremy Waldron, *Ego-Bloated Hovel*, 94 Nw U. L. REV. 597, 618–19 (2000).

[28] *Id.*

law to pursue those goals or whether law is well suited to achieve any one of them. At the same time, because there are valid arguments that there should be a connection between law and ethics, theories of legal responsibility that wander too far from well-settled views of moral responsibility run the risk of illegitimacy and redundancy.

THE MORAL RESPONSIBILITY OF THE INDIVIDUAL

Major Approaches

Responsibility has been defined as "the quality or state of being responsible,"[29] and in turn, to be responsible has been defined in part as being "liable to be called on to answer," "liable to be called to account as the primary cause, motive, agent," or "liable for legal review or in case of fault to penalties."[30] Wulf Loh and Janina Loh argue that responsibility has to do with an ability to account for one's actions, it is normative, and it implies certain psychological capabilities in a person to exercise judgment and to reflect on the implications of one's behavior.[31]

Such definitions reflect various understandings of responsibility common in the West. Andrew Eshleman describes the field as beginning with early Greek philosophers who wrestled with fatalism spurred by the gods' intervention in human affairs.[32] Aristotle's major work, the *Nichomachean Ethics*, however,

---

[29] *Responsibility*, MERRIAM-WEBSTER DICTIONARY (2015), www.merriam-webster .com/dictionary/responsibility.

[30] *Responsible*, MERRIAM-WEBSTER DICTIONARY (2015), www.merriam-webster .com/dictionary/responsible. On the idea that responsibility entails providing an explanation for oneself, *see* Andreas Matthias, *The Responsibility Gap: Ascribing Responsibility for the Actions of Learning Automata*, 6 ETHICS & INFO. TECH. 175, 175 (2004) ("When we judge a person responsible for an action, we mean ... that a person should be able to offer an explanation of her intentions and beliefs when asked to do so").

[31] Wulf Loh and Janina Loh, *Autonomy and Responsibility in Hybrid Systems: The Example of Autonomous Cars*, *in* ROBOT ETHICS 2.0, *supra* note 1, at 35, 35–7.

[32] Andrew Eshleman, *Moral Responsibility*, *in* STANFORD ENCYCLOPEDIA OF PHILOSOPHY (Edward N. Zalta ed., Summer 2014), http://plato.stanford.edu/entries/ moral-responsibility/. A distinction is sometimes made between metaethics, norma- tive ethics, and practical ethics. Metaethics asks broad questions, such as whether ethical norms are true in some objective sense or whether they are simply conventions of a society or whatever is chosen by an individual. Normative ethics asks questions like "what constitutes the good life?" Practical ethics explores what an ethical response should be in particular situations. *Introduction*, *in* THE BLACKWELL GUIDE TO ETHICAL THEORY 1, 1 (Hugh LaFollette ed., 2000). Most of the issues raised here are questions of metaethics.

articulates the problem in ways still used today. Aristotle conceives of responsibility as a person being subject to moral blame or praise for ones feelings or actions. Such blame or praise depends in part on whether such feelings or actions are voluntary or involuntary.[33] There is an epistemic component to responsibility: Aristotle argues an action done through ignorance is a form of involuntary action and thus not subject to moral blame.[34] He continues by asserting that an action is praiseworthy if done through rational choice, chosen as a way to achieve an end that has been determined through deliberation.[35]

Eshleman writes that Aristotle leaves unanswered a question still being debated: whether a person is subject to praise or blame because the individual in question herself has merited it, a merit-based view; or whether individuals are praised or blamed to influence their behavior, a consequentialist view.[36] This debate intertwines with another dispute about scientific or theological determinism, the idea that all events are determined by the physical laws of the universe or by an omniscient and omnipotent God. Incompatibilists believe that if determinism is true, no one can be morally responsible because one's actions are not voluntary. In contrast, compatibilists argue that a person can be morally responsible even if important aspects of one's identity and actions are determined outside of oneself.[37] Eshleman observes that merit-based views of responsibility tend toward incompatibilism, whereas consequentialists tend toward compatibilism. "[P]raising and blaming could still be an effective means of influencing another's behavior, even in a deterministic world."[38]

Peter Strawson tries to reconcile these debates by shifting focus from what justifies moral praise or blame (and whether it is coherent to do so) to the practice of moral praise or blame itself.[39] Strawson argues that in our relationships, we demand some degree of goodwill or regard on the part of those who stand in relation to us, and we have certain reactive attitudes, such as gratitude or resentment, when that demand is met or thwarted, as the case may be.[40] Sometimes those reactive attitudes can be suspended when a counterpart has an excuse, so his behavior is not a violation of the demand for goodwill, or when the person is for some reason not able to engage in everyday interper-

---

[33]   Aristotle, Nicomachean Ethics, bk. III, ch. 1, 37 (Roger Crisp trans. and ed., rev. edn. 2014) (330 BCE).

[34]   *Id.*, at 38–9.

[35]   *Id.*, chs 2–3, 40.

[36]   Eshleman, *supra* note 32.

[37]   *Id.*

[38]   *Id.*

[39]   Peter F. Strawson, *Freedom and Resentment*, 48 Proc. Brit. Acad. 1 (1962), *reprinted in* Peter Strawson, Freedom and Resentment and Other Essays 1 (Routledge edn. 2008).

[40]   *Id.*, at 6–7.

sonal relationships.[41] As Eshleman puts it, under this view, "[w]hereas judgments are true or false and thereby can generate the need for justification, the desire for good will and those attitudes generated by it possess no truth value themselves, thereby eliminating any need for an external justification."[42] Thus, one of Strawson's major contributions to ethics is to avoid metaphysical questions by locating praise or blame within the community in which judgments are made, a community in which certain expectations about one's behavior toward another have been adopted.[43]

In Eshleman's view, much of the contemporary literature has been devoted to responding to Strawson's contributions. Several strands are interesting for the purposes of this book. One is the distinction some scholars make between types of responsibility. Gary Watson, inspired by John Dewey, focuses on responsibility as a kind of self-disclosure: our actions express our commitments, morals, and so on.[44] This self-disclosure leaves people open to moral appraisal for the various ends they choose. As Angela Smith puts it, a person is responsible for something because "she is connected to it in a way that it can, in principle, serve as a basis for moral appraisal of that person."[45] *Attribution* is used to refer to the connection between the person and the act: "Conduct can be attributable or imputable to an individual as agent and is open to appraisal that is therefore appraisal of the individual as adopter of ends."[46] This is distinct from *holding* someone responsible, usually in the negative sense of blaming that person for something.[47] Fairness issues arise here because holding

---

[41]   *Id.*, at 7–10.

[42]   Eshleman, *supra* note 32. For Strawson, such responsibility need not be justified by its ability to achieve certain ends. "It is far from wrong to emphasize the efficacy of all those practices which express or manifest our moral attitudes, in regulating behavior in ways considered desirable … What *is* wrong is to forget that these practices, and their reception, the reactions to them, really *are* expressions of our moral attitudes and not merely devices we calculatingly employ for regulative purposes." Strawson, *supra* note 39, at 27.

[43]   *See* Philip Pettit and Michael Smith, *Freedom in Belief and Desire*, 93 J. PHIL. 429, 440–41 (1996). One implication of this approach is that any system of responsibility used to address the use of autonomous machines will necessarily be shaped by the communities in which moral judgments are made. As will be discussed in Chapter 5, this gives room for communities to consider new forms of responsibility to accommodate autonomous technologies.

[44]   Gary Watson, *Two Faces of Responsibility*, 24 PHIL. TOPICS 227, 227–8 (1996).

[45]   Angela Smith, *On Being Responsible and Holding Responsible*, 11 J. ETHICS 465, 465–6 (2007).

[46]   Watson, *supra* note 44, at 229.

[47]   As might be expected, various accounts can overlap. For example, R. Jay Wallace synthesizes Strawson's view of moral responsibility based on the reactive emotions and Kantian views of responsibility based on individual autonomy to suggest

someone responsible for something involves such negative consequences and entails the ability to make demands on that person. Hence, Watson argues that "[i]t is unfair to impose sanctions upon people unless they have a reasonable opportunity to avoid incurring them."[48] One result of there being different kinds of responsibility is that it might be possible to choose or reconcile various issues that arise from "harsher" forms of responsibility by making do with other, less problematic forms.

Finally, some commentators have focused on responsibility as requiring someone to give an account of her actions or attitudes. Marina Oshana is one of the proponents of this view. She writes, "[w]hen we say a person is morally responsible for something, we are essentially saying that a person did or caused some act (or exhibits some trait or character) for which it is fitting that she give an account."[49] This view presumes the individual in question meets some requirements of agency, has performed some act or exhibited a characteristic subject to certain moral standards, and has fallen short of those standards.[50] Finally, "the accountability interpretation assumes the actor possesses and is able to exercise certain capacities, rationality, self-awareness, an ability to appreciate and reply to telling questions, and the like."[51]

I will return to these differing views of moral responsibility in Chapter 5. For the purposes of this chapter, it is striking that despite the differences among these accounts of responsibility, each tends to focus on the human individual and all of them make similar assumptions about the persons who are subject to moral assessment. For example, the proponents of responsibility as answerability set out requirements that resonate with those required for Aristotelian moral praise or blameworthiness: it is fair to hold a person responsible for her actions if she is aware of the consequences of those acts and engages in them freely. This set of assumptions would also be consistent with certain criteria for the "rules" of interpersonal reactions in Strawson's terms, because actions that justify gratitude and resentment depend in part on at least weak assumptions about the rationality, freedom, and so on of the persons involved as they

---

it is reasonable to hold a person morally responsible (in the sense of subjecting that person to certain reactive emotions) if that person is capable of reflective self-control. R. Jay Wallace, RESPONSIBILITY AND THE MORAL SENTIMENTS 160–61, 226 (1994).

[48]   Watson, *supra* note 44, at 237. (Emphasis omitted.)

[49]   Marina A.L. Oshana, *Ascriptions of Responsibility*, 34 AM. PHIL. Q. 71, 77 (1997).

[50]   *Id.*

[51]   *Id.* These versions of responsibility can be mixed. David Shoemaker argues that a theory of ethics would encompass three understandings of responsibility: responsibility as attributability, answerability, and accountability. David Shoemaker, *Attributability, Answerability, and Accountability: Toward a Wider Theory of Moral Responsibility*, 121 ETHICS 602, 630–31 (2011).

live in relationship with each other. At a minimum these are assumptions that the practicing community would share. Further, scholars such as Watson and Smith agree that if one moves beyond attribution to holding someone responsible, some degree of freedom and control over one's circumstances is necessary before sanctions are appropriate. In large part, moral responsibility remains bound to the human individual and what we believe she is capable of doing.

CULPABILITY, FORESEEABILITY, AND CAUSATION

In law, the influence of ethical responsibility just discussed is reflected in several ways. Because they are so closely tied to legal responsibility, this section explores the extent to which the legal concepts of culpability (with foreseeability as a component) and causation reflect individual moral responsibility. Depending on which strands of jurisprudence one finds persuasive, culpability and causation can be viewed as reflecting something true about a defendant and about what he has done that justifies the imposition of legal consequences, or alternatively as constructions by legal decisionmakers that are used to achieve some end. I argued earlier that even if there are persuasive arguments that these legal doctrines should serve no moral function, there are equally persuasive arguments that they should. This is enough to support the conclusion that when we deploy the legal doctrines of culpability and causation in assessing legal responsibility, even if one is a pure constructionist, such analysis must at least jibe with understandings of moral responsibility. How this applies specifically to autonomous technology and its designers, owners, and users will be discussed later.

Culpability

It seems a commonplace that legal responsibility cannot attach without some form of culpability. This book does not discuss criminal liability in great detail, but it would be remiss to ignore culpability in the context of criminal law. Model Penal Code § 2.02(1) provides that, subject to a limited exception, a "person is not guilty of an offense unless he acted purposely, knowingly, recklessly or negligently, as the law may require, with respect to each material element of the offense." (Intentional, knowing, reckless, and negligent behavior are of course also forms of culpability in tort law.) The explanatory note to subsection 1 states:

> Subsection (1) articulates the Code's insistence that an element of culpability is requisite for any valid criminal conviction and that the concepts of purpose, knowledge, recklessness and negligence suffice to delineate the kinds of culpability that may be called for in the definition of specific crimes. The only exception to this general

requirement is the narrow allowance for offenses of strict liability in Section 2.05, limited to cases where no severer sentence than a fine may be imposed.[52]

In § 2.05 it is provided that culpability is not required for "violations" of the code, but such violations are not considered crimes subject to the "condemnatory aspect of a criminal conviction or of correctional sentence." Such condemnation and sentencing are "specifically precluded."[53]

Barry Feld links this insistence on culpability directly to moral responsibility and blameworthiness.[54] Feld writes that "[t]he criminal law assumes that rational actors possess free will and choose to violate the law based on their own preferences and values."[55] His point is well taken. The assumption of rationality and free will is reflected, for example, in the Model Penal Code's definition of acting purposely:

A person acts purposely with respect to a material element of an offense when:

(i)   if the element involves the nature of his conduct or a result thereof, it is his conscious object to engage in conduct of that nature or to cause such a result; and

(ii) if the element involves the attendant circumstances, he is aware of the existence of such circumstances or he believes or hopes that they exist.[56]

According to Feld, the determination that a person with full rationality has chosen to violate the law also subjects him to moral blameworthiness, which in turn "provides legitimacy to the criminal sanction."[57]

It is well accepted, therefore, that culpability is required for criminal liability (as well as for many forms of civil liability), but like many legal concepts, what culpability exactly is remains subject to debate. Klaus Roxin provides a thorough discussion of the concept.[58] He notes, as does Feld, that culpability has been conceived as having the power to comply with the law but deciding not to do so. This, however, makes a metaphysical presumption that people have free

---

[52]   MODEL PENAL CODE § 2.02 ex. note (AM. LAW INST. Proposed Official Draft 1962) [hereinafter MODEL PENAL CODE].

[53]   *Id.*, § 2.05 ex. note.

[54]   Barry C. Feld, *Competence, Culpability and Punishment: Implications of* Atkins *for Executing and Sentencing Adolescents*, 32 HOFSTRA L. REV. 463, 465 (2003).

[55]   *Id.*, at 465.

[56]   MODEL PENAL CODE, *supra* note 52, §2.02(2)(a).

[57]   Feld, *supra* note 54, at 465.

[58]   Klaus Roxin, DERECHO PENAL: PARTE GENERAL: FUNDAMENTOS. LA ESTRATURA DE LA TEORIA DEL DELITO (Diego-Manuel Luzón Peña, Miguel Díaz y Garcia Conlledo, and Javier de Vicente Remesal trans. 1997).

will.[59] Culpability has also been explained as having an internal attitude that manifests itself in an illegal action, but this again presumes there is a direct link between internal states and action.[60] It has also been associated with a person's character; however, it is not clear whether a person should be responsible for something innate, about which she might not have had any choice.[61]

Roxin continues by discussing views that culpability is a construction. Under one such theory, following Luhmann, culpability arises when juridical expectations about the requirements of the law are frustrated. The doctrine is then used instrumentally to encourage confidence in the legal system. The critique of this view is Kantian: a person should not be used as a means to an end, even if the end is to strengthen the law.[62] Roxin's own perspective is that culpability arises when a person commits an unjust action, taking into account the alternatives that were then psychologically available to the person.[63] For him, this is a legal assessment, not a truth proposition: a determination under law that a person acted with free will is a normative assertion made by the legal system independent of whether there is actual free will.[64] However, Roxin argues that even though culpability has a constructive aspect to it, it neverthe-less serves as an important check on state power;[65] presumably the state must make a plausible case in the view of the wider community that a defendant is indeed culpable. This type of theory has at least some similarities to Strawson's focus on the community practice of praise and blame.

Requiring culpability is ubiquitous, and has implications for law that pur-ports to address collections of people. As is well known, during the Nuremberg trials, the International Military Tribunal was authorized to hold groups such as the SS liable for international crimes as criminal organizations and to use membership in them to hold individuals criminally liable.[66] However, despite being given the power to do so, the tribunal declined to use it. The tribunal reiterated the principle that criminal liability requires some kind of personal

---

[59]   *Id.*, at 799–800.

[60]   *Id.*, at 802.

[61]   *Id.*, at 802–3.

[62]   *Id.*, at 805–6.

[63]   *Id.*, at 808.

[64]   *Id.*

[65]   *Id.*, at 811.

[66]   Charter of the International Military Tribunal, art. 9, Aug. 8, 1945, 59 Stat. 1544, 82 U.N.T.S. 279, http://avalon.lay.yale.edu/imt/imtconst.asp. *See also* Allison Marston Danner and Jenny S. Martinez, *Guilty Associations: Joint Criminal Responsibility, Command Responsibility, and the Development of International Criminal Law*, 93 CAL. L. REV. 75, 112–14 (2005) (discussing the strategy of holding organizations guilty of crimes and using such convictions as the basis for the summary conviction of individuals).

culpability and indeed was leery of the concept of a criminal organization. It cautioned that the discretion to hold groups criminal "should be exercised in accordance with well-settled legal principles, one of the most important of which is that criminal guilt is personal, and that mass punishments should be avoided."[67] This early decision in international criminal law establishes what has become a well-settled principle. As Fabian Remondo puts it, "no one may be held responsible for an act he has not performed, or in the commission of which he has not participated, or for an omission that cannot be attributed to him."[68] Two things result from this principle. "First, no one may be held responsible for crimes committed by others. Secondly, an individual may be held criminally responsible only if she is in one way or another culpable of any violation of criminal rules."[69] Current debates in this area of the law, particularly the doctrine of joint criminal enterprise, center on how far such theories of personal culpability can be extended before they limn into guilt by association.[70]

Foreseeability

Chapter 2 related at length Karnow's argument that when technology reaches a high degree of autonomy, it will be difficult to use the doctrines of negligence and product liability to hold designers and engineers liable for harms because they cannot foresee in sufficient detail what specific harms an autonomous machine might bring about. Some ethics scholars urge that foreseeability should serve as the test for determining whether software designers are morally or legally responsible for the harms caused by what they design.

That a person is not responsible for harm she could not foresee is justified on either fairness or pragmatic grounds. Some argue it is unfair to hold someone liable for a harm she was not aware (or should have been aware) could arise and thus had no opportunity to prevent or avoid. As a practical matter, it is unrea-

---

[67]   Judgment, *in* 1 TRIAL OF THE MAJOR WAR CRIMINALS BEFORE THE INTERNATIONAL MILITARY TRIBUNAL 171, 256 (1948).

[68]   Fabián O. Remondo, GENERAL PRINCIPLES OF LAW IN THE DECISIONS OF INTERNATIONAL CRIMINAL COURTS 80 (2008).

[69]   *Id.*

[70]   Attila Bogdan, *Individual Criminal Liability in the Execution of a "Joint Criminal Enterprise" in the Jurisprudence of the ad hoc International Tribunal for the Former Yugoslavia*, 6 INT'L CRIM. L. REV. 63, 75 (2006) (arguing that the extent to which a person can be held criminally responsible for the acts of others is unsettled at the international level, largely because this varies among legal systems); Jens Meirerhenrich, *Conspiracy in International Law*, 2 ANN. REV. L. SOC. SCI. 341, 346–53 (2006) (discussing the links between criminal organization, conspiracy, and joint criminal enterprise, and the issue of individual criminality).

sonable to ask someone to take precautions against harm that was beyond the contemplation of the defendant. Unsurprisingly, however, foreseeability poses conceptual problems. Where there is nothing new under the sun, everything is foreseeable. Therefore, one must distinguish between what is foreseeable for purposes of legal liability and what is not. Although most of this subsection concerns the role of foreseeability in tort, Judge Skelly Wright addresses this aspect of foreseeability in contract. In *Transatlantic Financing Corporation v. United States*,[71] an operator of a ship sought to be compensated when it was forced to round the Cape of Good Hope to deliver cargo instead of going through the Suez Canal, which had been nationalized and closed by Egypt. The issue was whether the operator's performance had been made impracticable because of the closure. Under that doctrine a contract party can be relieved of its obligations if performance of the contract is made impracticable by an event unforeseen by the parties. Judge Skelly Wright thought it was safe to assume that both parties were aware of tensions in the area, and that they might affect passage through the Canal. However, in his view, "[f]oreseeability or even recognition of a risk does not necessarily prove its allocation."[72] The judge then considered a number of factors to allocate that risk to the operator. In these kinds of situations, there is an argument that foreseeability is redundant.

In tort law, foreseeability is connected to debates about the nature of negligence itself, in particular whether torts must arise in relation to someone else. In that context, foreseeability determines whether a person is within the circle of persons to whom a person owes a duty of care. Judge Cardozo's construal of the facts of the *Palsgraf* case is the classic example.[73] In that case a passenger jumped aboard a train as it started to move away from the station. A guard on the train tried to pull him aboard and another on the platform pushed him from behind. This caused the passenger to drop a package of fireworks onto the tracks. The fireworks exploded, and the vibrations from the explosion caused some scales on the platform to fall on a woman, who sued for her injuries.[74] Judge Cardozo found that although the guards might have been negligent in relation to the passenger who boarded the train, in relation to the plaintiff their actions did not constitute negligence at all. For him this was not a matter of causation but rather one of culpability.[75] Because there was no indication that the package might pose a danger to the woman (and to others similarly situated to her), the guards' actions toward the man did not take on the nature of a tort

---

[71] 363 F.2d 312 (D.C. Cir. 1966).
[72] *Id.*, at 318.
[73] *Palsgraf v. Long Island R.R.*, 248 N.Y. 339 (1928).
[74] *Id.*, at 340.
[75] *Id.*, at 346.

with respect to her.[76] "The risk reasonably to be perceived defines the duty to be obeyed, and risk imports relation; it is risk to another or to others within the range of apprehension."[77]

Judge Andrews' dissent, joined in more recent times by scholars such as Heidi Hurd and Michael Moore (albeit on other grounds than Andrews'), took a different view of the issue. One of the principal components of Hurd and Moore's critique is that in essence, Cardozo's view of negligence is that it consists of putting at risk people who, given what the defendant can foresee about the consequences of his action, are those to whom he owes a duty. Instead, Hurd and Moore urge, "[o]ur legal rights are not rights against being hit by some risk; they are rights against actually being caused harm. They are rights only against risks that materialize, in other words."[78] In their opinion, breach should be analyzed under causation, while unreasonable risktaking goes to culpability.[79]

In a recent article, Avihay Dorfman grounds foreseeability within the relational, risk-based approach to negligence urged by Cardozo.[80] Foreseeability is necessary to this approach because "a duty to moderate one's risky activity can be intelligible only insofar as a sufficient measure of foreseeability *with respect to* potentially vulnerable others obtains."[81] At the same time, Dorfman argues that the current requirement that the tortfeasor be able to foresee possible plaintiffs—plaintiff foreseeability—is too limiting. His primary aim is to demonstrate how foreseeability can be used to encompass someone like Palsgraf as a person within the sphere of risk to whom the duty is owed. In a sense, then, he gives a rejoinder to Hurd and Moore. My purpose for discussing his work, however, is not to evaluate the success of his proposal, much less to resolve the debate between a risk-based or causal-based conception of negligence. Rather, the article is valuable because as part of his larger argument Dorfman discusses and assesses a number of theories of foreseeability, several of which can be understood as being premised on an individualistic view of responsibility, albeit framed in a certain way.

In one such explanation, foreseeability has to do with the agency of the defendant. "[F]oresight secures that the duty of due care will be predicated on control over one's practical affairs and the effects they ensue." Echoing Aristotle, we generally hold people responsible for actions and consequences

---

[76]   *Id.*, at 342.

[77]   *Id.*, at 344. (Citations omitted.)

[78]   Heidi M. Hurd and Michael S. Moore, *Negligence in the Air*, 3 Theoretical Inq. in Law 333, 352 (2002).

[79]   *Id.*

[80]   Avihay Dorfman, *Foreseeability as Re-Cognition*, 59 Am. J. Jur. 163 (2014).

[81]   *Id.*, at 168 (footnote omitted).

that are in some way under their control. Foreseeability helps make that possible by marking out the arena in which a person exercises his or her agency.[82] In another view, based on a Rawlsian concept of justice, negligence helps preserve the balance of primary goods, such as rights and liberties, powers, and so on, that each person in a liberal society is presumed to have. It does so by imposing a duty to avoid misusing one's own primary goods at the expense of another's and a duty to repair if one does so.[83] In this framework, "the capacity of a person to moderate her conduct in light of the equal claims of others to employ their respective primary goods presupposes (reasonable) foresight."[84] Under an efficiency approach, foreseeability is required because "tort law can generate incentives towards safety only insofar as risk-creators have available to them the information that is constitutive of deciding the optimal level of care."[85]

In service of Dorfman's attempt to criticize plaintiff foreseeability, although foreseeability is an important aspect of each of these approaches to negligence, he argues that it does not follow that persons outside the scope of foreseeability are excluded from the duty of care. Dorfman argues that a defendant's agency is not threatened if persons like Palsgraf are included in the sphere of care: in his view, all the information that the defendant needs to maintain his agency is already provided by those persons in the foreseeable range.[86] The same holds regarding negligence grounded on primary goods: "[t]he foreseeable passenger provides the railroad's employee with the requisite epistemic basis on which he could conduct his practical affairs in conformity with the general scheme of fairly distributed primary goods."[87] Dorfman concedes that the economic justification for plaintiff foreseeability is stronger: a person cannot rationally adjust his behavior with respect to someone he does not foresee; to hold a person nevertheless responsible "would make no practical difference in curbing inefficient behavior."[88] In these circumstances, requiring payment would be simply a wealth transfer that incurs transaction costs. Yet Dorfman argues such administrative costs might be incurred anyway since it is costly to determine if a plaintiff is indeed foreseeable, and those costs might be outweighed by the costs incurred to the injured party.[89]

---

[82] *Id.*, at 180.
[83] *Id.*, at 181–2.
[84] *Id.*, at 182.
[85] *Id.*, at 183.
[86] *Id.*, at 180.
[87] *Id.*, at 183.
[88] *Id.*, at 184.
[89] *Id.*

Dorfman's own concept of foreseeability is an ethical one. For him, the overarching problem with the other approaches to negligence and to foreseeability more specifically is that they are largely consequentialist, in service to abstract goals such as agency, liberty, and efficiency with little relationship to the plaintiff.[90] In contrast, Dorfman wants to ground negligence and foreseeability in terms of respectful recognition of others who might be affected by our behaviors:

> [R]espectfully recognizing persons as such requires the acknowledgement that, for any given act which is reasonably known to be risky, there is someone, whoever she is, who may be affected; that she is a person; and that she commands respectful recognition simply by virtue of being a person. The foreseeability requirement demands no more, but no less, than that.[91]

For Dorfman, therefore, it is not necessary that foreseeability be understood as marking out a sphere whereby a person exercises agency, balances primary goods, or takes efficient levels of care. Since foreseeability need not perform this function it is not necessary to restrict foreseeability to the plaintiff. Instead, to refer back to *Palsgraf*, it is sufficient that the guards know that by engaging in risky behavior, "there is someone, whoever she is, who may be affected."

As I wrote earlier, it is not the goal of this section to determine which of the above views of negligence and the role that foreseeability plays in them is the most persuasive. At the same time, as I will discuss presently, some attempts to hold engineers and designers responsible for harms caused by autonomous machines depend on foreseeable harms. Below I will explore more fully whether using foreseeability in this way impacts agency, liberty, or efficiency in some way. One could argue, as does Dorfman, that under these frameworks, foreseeability is not really concerned with individual responsibility or liability; it is concerned with furthering more abstract goals. Thus we have departed from the individualistic, moral foundations of responsibility discussed earlier in this chapter. However, I would argue differently: assuming arguendo that what is "really" taking place (to the extent that this can ever be determined) is the furtherance of goals that have little to do with specific individuals, still, each account is couched in terms of an individual who foresees how her actions might impact others or their primary goods, or who calculates how much care he should take. In Dorfman's own approach, one sees an individual who understands there might be people out there, even unforeseeable ones, who merit consideration. To evoke Strawson again, the individual continues to

---

90   *Id.*, at 185.
91   *Id.*, at 193.

play a role in determining how the community uses the concept of foreseeability in its process of praising and blaming.

Causation

Causation is another area in which the law's emphasis on individual liability surfaces. To repeat the standard elements of a negligence claim, a plaintiff who has been harmed must show not only that the defendant owed the plaintiff a duty of care and that the defendant breached that duty with some degree of culpability—intentionally, recklessly, or negligently—but also that the defendant's culpable act or omission caused the plaintiff's harm. As Richard Epstein puts it, "[Causation] is dominant in the law because it is dominant in the language people, including lawyers, use to describe conduct and to determine responsibility."[92] Ingebord Puppe writes: "All of someone's responsibility for an event is based on a relation of causality between his behavior (doing or omitting) and this event."[93]

Although there are variations, the standard approach to causation is to engage in two inquiries. The first is whether the defendant's culpable behavior did in fact cause the harm to the plaintiff. This first line of analysis often uses a "but-for" test: whether, but-for the defendant's act or omission, the harm would not have occurred. Another method is to ask whether the act or omission was a substantial factor in causing the harm. Since many events and actions can contribute to a harm, the second inquiry is to ask whether the act or omission in question was the "proximate cause" of the harm, culpable conduct which in the circumstances should be subject to legal responsibility. This second test requires some criterion for distinguishing between those causes that are legally significant and those that are not. Several have been offered: harms that are foreseeable to the defendant; conduct closely linked to the harm; and conduct which as a policy matter should be subject to liability. This two-part inquiry might not be so neatly divisible into an almost scientific inquiry about cause and effect and decision which, among several causes, the law should recognize as such. David Hamer argues that determining cause-in-fact involves some value judgments, and cause and effect necessarily plays some role in deciding whether a culpable action is a proximate cause.[94] In a sense, then, the distinction between cause-in-fact and proximate cause can itself be viewed as a legal

---

[92] Richard Epstein, *A Theory of Strict Liability*, 2 J. LEG. STUD. 151, 164 (1973).

[93] Ingebord Puppe, *The Concept of Causation in the Law, in* CAUSATION AND RESPONSIBILITY: CRITICAL ESSAYS 67, 67 (Benedikt Kahmen and Markus Stephanians eds., 2013).

[94] David Hamer, *"Factual Causation" and "Scope of Liability": What's the Difference?* 77 MOD. L. REV. 155 (2014).

construction.[95] Regardless, the two-part analysis is in turn subject to variations. For example, there are concurrent causes: another cause that simultaneously contributes to the injury. There is the possibility of an intervening or superseding cause. Although one person might have been negligent, another person's negligence might break the causal connection and cause harm to the plaintiff.

Causation as a legal concept has been defended, criticized, or dismissed on a number of grounds, which in turn has led to different views on how terms like cause-in-fact, proximate cause, and so on should be construed and applied. For example, Moore argues criminal law and tort are "causation drenched."[96] This is appropriate for Moore because he believes that the primary goals of criminal law and tort are retribution and corrective justice, respectively, which require the support of moral responsibility, which in turn entails causation. Moore argues: "we all have primary moral duties not to hurt others; when we culpably violate such primary moral duties, we then have a secondary duty to correct the injustice we have caused."[97] Moore argues that the moral responsibility to correct culpable violations of those moral duties involves causation: for him this is evident from the fact that we feel more guilt for causing a harm than we do when we merely attempt to do so.[98] As a result, Moore would distinguish between foreseeing or allowing a morally blameworthy act on the one hand, and causing that blameworthy act on the other.[99] (In contrast to scholars such as Dorfman, to the extent that torts are relational, it is causation—not foreseeability—that links a plaintiff to the tortfeasor.) Other scholars, however, do not tie causation to ethics. Informed by legal realism, Wex Malone argues that causation, like other doctrines, is used by judges to further a number of policies.[100] According to some scholars influenced by law and economics, causation is unnecessary because the primary goal of liability rules is to assign liability to the party who is the least costly risk avoider.[101] Causation has no role to play in this assignment.

As is true with foreseeability, for the purposes of this book it is not necessary to resolve debates about the validity of causation. What is important for my argument is that causation, even if it is in fact theoretically flawed and

---

[95]   Epstein, *supra* note 92, at 160–65.

[96]   Michael S. Moore, Causation and Responsibility: An Essay in Law, Morals, and Metaphysics 22 (2009).

[97]   *Id.*, at 95.

[98]   *Id.*, at 33.

[99]   *Id.*, at 77.

[100]   Wex S. Malone, *Ruminations on Cause-in-Fact*, 9 Stan. L. Rev. 60 (1956).

[101]   *See, e.g.,* Guido Calabresi, *Concerning Cause and the Law of Torts: An Essay for Harry Kalven, Jr.,* 43 U. Chi. L. Rev. 69 (1975); William M. Landes and Richard A. Posner, *Causation in Tort Law: An Economic Approach,* 12 J. Legal Stud. 109 (1983).

applied imperfectly, cannot be ignored as a means of assigning responsibility. It might be because attempts like those of Hart and Tony Honoré,[102] and of Moore, to justify causation are successful, or because, as I argued earlier in this chapter, law cannot become untethered from our moral understandings of morality. As Epstein puts it, "[Causation's] presence reminds us that a system of law which tries to banish it from use may not respond to ordinary views on individual blame and responsibility."[103]

IMPLICATIONS FOR AUTONOMOUS TECHNOLOGIES

Having reviewed moral responsibility and the ways in which it is reflected in the legal concepts of culpability, foreseeability, and causation, it is possible to return to some of the concerns raised in Chapter 2 with a broader perspective. Chapter 2 considered debates as to whether negligence and product liability law will be able to reach harms caused by autonomous machines. To the extent that there are doubts that they will, these arise in part because unless there are egregious facts, there are valid arguments that the likely defendants in an action involving autonomous technology—the software engineer, the designer, or the manufacturer—were not culpable in the sense that they intended harm or were reckless or careless in fulfilling their individual roles.

Such legal culpability reflects the link between moral blameworthiness and Aristotelian ideas of autonomy. As Robert Sparrow puts it:

> [A]utonomy and moral responsibility go hand in hand. To say of an agent that they are autonomous is to say that their actions originate in them and reflect their ends. Furthermore, in a fully autonomous agent, these ends are ends that they have themselves, in some sense, chosen. Their ends result from the exercise of their capacity to reason on the basis of their own past experience.[104]

Sparrow is concerned with whether a robot itself can be considered morally responsible, a topic discussed in Chapters 8 and 9. Here, Sparrow views responsibility at present as associated only with human beings. Under this view, it follows that an act for which someone is responsible must somehow be one's own.

Where an agent acts autonomously, then, it is not possible to hold anyone else responsible for its actions. Insofar as the agent's actions were its own and stemmed from its own ends, others cannot be held responsible for them.

---

[102] H.L.A Hart and Tony Honoré, Causation in the Law (2nd edn. 1985).
[103] Epstein, *supra* note 92, at 164.
[104] Robert Sparrow, *Killer Robots*, 24 J. Applied Phil. 62, 65–6.

Conversely, if we hold anyone else responsible for the actions of an agent, we must hold that, in relation to those acts at least, they were not autonomous.[105]

Sparrow is agnostic as to whether machines will ever achieve the highest levels of autonomy such that they are acting for themselves. However, he argues that the closer such machines come to the ability to form their own ends based on their experiences of the world, "the less it seems that those who program or design them, or those who order them into action, should be held responsible for their actions."[106]

The issue can be reframed in legal terms by applying the principles of foreseeability and causation. Earlier in this chapter, I discussed a working group of scholars who produced a set of rules regarding the moral implications of autonomous technology, "computing artifacts," in their terms.[107] Rule 2 reads:

> The shared responsibility of computing artifacts is not a zero-sum game. The responsibility of an individual is not reduced simply because more people become involved in designing, developing, deploying or using the artifact. Instead, a person's responsibility includes being answerable for the behaviors of the artifact and for the artifact's effects after deployment, to the degree to which these effects are reasonably foreseeable by that person.[108]

Such a rule of moral responsibility indicates that at least some commentators feel the circle of responsible actors can be expanded and could form the basis for legal doctrines that could reach large groups of programmers and engineers who will contribute to the design and manufacture of intelligent machines, as well as reaching the human members of groups who use them.

Note, however, that Rule 2 ties responsibility to foreseeability. In Chapter 2, I related Karnow's concerns that designers will not be able to foresee behaviors of machines that emerge from their complex interactions with their environment. Wendell Wallach and Colin Allen argue that the design process itself, discussed briefly in Chapter 1, makes prediction very difficult. Given the complexity of modern computers, engineers commonly discover that they cannot predict how a system will act in a new situation. As set out in Chapter

---

[105]   *Id.*, at 65–6.

[106]   *Id.*, at 66. Bertolini shares similar doubts that machines will achieve what she calls "strong autonomy." Andrea Bertolini, *Robots as Products: The Case for Realistic Analysis of Robotic Applications and Liability Rules*, 5 LAW INNOVATION & TECH. 214, 222–3 (2007). Andreas Matthias shares this concern, arguing that "there is an increasing class of machine actions, where the traditional ways of responsibility ascription are not compatible with our sense of justice and the moral framework of society because nobody has enough *control* over the machine's actions to be able to assume the responsibility for them." Matthias, *supra* note 30, at 177.

[107]   Miller, *supra* note 4, at 57.

[108]   *Id.*, at 58.

1, hundreds of engineers contribute to the design of each machine. Different companies, research centers, and design teams work on individual hardware and software components that make up the final product. The modular design of a computer system can mean that no single person or group can fully grasp the way the system will interact with or respond to a complex flow of new inputs.[109]

This modular approach to computer design casts doubt on Rule 2's proposition that the responsibility of an individual is not reduced by the fact that more people are involved in the development of computational technologies. Put another way, to limit responsibility through foreseeability is to undermine the claim that responsibility cannot be diluted.

In such situations, there is a strong argument that foreseeability should win out. The "factual" problems concerning foreseeability in computer design are joined by somewhat more abstract ones. In the previous subsection I discussed Dorfman's argument that foreseeability is necessary in agency-based, liberty-based, and efficiency-based views of negligence, as well as his own view that foreseeability recognizes that when one engages in risky behavior "there is someone, whoever she is, who may be affected." I also argued that each such account is couched in terms of an individual who foresees how her actions might impact others or their primary goods, or who calculates how much care he should take, or, with respect to Dorfman's own approach, who understands there might be people out there, even unforeseeable ones, that merit some consideration. Consider a programmer who contributes a few lines of code for a subroutine among tens of thousands of them. It is hard to argue that such an individual's agency, ability to balance public goods, or ability to assess the proper level of care would not be adversely affected, unless foreseeability limited moral or legal responsibility. Perhaps under Dorfman's approach it could be argued that the programmer should be aware when writing those lines of code that there is someone out there who might be affected. But this result shows the breadth of Dorfman's concept of foreseeability and responsibility more generally. It comes close to a form of strict liability, which I will assess in more detail in Chapter 5.

The same problems arise if we use concepts of causation as the basis for liability. Suppose, for example, that we agree with Moore that the purpose of criminal law is retributive justice and that the purpose of tort law is restorative justice. An argument can be made that viewing criminal law and tort law in this way increases the likelihood of a gap in responsibility when an autonomous system is involved. This is because a test for causation tied to moral respon-

---

[109]   Wendell Wallach and Colin Allen, MORAL MACHINES: TEACHING ROBOTS RIGHT FROM WRONG 39 (2010).

sibility is likely to be exacting, as a finding of causation makes a defendant open to criminal or civil sanctions. Consider Moore's recommendations for proximate cause tests:

> Proximate-cause tests ... should serve the function of grading offenders between the more blameworthy causers of harm, and the less blameworthy riskers or intenders of such harm. Analogously, in tort law the function of proximate-cause doctrines is to serve corrective justice. That justice demands that one pay for all and only the harms one has caused.[110]

What happens if, when transporting a passenger, an autonomous vehicle that is being used in a ride sharing service like Uber harms a pedestrian? It seems hard to argue that the passenger or the ride sharing service caused the harm as Moore understands cause; nor would they have allowed the harm to occur. Perhaps it might be appropriate to conclude that the software engineer or designer was a risker of such harm, again to use Moore's terms, because they should have been aware there was some chance that the machine would malfunction and harm someone, but that is likely all we could say of them. It would be reasonable, even if one was not wedded to Moore's view of causation as linked to morals, to conclude that the engineers and designers did not cause the harm. Within Moore's framework, causation must correspond to the state of affairs in the world; in this case it seems plausible to describe that state of affairs by saying the autonomous vehicle caused the accident.

On the other hand, suppose we adopt a constructive view of causation. This would enable a decision maker to use a multifactor analysis, including the aim of the tort law to create incentives for people to reduce risk, to leapfrog the autonomous vehicle and find that the designers proximately caused the accident, so that the designer is legally responsible. This perhaps could be justified because such a finding meets certain societal goals such as efficiency. The rub, however, is that this ignores the fact that the law serves other ends, including to do justice. This chapter has argued that, when it comes to a just finding of legal responsibility, the autonomous individual remains the paradigm as the responsibility bearer. This raises questions whether law is equipped to respond to some of the associational problems that will arise when autonomous machines or systems cause harm. To respond to those questions more fully, the next chapter explores the literature of group responsibility.

---

[110] Moore, *supra* note 96, at 97.

4. The legal and moral responsibility of groups

Chapter 3 concluded by arguing that legal principles essential to legal responsibility, such as culpability, foreseeability, and causation, reflect common conceptions of individual moral responsibility, which is premised on the autonomous individual. Although commentators urge us to consider spreading responsibility for harms caused by autonomous technology, the requirements of culpability, foreseeability, and causation challenge that effort. The more sophisticated the machine, the harder it is to allocate responsibility beyond the machine to its designers and owners because of the limits to responsibility imposed by those legal principles. Such an argument, however, is incomplete without returning to the question of responsibility beyond the individual. As Mark Coeckelbergh argues, "technological action is often distributed and collective rather than individual."[1] What, if anything, should we make of the fact that the designers, manufacturers, owners, and users of autonomous machines and systems will almost always be associated with groups, and that, as I have said earlier, as machines achieve greater autonomy, it will become valid to speak of groups of humans and machines working together? To bring attention once more to White and Blum's point, at some point the law will need to consider how to allocate responsibility between human and machine.

The main purpose of this chapter is to introduce major themes in the literature of group responsibility and the relevance of those themes to autonomous technologies. The first part of this chapter is organized along four areas of concern for the field. One is whether one can meaningfully ascribe responsibility to groups or whether doing so is simply shorthand for assigning responsibility to the individual members of those groups. If it does makes sense to do so, a second area of debate is what types of groups can be held responsible. A third area of inquiry is when and how the responsibility of a group can be distributed to its members. Finally, there are pragmatic issues about whether distributing group responsibility to its members is workable or creates the wrong incentives for the members involved. As will be discussed in this chapter and elaborated

---

[1]   Mark Coeckelbergh, *Moral Responsibility, Technology, and Experiences of the Tragic: From Kierkegaard to Offshore Drilling*, 18 SCI. & ENG'G. ETHICS 35, 36 (2012).

in more detail in Chapter 6, all four questions have implications for the responsibility of autonomous machines and those who design, manufacture, use, or
work with them. At the same time, in part because of differences between law
and ethics and in part because of the nature of the problem, the ethical literature
does not provide completely satisfactory answers to those questions. Finally,
this chapter will conclude with a discussion of the implications of complexity
theory for these issues. Concepts from that theory suggest the problems we are
considering will remain intractable; thus, we may find ourselves consigned to
applying second-best solutions to the question of how to attribute responsibility from machine to human.

THE MORAL RESPONSIBILITY OF GROUPS AS SUCH

Whether a group itself can be morally accountable for a harm involves an
ontological or conceptual decision as to whether a group can exist in and of
itself as more than the sum of its parts, or whether in reality group behavior
is simply a metaphor for the actions of the individual members of that group.[2]
Of course, as discussed in the previous chapter, the law has already answered
this question, at least in some circumstances. It is well settled that entities such
as corporations and nation states have legal personality and can incur legal
obligations and duties and enjoy certain rights. But the issue persists. In some
jurisdictions, business entities are not charged with crimes because they are
considered incapable of committing them, although their human agents are.
The debate in corporate law between Adolf Berle and Gardiner Means on the
one hand, who argue that the corporation should be understood as an entity in
itself, and Michael Jensen and William Meckling on the other, who view the
corporation as a nexus of contracts between and among its constituents, is one
manifestation of the larger issue.[3]

The issue endures in part because of the structure of groups. By their nature,
no group can act for itself and must instead do so through its agents. Colin
Wight thus argues that although the state is recognized as a legal subject under

---

    [2]   For example, David Copp believes that under some circumstances, a group can
be found to be morally responsible for an action or outcome even though its members
are not. David Copp, *The Collective Moral Autonomy Thesis*, 38 J. Soc. Phil. 369
(2007).

    [3]   *See* Adolf A. Berle, Jr. and Gardiner C. Means, The Modern Corporation and
Private Property 353–7 (1933); Michael C. Jensen and William H. Meckling, *Theory
of the Firm: Managerial Behavior, Agency Costs and Ownership Structure*, 3 J. Fin.
Econ. 305 (1976). As discussed below, the question whether corporations can commit
crimes is another example of this issue. For a discussion, *see* Edward B. Diskant,
*Comparative Corporate Criminal Liability: Exploring the Uniquely American Doctrine
through Comparative Criminal Procedure*, 118 Yale L. J. 126 (2008).

international law, it is not in itself capable of independent action and should not be treated as a person for moral evaluation.[4] For Wight, even though the state has structures and causal powers that facilitate collective action, "such causal power that does emerge can only be accessed by individuals acting in cooperation with others."[5] John Hasnas argues the same is true for corporations.[6] On the other hand, scholars such as J. Angelo Corlett argue that at least in some organizations, the structures of control and decision which Wight concedes exist are strong enough that it is appropriate to speak of the organization itself as having a sufficient level of intentionality and ability to, under the individualistic view of moral responsibility, allow us to hold it responsible for its actions, separately and apart from its members.[7]

Despite these ontological concerns, the assumption under law that certain groups as such can be held legally responsible for harms means that assigning legal responsibility to a group for an autonomous machine's behaviors will not be a major leap in current views of legal responsibility, as long there is a strong enough connection between the group and the machine. For example, it would seem uncontroversial to hold a state responsible for harm caused by a robot weapon under its command, as was suggested in Chapter 2. Such a weapon would be the property of the state and would presumably be engaged in activities for the state. It would be equally unremarkable to hold a corporation liable for harms caused by a defectively designed autonomous vehicle. A somewhat more difficult issue arises, however, when one asks what kinds of groups are subject to legal responsibility.

TYPES OF COLLECTIVES

If we assume that groups as such can be subject to legal and moral evaluation, the question emerges as to what kinds of groups qualify. Several ethicists, again informed by the requirements of individual moral responsibility, argue that longlived groups with centralized decision-making systems and structures,

---

[4] Colin Wight, *State Agency: Social Action without Human Activity?*, 30 REV. INT'L STUD. 269, 278 (2004).

[5] Colin Wight, *They Shoot Dead Horses Don't They? Locating Agency in the Agent-Structure Problematique*, 5 EUR. J. INT'L REL. 109, 128 (1999).

[6] John Hasnas, *Where Is Felix Cohen When We Need Him? Transcendental Nonsense and the Moral Responsibility of Corporations*, 19 J. L. & POL. 55 (2010) (arguing that the corporation cannot bear moral responsibility because it is a legal fiction). *See also* Pekka Mäkelä, *Collective Agents and Moral Responsibility*, 38 J. SOC. PHIL. 456 (2007) (arguing against collective responsibility).

[7] J. Angelo Corlett, *Collective Moral Responsibility*, 32 J. SOC. PHIL. 573, 575 (2001). *See also* Philip Pettit, *Responsibility Incorporated*, 117 ETHICS 171 (2007) (arguing that certain groups meet criteria for being held morally responsible).

such as an army or a corporation, can be subject to moral evaluation because those structures enable such groups to "think" and "plan" and to form and pursue goals. In contrast, more amorphous collectives such as spectators at a sporting event or patrons in a restaurant should not be subject to moral evaluation. If some harm occurs at such an event or at the restaurant, individual spectators or customers will be subject to evaluation, not the "group" itself.

Philip Pettit argues that business firms would qualify as a group capable of bearing moral responsibility. Pettit begins by setting out the conditions under which a group as such might bear responsibility, analogous to the requirements for the individual: a sense in which the group is faced with a decision of moral significance; access to information necessary to make judgments about the value of options; and some degree of control in an organization to choose between various options.[8] Pettit argues that such conditions are met in corporations. First, he urges that corporate judgment is distinct from the judgment of its constituents; similarly, group members can weigh different options for the group, as opposed to simply doing so from an individual perspective. (Thus in his view, a board of directors decides as a board, not as individual directors.) Finally, the control element is met because some groups, such as firms, "program" how their agents will act: the firm's objectives, culture, and so on engender policies and incentives that create the conditions for its agents to act in particular ways.[9] Under this view: "The members will have responsibility as enactors of the corporate deed, so far as they could have refused to play that part and didn't. The group agent as a whole will have responsibility as the source of that deed: the ultimate, reason-sensitive planner at its origin."[10]

Other scholars propose an intermediate step that holds individuals subject to moral responsibility as members of teams. Ian Lee suggests:

> [W]e think of a collectivity as being constituted and maintained by the self-identification of its members with the group. In this definition, the key concept is neither the group's identity nor its institutional features but the fact that its members regard themselves as the members of a collectivity. Collectivities are not quasi-persons, but *teams*.[11]

For Lee, a team exists when "its members regard themselves as the members of a team and adopt collectively rational principles as principles of action."[12] A team member can be held responsible for the actions of other team members

---

[8]   Pettit, *supra* note 7, at 177.

[9]   *Id.*, at 191.

[10] *Id.*, at 192.

[11] Ian B. Lee, *Corporate Criminal Responsibility as Team Member Responsibility*, 31 OXFORD J. LEGAL STUD. 755, 772 (2011).

[12] *Id.*

because he or she has contributed to the goals of the team (thus having some degree of moral culpability), even though he or she was not directly involved in the harm caused by a team through one of his or her teammates. Lee feels it is also appropriate to condemn the team as such, over and above its members. He argues that "[c]ondemnation of the team draws attention to the contributory role that the team's norms played in producing the wrongdoing and to the responsibility of the member in relation to the content of those norms."[13] This is important because in Lee's view, focusing only on the individual in effect absolves the team, with no impact on the norms and structures of the team that contributed to the harm.[14]

For the law and for autonomous machines, the issue is whether as a legal matter one should be able to attribute legal liability to looser associations that are not already legal entities in themselves and thus already subject to liability. Perhaps a software design team might qualify. The British Standards Institution identifies an interesting issue in this regard. As part of its definition of an autonomous system, the BSI states that a system is a "set of parts which, when interoperating, has behavior that is not present in any of the parts them-selves."[15] It explains that this "includes systems of fleeting duration, such as cars passing by each other and behaving appropriately during this moment, to long-lived systems such as Voyager II."[16]

Including systems of fleeting duration within these design standards (pro-vided they are autonomous, that is, with the "ability to perform intended tasks based on current state, knowledge and sensing, without human intervention")[17] recognizes that even fleeting groups have causal effects in the world. The example of cars passing by each other and behaving appropriately at that time is a good one. An autonomous car will be designed to sense and interact with other cars, as well as with the road itself, to regulate traffic flow and of course to avoid collisions. It is possible that unique configurations of autonomous cars that are interacting with one another will engage in what would plausibly be called collective action that could cause harm in particular instances; such configurations will have exhibited behaviors not present in any of the individ-ual cars themselves.

---

[13] *Id.*, at 778.

[14] *See id.* Amy Sepinwall also uses team ethics to argue that it is appropriate for corporate officials to be held morally responsible for crimes committed by corpor-ations. Amy J. Sepinwall, *Guilty by Proxy: Expanding the Boundaries of Responsibility in the Face of Corporate Crime*, 63 Hastings L.J. 411, 435–45 (2011).

[15] British Standards Institution, Robots and Robotic Devices: Guide to the Ethical Design and Application of Robots and Robotic Systems, standard 3.9.

[16] *Id.*

[17] *Id.*, standard 3.1.

Such fleeting systems have much shorter duration than the teams which Lee proposes can be subject to moral evaluation and are much more loosely organized. Yet, if individual cars have been designed for traceability and transparency, presumably we should be able to discover why they "chose" to act in concert and why they chose to exhibit a particular behavior. For at least a brief moment, there will have been organizing principles for the fleeting system. Artificial intelligence is already being used to detect heretofore unnoticed patterns in large crowds of people in public places such as stadiums, to help businesses better understand where to place advertisements and vendors.[18] Under the BSI standards, such fleeting systems would be considered capable of causing moral harms and the system would be subject to moral evaluation. Greater acceptance of the "reality" of such systems for moral evaluation might pave the way for subjecting those fleeting groups to legal claims and potential liability.

More generally, factors such as a group's duration, its internal structures, and a common purpose might help determine when it is appropriate to attribute liability among a wider group of human "participants," in the case of autonomous vehicles, among manufacturers, software programmers, and engineers, as Vladek and others propose. Team concepts such as those suggested by Lee would make it possible to hold somewhat looser associations of individuals or groups responsible for harms caused by autonomous machines. This would encompass the associations themselves and team members. However, the issue of which kinds of groups can be subject to responsibility never completely disappears. Teams and systems of fleeting duration that allow for looser affiliations of individuals to be held responsible simply raise the issue to another level. Whether there are enough coherent norms and structures in a collective to constitute a team will always be subject to debate. For example, some might argue that contractual relations that define the rights and duties of a production team allow us to characterize that loose affiliation as a team. Others, however, would argue that those "norms" are too thin to create a common ethos and goals that are associated with sports teams. The problem is even more difficult with systems of fleeting duration because any ties between interacting individuals seem even looser.

---

[18] For example, WaitTime offers crowd intelligence services to help venues monitor crowd movement and density and to provide customers with information about the shortest wait times. WaitTime, Product, http://thewaittimes.com/product/.

THE DISTRIBUTION OF RESPONSIBILITY FROM A GROUP TO ITS MEMBERS

One of the reasons why questions about whether and what kinds of groups are subject to moral and legal evaluation are so difficult is that they have implications for the distribution of responsibility from groups to their members. This perhaps is the most knotty problem for autonomous machines and systems. In ethics, recalling Chapter 3's discussion of individual moral responsibility, there seems to be general agreement that since "judgments about the moral responsibility of [a collective's] members are not logically derivable from judgments about the moral responsibility of a collectivity,"[19] the member herself must be culpable in some way before moral judgments about the collective can be transferred to her. Otherwise, the individual will be held responsible by association. As will be recalled from Chapter 3, concerns such as these explain the International Military Tribunal's caution in using its power to hold that a group is a criminal organization and to use that finding to hold individual members responsible as well.

Despite these concerns, ethicists have explored several reasons why it might be appropriate to hold members responsible for the actions of a group. Some argue that if a member shares the objectives of a group, it is appropriate that she share responsibility for the group's actions to further them. This is reflected in Lee's argument that a member of a team can be held responsible for the actions of other teammates because they share a common goal. Another approach focuses on shared benefits: if a member benefits from the group it is fair that she share its burdens, including responsibility for harms committed by the group or other group members. Yet another argument for personal responsibility stems from whether a person has joined a group voluntarily; the act of joining a group is a form of consent to bear the consequences of things done by the group. Each of these approaches provides plausible reasons for when it is fair to hold someone liable for a group action and is reflected in the law. At the same time, each approach is limited.

Common Purpose

Legal doctrine is quite familiar with the concept of common purpose, as is evident in the crimes of conspiracy and joint criminal enterprise, in particular types one and two. Common purpose in the context of those crimes makes each participant in the conspiracy individually culpable, thereby creating a predi-

---

[19] Virginia Held, *Can a Random Collection of Individuals be Morally Responsible?*, 67 J. PHIL. 471, 475 (1970).

cate for individual criminal liability. In ethics, common purpose also serves to create at least a modicum of personal culpability that would justify distributing moral blame on the group level to its members. If for example, software developers, manufacturers, and engineers share a common goal of producing an autonomous machine, under this view it is not unfair to find them liable for harms caused by that machine. For example, in the context of autonomous vehicles, Loh and Loh propose using common purpose to constitute car and driver as a group subject to moral responsibility. In their view, autonomous vehicles themselves have not reached a sufficient level of autonomy to be considered ethical subjects themselves. This means that responsibility has to be located within a broader network:[20]

> Autonomous driving systems fulfill the given prerequisites for hybrid systems [subject to moral responsibility] since they consist of a set of collaborating but clearly distinguishable subsystems that are categorically different: the car and the driver. Each subsystem is at least operationally autonomous, and together they form a plural subject ... with the common goal of getting safely from *A* to *B* in the most efficient way possible.[21]

As discussed, the authors view common purpose as constitutive of the group. They foresee the division of responsibility by tasks. As between the driver and the car, the "artificial system" is responsible for safe driving operations.[22] Much of the authors' approach assumes a human operator will be present in an autonomous vehicle and will have some degree of control over it: "As long as there is something like a driver in autonomous cars, however, she will have to bear the responsibility for making the morally relevant decisions that are not covered by traffic rules, as part of the hybrid system."[23] They also agree with what appears to be the consensus discussed in Chapter 2 that most accidents involving autonomous vehicles in normal operations will be handled by product liability laws, and that on rare occasions, specific programmers and engineers might become involved.[24]

---

[20]   Wulf Loh and Janina Loh, *Autonomy and Responsibility in Hybrid Systems: The Example of Autonomous Cars*, *in* ROBOT ETHICS 2.0: FROM AUTONOMOUS CARS TO ARTIFICIAL INTELLIGENCE 35, 41 (Patrick Lin, Ryan Jenkins, and Keith Abney eds., 2017).

[21]   *Id.*, at 42–3. The term "plural subject" stems from the work of Margaret Gilbert. *See, e.g.*, Margaret Gilbert, *Who Is to Blame? Collective Moral Responsibility and Its Implications for Group Members*, 30 MIDWEST STUD. PHIL. 94, 98–102 (2006).

[22]   Loh and Loh, *supra* note 20, at 45.

[23]   *Id.*

[24]   *Id.*, at 43.

Shared purpose therefore does have some plausibility as a reason for distributing responsibility from a group to its members, but this is not always obvious. It seems justified in the case of conspiracy to hold each member responsible for a crime everyone intended to be committed. However, this is less clear if the shared purpose is not prohibited. It could be argued that a manufacturer, software developer, and engineer pursue the common goal of creating an autonomous machine, but that goal is desirable. At a minimum, they do not work together for the purpose of causing harm, and if they do not intend to cause harm, why should they be held responsible for it? In law, the answer is obvious: tort law sidesteps problems related to intent and the appropriateness of goals by finding that it is enough that people foresee their activities could cause harm and do not take reasonable steps to avoid it. This is the impulse that informs Rule 2 discussed earlier. But foreseeability stands to cut off shared intentions or goals as a form of complicity: as Wolfgang Sohst puts it, large collectives "are usually organized so very complexly that hardly any relationship can be traced between the individual intention and the actually realized collective action, especially over longer periods of development."[25] Moreover, once we use foreseeability to distribute responsibility, we have moved away from a common goal approach. Further, as discussed in Chapter 3, foreseeability poses its own conceptual problems.

A related shortcoming of the common purpose approach is that it ignores differences between a goal and the means to achieve it. Soldiers might share the same military objective while on a mission yet disagree about the means to fulfill it. Under current understandings of liability, that one solider commits a war crime is not imputed to fellow soldiers even though their primary goal is the same. Thus, one must go beyond shared goals and differentiate between legitimate and illegitimate ends and between legitimate and illegitimate means, implying that shared goals alone are not sufficient conditions for distributing liability from the group to individual members.

Personal Benefit

If individuals have benefited from the design, manufacture, and sale of autonomous technology, it seems appropriate they share any costs incurred by them. Notice that the shared goals and benefits approaches do not necessarily require the individuals to be part of a particular kind of group, so long as there are goals and benefits common among the individuals involved. Shared goals or benefits also provide some of the moral underpinnings of agency law. The

---

[25] Wolfgang Sohst, COLLECTIVE MORAL RESPONSIBILITY 78 (Susan Rose trans., 2017).

principal and agent are supposed to have the same aims and both gain from their relationship, so in most cases, it seems appropriate that the principle shares legal responsibility for the agent's actions and sometimes bears full responsibility. Applied to autonomous machines, even though it is likely under current tort law that the manufacturer, and by extension the software developer and the engineer, will be the primary defendants in any action, it could also be argued that the owner/passenger of an autonomous vehicle should also bear some responsibility since he or she has employed the vehicle for his or her benefit.

Similar problems arise with benefits as a basis for associational responsibility. Reiff points out that benefits are not shared evenly among group members.[26] Further, culpability arising from receiving a benefit is not the same as culpability that arises from causing harm.[27] These problems lead to two consequences. A benefit-based system requires a method to share responsibility according to the benefit received. This might be possible in some cases, but not in others. A benefit might come from several sources that cross group boundaries, thus making it hard to use a group member, benefit-burden schema. Further, the difference between group-caused harm and the group benefit received raises several subissues. As Richard Vernon points out, one is the concern that any costs of sanctions for the original wrong will be disproportionate to any such benefit.[28] Moreover, it is not always the case that a person who receives benefits should share costs; for example, although citizens of a state certainly benefit from it, some vulnerable individuals are protected with no expectation of return.[29]

Voluntary Association

Another way to justify distributing group responsibility to group members is voluntary association. If a person freely agrees to join a group, it can be argued he has implicitly agreed to bear any consequences that arise from membership in that group, or has agreed to play a role within that organization—a role

---

[26] *See* Mark R. Reiff, *Terrorism, Retribution, and Collective Responsibility*, 34 Soc. Theory & Prac. 209, 218–19 (2008).

[27] *Id.*, at 219.

[28] Richard Vernon, *Punishing Collectives: States or Nations?*, in Accountability for Collective Wrongdoing 287, 300 (Tracy Isaacs and Richard Vernon eds., 2011) hereinafter Accountability for Collective Wrongdoing]. (*Citing* Richard Vernon, *States of Risk: Should Cosmopolitans Favor Their Compatriots?*, 21 Ethics & Int'l Aff. 451, 451–69 (2007).)

[29] *Id.* (*Citing* Robert Goodin, *What Is So Special about Our Fellow-Countrymen?*, 98 Ethics 663, 663–86 (1988).)

that will contribute to corporate acts that will have impacts in the world. Saba Bazargan makes the latter argument in connection with ethics in warfare.[30] Bazargan contends that any person who volunteers to participate in a cooperative project agrees to perform a role or function that will help fulfill the purpose of the project. She can thus be considered a coauthor of that function's end. That end is the cooperative act that the participants in the group do together. If that act is wrongful, the participant is complicit as a coauthor of that act.[31] For Bazargan, a person is not liable according to her effectiveness in the role; rather, it is the nature of the role itself that is the issue. The more important a role is in a cooperative project, the more culpable is the person who agrees to perform that role.[32]

If we want to expand the pool of people who could be held responsible for harms caused by autonomous machines and systems, voluntary association is perhaps the most persuasive reason to do so. As a rule, people choose to work for manufacturers and designers. Participants in a supply chain agree to enter into contractual relationships that form that chain. Everyone consents to perform a function they know contributes to the work of a specific group that leads eventually to the production of some autonomous technology. Similarly, if a group of humans and machines and systems work together, in most cases, the humans will have agreed to fulfill particular roles as the artificial agents fulfill theirs. Under Bazargan's approach, each participant in the design, manufacture, and training of autonomous machines becomes a coauthor of the various acts that resulted ultimately in that design, manufacturing, and training. If a harm arises and such individuals are held liable, this would not be a matter of distributing group liability to them; each person would be culpable individually because she agreed to perform her function.

On balance, voluntary association with a group and agreeing to play a particular role within it is an attractive justification for extending responsibility for harms attributable to groups to their members. At the same time, it has its own limitations. By definition, voluntary association leaves out people who do not freely associate with a group. Bazargan argues in this regard that persons who are drafted into the military are not culpable for acts done in concert with others because they were compelled to perform their respective functions.[33] In this regard, Sohst argues that voluntary association has the odd effect of leaving out the most important types of collective responsibility. "All situations of fundamental import, including collective responsibility for such huge

---

[30] Saba Bazargan, *Complicitous Liability in War*, 165 PHIL. STUD. 177 (2013).
[31] *Id.*, at 188.
[32] *Id.*
[33] *Id.*, at 192–3.

events as a military attack[], genocide or similarly serious macro-social crimes, cannot be decided with this criterion."[34] On the other end of these macro-social crimes, under this approach, humans who are associated with at least some autonomous systems of fleeting duration contemplated by the BSI would also likely be free from complicity. Further, it seems difficult to argue that the human designers and manufacturers of self-driving cars agreed to fulfill any function relevant to a cooperative act arising from a brief configuration of cars. Nor does it seem that any human passenger in the configuration of cars consented to fulfill a role that would have contributed to the group act.

One could respond that the voluntary association criterion is simply doing its job in the case of military conscription or the brief configuration of cars. Bazargan uses his theory to answer a particular question in the ethics of war: whether it is ethical to use deadly force against low ranking personnel in an army that is waging an unjust war. He argues that whether compulsion excuses a person from complicity depends on the nature of the threat and wrongfulness of participating in the cooperative project, so there is still room to hold draftees liable for serious violations of human rights. However, with regard to systems of fleeting duration, presumably the BSI felt there were good reasons to find that such systems could cause ethical harm. If so, a strictly voluntary approach would leave a vacuum in which some systems would cause harm but in which it would be hard to find its human participants responsible.

Sohst's major criticism of voluntary association as a basis for responsibility is tied to foreseeability. Even if a person does in fact join a group, Sohst argues that the member needs to be able to predict that the group will engage in morally blameworthy behavior in the future. This might be possible in some cases, such as where entities are expressly organized to commit crimes, but not in most organizations.

Finally, another issue raised by the voluntary association approach is that, like the benefits approach, there might need to be gradations of responsibility. Bazargan acknowledges, for example, that although a person is culpable if she agrees to perform a particular role in a cooperative project, some roles are more important in completing it than others.[35] If, then, there are such gradations in roles, then as a pragmatic matter, if the goal is to expand responsibility to a wider range of participants in a group, it is unclear if voluntary association improves on other justifications in reaching that goal.

---

[34]   Sohst, *supra* note 25, at 70.
[35]   Bazargan, *supra* note 30, at 188.

THE "PRAGMATICS" OF GROUP RESPONSIBILITY

The question of consequences, the fourth major area of concern in the group responsibility literature, is conceptual and pragmatic. Several concerns that fall under this major area of inquiry were alluded to earlier. Whether a group itself should suffer consequences for a wrong depends in part on the purposes of moral sanctions and whether such consequences serve them. Sanctions are used for several purposes, including corrective justice, retribution, societal condemnation, or deterrence of future wrongs. Determining which purpose should be served and whether a particular sanction will be effective in furthering it is hard enough in the case of individuals but becomes harder still when groups are involved. Since the group "has no soul to be damned and no body to be kicked," it is not possible to literally imprison a corporation or cause it to feel regret.

Nevertheless, one would expect that as a social tool, collective responsibility has various uses and will have varying effects depending on the social environments in which it is used. On the positive side, Melody Manchi Chao and her coauthors point out that people do in fact engage in what they term collective culpability: "blaming the collective or its members for a negative event caused by another member of the collective."[36] Such culpability is thought of as performing two functions. First, it might have a deterrent effect. Societies may hold groups or individuals responsible for someone else's actions because they are in the best position to control that person.[37] Second, collective culpability might also contribute to group solidarity if the group or its members believe they will be responsible for what someone does.[38] On the negative side, if an individual believes she will be held responsible for a wrong even if that responsibility is primarily someone else's, she will have little incentive to take care. Or if she is in a position to prevent another person from doing harm, she has less incentive to do so, since she will be held responsible by association anyway. Indeed, Mark Reiff argues that if an individual believes he will be found liable for wrongdoing committed by someone else, he will have an incentive to engage in such wrongdoing himself and reap its benefits, since he can no longer avoid punishment by refraining from the wrongful act.[39]

---

[36] Melody Manchi Chao, Zhi Xue Zhang, and Chi-Yue Chu, *Personal and Collective Culpability Judgment: A Functional Analysis of East Asian—North American Differences*, 39 J. CROSS-CULTURAL PSYCHOL.730.

[37] *Id.*, at 732.

[38] Philip E. Tetlock, *Social Functionalist Frameworks for Judgement and Choice: Intuitive Theologians, Politicians, and Prosecutors*, 109 PSYCHOL.REV. 451, 464 (2002).

[39] Reiff, *supra* note 26, at 242.

Under these circumstances, assigning responsibility to groups can be viewed as balancing the purposes of group sanctions with the fairness of distributing those sanctions downwards from group to individual. It follows that the type of group sanction or the specific consequence could be relevant to whether they should be shouldered by members of the group. For example, Avia Pasternak distinguishes between punishment and liability for harms. She considers punishment an expression of anger and moral judgment that should not be directed to individuals unless they are personally culpable.[40] As Pasternak puts it, "When the group itself is the agent that behaves wrongly but its members are the ones who end up being condemned, then the necessary connection between responsibility and punishment ... is broken."[41] Therefore it would be inappropriate to punish members for the wrongdoing of the group itself. In contrast, liability does not carry with it the same sense of condemnation as punishment carries.[42] Although liability also imposes costs on members, it is not based on personal culpability; rather, it is based on the need to pay for the costs incurred when the law is broken and to compensate victims for harms.[43] Hence, Pasternak argues that it would be appropriate to distribute liability to group members even though it would be inappropriate to punish them.

IMPLICATIONS

I have argued several times that the law does not hesitate to hold groups responsible for actions. But this must be qualified to some extent in light of the foregoing discussion of collective responsibility. The concerns of collective responsibility do influence the law.

In the corporate area, I mentioned earlier that there is debate as to whether business entities can be convicted of crimes.[44] In a three-volume report on corporations and international criminal law, the International Commission of Jurists notes that despite recent legislation in some states that enables corporations to be convicted of crimes, significant opposition persists. The Commission's Panel of Experts summarizes the conceptual reasons for this opposition:

> National criminal laws were developed many centuries ago, and they are built and framed upon the notion of the individual human being as a conscious being

---

[40] *See* Avia Pasternak, *The Distributive Effect of Collective Punishment*, in ACCOUNTABILITY FOR COLLECTIVE WRONGDOING, *supra* note 28, at 210, 215–16.

[41] *Id.*, at 216.

[42] *Id.*, at 216–18.

[43] *Id.*, at 213.

[44] *See* Diskant, *supra* note 3.

exercising freedom of choice, thought and action. Businesses as legal entities have been viewed as fictitious beings, with no physical presence and no individual consciousness. As such, many perceive it to be impossible to prove that a business entity had criminal intent, or knowledge. Furthermore, many believe that punishing individuals who commit crimes with the aim of imbuing a sense of wrong done, shame and remorse, is a central purpose of any criminal justice system. Questions arise as to how this can be achieved when the target is an artificial entity without the attributes of a human being.[45]

Notice that the Panel wrestles with the set of questions that occupy the attention of the literature of group responsibility. For example, the Panel considers the pragmatic reasons for refusing to convict business entities of crimes:

Another perceived obstacle is the fact that traditional criminal sanctions may not always be appropriate in respect of business. A business cannot be put in prison. A fine may not have a serious impact on the behavior of a large wealthy business, particularly if financial sanctions can be passed on to customers, thus attenuating although not obliterating their punitive effects. Other punishments tailored for business entities may include steps such as revoking the corporate charter or registration. However it will not always be clear whether it is in the interest of society to close a business down because it commits a crime.[46]

Again, these concerns echo a more general set of issues. If it is perceived that the law or a moral system's purposes are not served by addressing collectives as such, or that the consequences of legal or moral sanctions on a group are meaningless or minimal, then the legitimacy of that system would be brought into question. However, the Commission's Panel of Experts takes the view that these conceptual and pragmatic objections can be overcome.[47] It points out again that several jurisdictions now hold corporations liable for criminal acts. "In some jurisdictions," it writes, "the business can be held criminally liable for the acts of its employees, in others a business is directly responsible for the acts of senior management because the law considers them to be the 'brain' of the business, and as such the guilt of the business is inferred from their intention and knowledge."[48]

Giovanni Sartor argues in this regard that organizations such as corporations can be deemed to have intentionality for purposes of the law.[49] He uses Daniel

---

[45] INT'L COMM'N OF JURISTS, CORPORATE COMPLICITY & LEGAL ACCOUNTABILITY: VOL. 2: CRIMINAL LAW AND INTERNATIONAL CRIMES 57–8 (2008).

[46] *Id.*, at 58.

[47] *Id.*

[48] *Id.*

[49] Giovanni Sartor, *Cognitive Automata and the Law: Electronic Contracting and the Intentionality of Software Agents*, 17 ARTIFICIAL INTELLIGENCE L. 253 (2009).

Dennett's concept of the intentional stance: an observer cannot see another person's internal states, but nevertheless can make predictions about the person's likely behavior by treating the person as a rational agent, determining what desires that person ought to have, and then making those predictions.[50] Since the intentional stance is neutral as to what that person's internal state is, the stance can be taken with regard to other entities such as corporations.[51] It can also apply to advanced computer programs, such as Deep Blue, as well as to autonomous machines and systems.[52] The intentional stance can also be taken toward "a combination of human, electronic, and organizational components."[53] In each case, the intentional stance enables observers to say coherently that the actor in question has intentions.[54]

What are the implications of this debate for using legal responsibility to address as a whole the large number of participants in the design, manufacture, and use of autonomous technologies? One conclusion is that there are some grounds for identifying new or more loosely organized collections or groups that can be the subjects of moral and legal responsibility, but it still remains the case that, given the individualistic nature of moral and legal analysis, the best candidates for responsibility will always be organizations with the kinds of structure that enable them to exercise autonomy that matches roughly that of human beings. This means that attempts to address supply chains or other loose affiliations of business entities and human individuals will always be subject to criticism, unless a concept like Dennett's intentional stance can be applied cogently to those more amorphous groups. A second lesson is that the distributional issues that arise when moving from group to individual member create challenges if one tries to reach the many subgroups and individuals involved in the development of autonomous machines (this problem is explored in more detail in Chapter 6). Shared intention, shared benefits, and voluntary association each provide plausible grounds for penetrating larger entities, but they are not dispositive. Finally, to return to Balkin's insight that cultural tools have unintended consequences, the law would need to be cautious about the incentives that would be created if society chose to expand liability in this way.

---

[50]   *Id.*, at 261. (*Citing* Daniel C. Dennett, THE INTENTIONAL STANCE 17 (1989).)

[51]   *Id.*, at 263–4.

[52]   *Id.*, at 262.

[53]   *Id.*, at 264.

[54]   Pedro Freitas, Francisco Andrade, and Paulo Novais argue that reconceiving concepts such as intentionality so that criminal law can be extended to legal entities such as corporations shows how criminal law might be used to apply directly to autonomous agents. Pedro Miguel Freitas, Francisco Andrade, and Paulo Novais, *Criminal Liability of Autonomous Agents: From the Unthinkable to the Plausible*, in REVISED SELECTED PAPERS OF THE AICOL 2013 INTERNATIONAL WORKSHOPS ON AI APPROACHES TO THE COMPLEXITY OF LEGAL SYSTEMS 145 (Pompeu Casanovas et al. eds., 2013).

COMPLEXITY THEORY AND ITS MEANING FOR GROUP AND INDIVIDUAL RESPONSIBILITY

In the Preface I wrote that this project is informed by three intersecting areas of interest. The first is artificial intelligence and the machines and systems it will power. The second is the responsibility of groups, which has just been discussed. The third is complexity theory and its implications for legal responsibility. Recall that concepts from that theory inform Karnow's argument that once machines reach full autonomy, their complex interactions with their environment will make it impossible for humans to foresee their possible behaviors, thus making it impossible for human individuals, designers, and manufacturers to be held liable for negligence, for product liability, or even under strict liability. Here I discover complexity theory in more detail.

Concepts

As I have done in other contexts, I suggest complexity theory helps us better understand the nature of the problems involving collective responsibility, as well as the limits of our ability to respond to them. Complexity theory is relatively new, comprising a set of related concepts that have arisen from a number of disciplines. Two concepts in particular are pertinent to this discussion. The first is that, under the right conditions, the interactions of individuals can give rise to "higher level" phenomena that would not be predicted from the individuals themselves. The flock of birds is a much used example: individual birds need not be "programmed" to flock in Vs; as it happens, when a sufficient number of individual birds, programmed to follow simple instructions such as to keep up or to avoid collisions, interact, such patterns simply "emerge." Something, in this case the V, comes about that is greater than the sum of its parts.[55] With the flock of birds, it is the "micro" level interactions among individual birds which give rise to complex behavior, but in more complex systems discussed below, such behavior can also arise from the interaction of the components or rules of a single system.[56]

A second concept from complexity theory is that sometimes an emergent phenomenon will persist in its environment as a complex adaptive system.

---

[55] Craig W. Reynolds, *Flocks, Herds, and Schools: A Distributed Behavioral Model*, 21 COMPUT. GRAPHICS 25 (1987).

[56] Dirk J. Bezemer, *The Economy as a Complex System: The Balance Sheet Dimension*, 15 ADVANCED COMPLEX SYS, Supp. 2 1250047-1-1250047-22, at 1250047-2 (2012). Bezemer argues, using a flow of funds model, that complex changes in the economy can be accounted for by the structure of leverage within that economy. *Id.*, at 1250047-10.

Melanie Mitchell proposes two definitions for the term. A complex system is one "in which large networks of components with no central control and simple rules of operation give rise to complex collective behavior, sophisticated information processing, and adaptation via learning or evolution."[57] Put another way, it is "a system that exhibits nontrivial emergent and self-organizing behaviors."[58] According to the theory, such systems are readily observable in nature: the flock of birds discussed above, hurricanes, the immune system, the economy, and human societies have all been described as complex adaptive systems.[59] Such systems are distinct from the individuals from which they emerge and from their environment, although such systems are impacted by that environment. They are thus "inherently anti-reductionist."[60]

Complexity Theory and Collective Responsibility

The ontology of complex adaptive systems has several implications for collective responsibility. As an initial matter, because it accepts the reality of complex adaptive systems, complexity theory appears to side with those who argue that collectives are ontologically distinct from their members; thus, to the extent that responsibility requires that there be some actor to which responsibility can be attributed, complexity theory suggests that groups such as corporations, military organizations, and the state qualify as such actors because they persist in the world, have causative effects, and do not dissolve into constituent parts. Complexity theory is thus consistent with a basic assumption of law, that corporations and the like are appropriate units to which to ascribe legal responsibility; they are not simply extensions of the individual.

At the same time, the ontology of complex adaptive systems suggests that there are gaps between the individuals and the complex adaptive systems of which they are a part. First, complexity theory confirms that relatively innoc-

---

[57] Melanie Mitchell, COMPLEXITY: A GUIDED TOUR 13 (2009). (Emphasis omitted.)
[58] *Id.* (Emphasis omitted.)
[59] Reynolds, *supra* note 55 (birds); Matthew R. Lear, *A Complex Adaptive System Approach to Forecasting Hurricane Tracks*, (2005) (Master's thesis, Naval Postgraduate School), www.dtic.mil/dtic/tr/fulltext/u2/a435522.pdf (hurricanes); Debashish Chowdhury, *Immune Network: An Example of Complex Adaptive Systems* (1998), http://arxiv.org/pdf/cond-mat/9803033v1.pdf (immune system); W. Brian Arthur, COMPLEXITY THEORY AND THE ECONOMY (2014) (the economy), R. Keith Sawyer, SOCIAL EMERGENCE: SOCIETIES AND COMPLEX SYSTEMS (2005) (human societies).
[60] David Byrne, COMPLEXITY AND THE SOCIAL SCIENCES: AN INTRODUCTION 15 (1998).

uous individual behavior can contribute to unwanted actions or results at the group level. David Bella argues:

> To merely blame individuals … is to avoid … the essential claim of emergence: that the character of wholes should *not* be reduced to the character of parts[.] … [E]vil … outcomes can emerge through the efforts of normal, competent, and well adjusted people much like ourselves.[61]

Bella uses as an example scientists who worked for a government organization responsible for producing biological weapons. He shows how the interactions among individual scientists under relatively simple working rules and incentives could nevertheless result in the production of these weapons of mass destruction.[62] If Bella is right, complexity theory again confirms that in many circumstances, collectives as such must be the focus of responsibility, if only because individual actions that contributed to emergent collective behavior can seem unremarkable.

However, if an individual's actions are indeed innocuous, yet unlawful behavior at the group level can result from them, the distributive problem discussed earlier in this chapter becomes even more vexing. The nonlinear relationship between the complex interactions of individuals and the phenomena that emerge from those interactions means that in most cases it will be impossible to trace direct connections between an individual and the complex adaptive system of which she is a part and the impacts that system may have in the world. Since the phenomena that form and occur in complex systems emerge, how can an individual be said to have caused them? This suggests that even if an individual agrees with the complex system's actions, there may still be no meaningful connection between that agreement and what the system does. The nonlinearity between member and group suggests that the gap between the two cannot be bridged, and to the extent that the distribution of responsibility depends on some connection between a group and its members, the theory explains why the problem of distribution might be intractable.

Complexity Theory and Individual Responsibility

Complexity theory also has implications for responsibility itself. Again, under the standard model of responsibility, it is appropriate to hold an individual responsible when she has committed a proscribed act with some appreciation of the consequences and did so freely, and such act caused harm. But if either

---

[61] David Bella, *Emergence and Evil*, 8 EMERGENCE: COMPLEXITY & ORG. 102, 103 (2006).

[62] *Id.*, at 104–11.

action or inaction can lead to unanticipated consequences in the long run, how
can a person be responsible for them? "Self-organization ... strongly counsels
for a wider denotation for the term *cause*, one reconceptualized in terms of
'context-sensitive constraints' to include those causal powers that incorporate
circular causality, context-sensitive embeddedness, and temporality."[63] Klaus
Mainzer agrees that in a linear model of causation, "the extent of an effect is
believed to be similar to the extent of the cause. Thus a legal punishment of
a punishable action can be proportional to the degree of damage effected."[64]
However, since under complexity theory many phenomena result from random
events, the belief in proportionate responsibility is called into question.
Complexity theory suggests that most of the issues of concern to us have nonlinear characteristics. "As the ecological, economic, and political problems of
mankind have become global, complex, nonlinear, and random, the traditional
concept of individual responsibility is questionable."[65]

Responsibility also entails some measure of freedom. Up to this point, this
book has not delved into debates about that concept, but it is appropriate to do
so in more detail here. Alicia Juarrero uses complexity theory to reconstruct
the classic criteria of action, knowledge of consequences, and freedom required
for individual responsibility.[66] Juarrero argues that complex interactions with
her social environment have resulted in the human being developing certain
capacities that give her some measure of autonomy vis-à-vis that environment.
First, a person can interpret her environment, thus imposing order on and to
some extent freeing herself from it.[67] Second, as a complex system herself, the
human being "has new and different states to access."[68] Psychological states
such as attraction, self-awareness, and so on emerge from "complex neurological dynamics constructed as a result of the coevolution of human beings
and the complex social organization that they both structure and are structured
by."[69] These higher states enable a person to act as an autonomous agent. "In
humans," Juarrero writes, "there emerges both the remarkable capacity for
self-awareness and the sophisticated ability to think of, describe, judge and act
in terms of the meaningfulness of our choices."[70] This second aspect of freedom

---

[63] Alicia Juarrero, *On Philosophy's "To Rethink" List: Causality, Explanation, and
Ethics*, 20 ECOLOGICAL PSYCH. 278, 280 (2008).

[64] Klaus Mainzer, THINKING IN COMPLEXITY: THE COMPUTATIONAL DYNAMICS OF
MATTER, MIND, AND MANKIND 435 (5th ed. 2007).

[65] *Id.*

[66] Alicia Juarrero, DYNAMICS IN ACTION: INTENTIONAL BEHAVIOR AS A COMPLEX
SYSTEM 150, 173–4, 192–74, 211–13 (1999).

[67] *Id.*, at 231.

[68] *Id.*

[69] *Id.*, at 247.

[70] *Id.*

is closely related to a third. Just as the individual's freedom to access new and different states emerges from the constraints of other humans and social organizations, so too a human person is free when she is able to constrain her own behavior. "[I]ntentional human action is free to the degree that context-ual constraints put the most complex levels of its neurological organization, those governing meaning, values and morals, in control."[71] Juarrero explains: "[I]f you're going to behave ethically, there are some things you just can't do. At the same time, however, together with the decision to be ethical, other new possibilities appear, thus making the agent freer within that context."[72]

The ability to interpret one's environment, access various emotional and cognitive states, and constrain one's behavior does give the individual some measure of freedom. However, Juarrero urges that a full understanding of an individual's behavior cannot be divorced from its organizational context: the interactions between the individual and her environment that form the cogni-tive and psychological states make meaningful choice possible.[73] However, for other scholars, these constraints lead them to doubt whether an individual enjoys much freedom at all:

> We are shaped by environment, genetics, and experience in a way that affects what we perceive as reasons and narrows the horizon of possibilities for action. Environmental, genetic and psychological factors all shape what count as reasons for a person. Recognizing this should challenge our confidence that a given wrong-doer was morally capable of doing better.[74]

For these reasons some who want to retain some concept of responsibility are led to conclude that such responsibility must be constructed. "Responsibility ... does not exist prior to its assignment."[75]

Juarrero, however, continues to hold that a person's character, understood as the accretion of constant interactions between a person's original internal dynamics with her past and present social environment, influences how a person will behave.[76] In her view, complexity theory thus leaves room for

---

[71] *Id.*

[72] *Id.*, at 248.

[73] *Id.*, at 249–50. Elsewhere, she writes: "Moral agents ... can no longer be thought of as Newtonian atoms. They are inextricably embedded in a network of feedback loops that become aspects of the agent's reflection and even of his or her identity." Juarrero, *supra* note 66, at 278–82, 281.

[74] Erin I. Kelly, *Reparative Justice, in* ACCOUNTABILITY FOR COLLECTIVE WRONGDOING, *supra* note 28, at 193, 193–4.

[75] Anton Schütz, *Desiring Society: Autopoiesis beyond the Paradigm of Mastership*, 5 LAW & CRITIQUE 149, 160 (1994).

[76] Juarrero, *supra* note 66, at 250. Similarly, Mainzer writes, "Individual freedom is not abolished, but restricted by collective effects of complex systems in nature and

individual responsibility, but pays more attention to one's past history and social environment. "[W]e cannot start afresh, halfway through our lives, as if the previous years had never happened. On the other hand we are not, for the same reason, condemned to a predetermined future."[77] This is because the social environment coevolves with individuals, such that over time, human beings have the ability to select and to change the environments within which they live:

> Once we are mature and aware, we can self-consciously select the stimuli to which we will respond and that will affect what and who we are in the future. At that point we are as responsible for who we will become as is the environment. And once again, that is true for each of us both as members of a community and as individuals.[78]

Over the long run, however, interactions with the environment do cause us to engage in behaviors that become more or less fixed: we become set in our ways as we grow older.[79] For this reason Juarrero urges that a society must pay attention to an individual's earliest experiences with social organizations.[80] This also highlights the importance of choosing carefully the social environments with which one will interact.

The idea of freedom acting within and perhaps contributing to constraint resonates with Coeckelbergh's idea of the tragic, informed by Kierkegaardian concepts of tragedy and responsibility. Complexity theory's recognition of emergent phenomena has also been used to explain cascading events such as stock market crashes or disasters, in which interactions among agents lead to abrupt breaks. Coeckelbergh argues that engineering disasters such as Deepwater Horizon are born out of a combination of complex technology, cascading events, and unexpected consequences that make it impossible to apply conventional methods for allocating blame that presuppose that someone has knowledge and control.[81] He suggests that those kinds of event should be viewed through the lens of tragedy and responsibility in which it is understood that the actors have some ability to act (indeed have a responsibility to do so) and some measure of control, in the face of something that is out of one's control.[82] "[T]tragedy is not the word we normally use to express concrete experi-

---

society which cannot be forecast or controlled in the long run. Thus it is not enough to have good individual intentions." MAINZER, *supra* note 64, at 435.

[77]   Juarrero, *supra* note 66, at 252.

[78]   *Id.*, at 260.

[79]   *Id.*, at 254.

[80]   *Id.*, at 254–5.

[81]   Coeckelbergh, *supra* note 1, at 35.

[82]   *Id.*, at 40.

ences of limitations to human control (e.g. when an accident happens in which we had a hand), but rather the condition of possibility for such experiences."[83] This tragic aspect of human experience, however, does not absolve individuals of responsibility; rather, it tempers it:

> Technological action is not a matter of having either full control or no control. We usually have some control. Similarly, knowledge is a matter of degree. Therefore, where technological action is concerned the question is not whether or not a person is responsible, but to what extent a person is responsible.[84]

This kind of approach to responsibility matches well with Juarerro's use of complexity theory to argue for human freedom within the complex adaptive system which is the human individual and the large system of human society.

Complexity Theory and Organizations

Earlier I argued that because complexity theory takes seriously the possibility of complex adaptive systems, it confirms law's application to organizations such as corporations and states as such. At the same time, if it is true that complexity theory makes concepts such as foreseeability and causation less effective as tools for ascribing responsibility, this suggests that theory poses challenges for collective responsibility as well, given that it models itself on individual responsibility. The work of William Frederick is interesting in this regard. Frederick uses complexity theory to show how corruption among corporate management might emerge.[85] He argues that corporate wrongs are a "natural" outcome of a set of dynamics that involve more than rogue members of the firm. Instead, they emerge from complex interactions of competing norms that exist in every firm. As just mentioned, Frederick focuses on corporate wrongdoing, but this analysis can be generalized to many corporate behaviors. Frederick also uses a biological framework, but in my view, one need not accept the validity of the analogy to understand the more general argument.

For Frederick, corporate behavior is driven by a set of values that stem from biological impulses that inform all human societies. Like a cell that fights entropy by drawing in food for energy so that it can draw in more, a firm draws "resources from its environment and convert[s] them to fungible products and services" so it can continue in business.[86] (Frederick refers to this

---

[83] *Id.*, at 41.

[84] *Id.*, at 42.

[85] William C. Frederick, *Emergent Management Morality: Explaining Corporate Corruption*, 5 EMERGENCE 5 (2003).

[86] *Id.*, at 7.

activity as "economizing.") To do so, firms and their agents try to find niches in the market and in the corporate organization itself to increase chances of survival.[87] This economizing becomes a value in itself. Human societies are often marked by hierarchies of dominance and this shows itself in the firm, yet differences in power among members are tempered somewhat by reciprocal social exchanges that create rough expectations of fairness.[88] Thus, a form of business morality, a second source of values, comes to be associated with these dynamics. At the same time, the firm is also influenced by the values and behaviors which individual employees and managers bring to the firm. This third source is less predictable. These drivers of corporate behavior—the need to survive in the business environment, rough expectations of fairness, and individual values—can conflict and lead to "unexpected" behavior.

Contradictions arise from simultaneous efforts to achieve adaptive economizing outcomes for the firm, power aggrandizement for coalition members, and deontic obligations stemming from symbiotic social contracts with internal and external stakeholders. Management morality is therefore the emergent consequence of autonomous agents acting out the morally contradictory behavioral predispositions of genetically embedded neural algorithms.[89]

Frederick thus argues that corporate wrongs are a "natural" outcome of a set of dynamics that involve more than individual caprice:

> Shocking and ugly as they are, such behaviors are entirely consistent with what is otherwise a normal agent-environment, self-reinforcing, feed-back interaction … Executive behavior at rogue corporations was precisely what one can expect of adaptive agents responding to environment opportunities on their "fitness landscapes."[90]

To be fair, Frederick does not excuse such behavior. Like Juarrero, he argues that although firm dynamics might predispose an individual toward a particular behavior, they are not determinative; a person can still choose to act against her environment.[91] Even so, the work of both theorists leaves the strong impression that the environment, that is, the firm itself, is crucial in encouraging and enabling unwanted behaviors.[92] Moreover, one could extend the fitness land-

---

[87]   *Id.*, at 8–10.

[88]   *Id.*, at 12.

[89]   *Id.*

[90]   *Id.*, at 25–6.

[91]   *Id.*, at 26.

[92]   *See* also Minka Woermann, *Corporate Identity, Responsibility and the Ethics of Complexity, in* COMPLEXITY, DIFFERENCE & IDENTITY: AN ETHICAL PERSPECTIVE 67 (Paul Cilliers and Rika Preiser eds., 2010). Woerman argues that "since we are dynamically differentiated across contexts, our individual responsibilities within a corporation

scape analogy to apply to firms who must compete within a particular market, for whom the choice of environment is not always an option, short of entering or leaving the market.

Implications for Responsibility for Autonomous Technologies

Complexity theory places the actions of major firms and organizations that are involved in the development of autonomous technologies into a broader context. As discussed earlier, complexity theory gives further credence to holding collectives responsible as such. However, the theory does not resolve the problem of the pragmatics of responsibility, particularly as applied to large, complex systems. Complexity theory suggests that firms will always adapt to and coevolve with the very norms that seek to guide them, ensuring that organizations will remain elusive targets for regulation. This resonates with Iris Chiu's description of the regulatory landscape that includes in its features forms of private and public ordering, in which firms have power to affect that landscape. One would expect large technology firms, driven by their own internal dynamics, to act as their earlier predecessors did. But perhaps the most important implication stems from complexity theory's view that there is no linear connection between the emergent structures, cultures, or behaviors that comprise collectives and the complex interactions of the individuals from which they arise. This could mean that an attempt to derive collective responsibility from the acts of culpable individuals at the lower level or to derive individual responsibility from the acts of the collective might not be a derivation at all; it might be an assignment of responsibility. This suggests that although there might be a desire to hold a larger group of people and machines acting together responsible for the harms they cause, any such responsibility will be constructed.

If responsibility is more in the nature of an assignment than a derivation, it calls into question our need to rely on the individualistic conception of moral and legal responsibility. Perhaps responsibility can be modified or reconceived to better account for responsibility in general and to better address harms caused by autonomous machines and systems in particular. That is the purpose of the next chapter.

---

cannot be equivalent to our responsibilities as people. This is because our corporate responsibilities are determined by our roles and identities within corporations and are, therefore, framed within practice." *Id.*, at 179.

PART III

Reimagining responsibility and the responsible agent

5. Reframing responsibility

Chapters 3 and 4 argued that many of the core issues that arise from using the law to address harms caused by autonomous technologies stem from our reluctance to find someone responsible if she is not personally culpable in some way, a problem exacerbated when collectives are involved. We have seen that our ethical impulses inform the law's approach to associational responsibility, but conceptual problems with such responsibility create tensions within law and ethics and between each other. The felt need to use law to address harms caused by autonomous machines and systems on the one hand, and a deep aversion to liability by association on the other, make it likely we will perceive gaps in responsibility, moral and legal, as autonomous technologies become more prevalent and we use our current moral and legal concepts to address harms they cause. Finally, themes taken from complexity theory suggest that some of these issues might be intractable.

The concern that there will be gaps leads to two broad, interrelated strategies. The next two chapters explore two aspects of the first strategy: to change the way we understand responsibility or the way we understand the responsible agent. This chapter discusses how societies might emphasize other ways of applying responsibility or of distributing it, to help ease the tensions raised by the individualistic, Aristotelian conception of responsibility, or to mitigate harms without concerning ourselves with who is responsible for such harms. This chapter argues that just as these other ways of understanding responsibility and responding to injuries already play a role in addressing wrongs to others, so too they will figure into responses to harms caused by autonomous technologies, perhaps more so. Chapter 6 explores more speculative ideas about possible changes in the way we understand agency and autonomy. Ultimately, however, the strategy of recasting responsibility or responsible agents does not provide a complete answer to the problems of harm, in particular because the idea of individual responsibility is so persistent.

STRICT LIABILITY AS AN ALTERNATE FORM OF RESPONSIBILITY

Chapter 2 discussed recommendations that strict liability be used as a means to avoid issues involving ordinary negligence and product liability law as they apply to autonomous machines and systems. I return to that doctrine now in more detail, in light of the concerns about individual and collective responsibility discussed in the preceding two chapters. Strict liability has existed for centuries, and its longevity indicates that some moral justifications can be given for using it to hold people liable for harms, that it performs some desired function, or both. Criticisms and defenses of the doctrine have tended to center around the ethics of strict liability, doctrinal coherency and feasibility (often in comparison to negligence), and the incentives strict liability might or might not create.

Moral Considerations

With regard to the moral issues raised by strict liability, under the doctrine, culpability—at least in its stronger aspects found in criminal law and tort—is not taken into account; it is sufficient that there is some relevant association between the respondent and the harm, such as ownership of the reservoir in the paradigmatic *Rylands v. Fletcher* case.[1] At the same time, commentators acknowledge that this approach is problematic precisely because of strict liability's disregard for the blameworthiness of the defendant. Although Stephen Cohen defends the doctrine, he is aware of the issue: "The heart of the doctrine of strict liability (unlike any doctrine of negligence) holds that someone can be liable even if he has exercised all required, reasonable, or even (all) possible care that a certain event not occur."[2] This seems to run counter to the Aristotelian conception of responsibility explored in Chapter 3.

Cohen responds to this objection by pointing out that the principle of personal responsibility is just one of several principles relevant in cases of harm. Moral principles can be overridden by others, and as there is no generally acceptable hierarchy of moral norms, there is no reason why personal responsibility should take precedence on moral grounds alone.[3] As Cohen points out, another moral framework shifts the question from the fairness of holding a person responsible to the fairness of having someone bear the costs of a harm. "[T]he issue is not so much whether it is fair to the … defendant … to be held responsible for a harm he has caused, but whether it is fairer for him or … the plaintiff to bear those costs."[4] Epstein shares this view. He writes:

> In any system of common law liability, a court must allocate, explicitly or implicitly, a loss that has already occurred between the parties—usually two—before it. It

---

[1]   *Rylands v. Fletcher*, L.R. 3 H.L. 330 (1868).

[2]   Stephen Cohen, *Justifications for a Doctrine of Strict Liability*, 8 Soc. Theory & Prac. 213, 215 (1982).

[3]   *Id.*, at 216.

[4]   *Id.*, at 220.

could turn out that neither of the parties acted in a manner that was unreasonable or improper from either an economic or a moral point of view, but a decision that the conduct of both parties was "proper" under the circumstances does not necessarily decide the legal case; there could well be other reasons why one party should be preferred to another.[5]

In this regard, Epstein points out that negligence itself is not free of moral issues. The reasonable person standard as the measure of the required standard of care is the most obvious example: people who in fact cannot act with such care are nevertheless found liable for negligence.[6] Since the standard does not take into account the particular capacities of the individual, it departs from a pure version of individual responsibility.

Strict liability can be justified on fairness grounds, Cohen contends. He argues that most parties who are now subject to strict liability already know they are. They tend to be large entities that can take precautions against risk. Moreover, strict liability usually applies in cases where such entities' activities affect large numbers of people. Strict liability requires these entities to give an "unconditional guarantee for their products or activities."[7] Not only might this encourage buyers, but it also might encourage entities to come up with even safer products or services. Finally, in Cohen's view, strict liability does not rob parties of choice. Earlier, in Chapter 4, I argued in my discussion of complexity theory that the decision to enter or leave a market might be one of the few choices that a firm can exercise: once in the market the firm's degrees of freedom become constrained. That choice is enough for Cohen, at least with regard to strict liability. He argues that large entities take on a special position in society, again because of the broad impact they have, but also because people often cannot avoid those impacts. The decision to take up that special position becomes a form of choice. "Given that there are some benefits which stem from a system of strict liability, the fact that one chooses to occupy a position in which he is strictly liable strengthens the claim that that system is justified, that is, since it is not forced upon someone."[8]

---

[5]   Richard Epstein, *A Theory of Strict Liability*, 2 J. Leg. Stud. 151, 157 (1973).
[6]   *Id.*, at 153.
[7]   Cohen, *supra* note 2, at 225.
[8]   *Id.*, at 226.

Coherency and Feasibility

With regard to the doctrinal coherency of strict liability and feasibility of use, Epstein makes the case that strict liability has the benefit of avoiding the problems raised by negligence:

> [T]he rules of liability should be based upon the harm in fact caused and not upon any subsequent determination of the reasonableness of the defendant's conduct. The question of liability is thereby severed from both general cost-benefit analysis of the defendant's conduct and a moral examination of his individual worth[.] ... [T]he rules of strict liability avoid both the unfairness and complications created when negligence, in either its economic or moral sense, is accepted as the basis of tort law.[9]

I have already discussed Epstein's concerns about the moral implications of negligence. He adds to this criticism by arguing that the general cost-benefit analysis used as a measure of negligence, most famously represented by Learned Hand's BPL formula (there is liability if the burden (B) of taking care is less than the amount of loss (L) from the failure to do so, times the probability (P) of that loss),[10] does not help resolve certain coordination problems, that is, the formula does not help two parties determine the required amount of care when that amount depends in part on the level of care the other party is taking.[11]

As to the advantages of strict liability in terms of fairness and feasibility, Epstein rests much of his conception of strict liability on causation as one of the reasons a court might prefer one party over the other. As related in Chapter 3, Epstein recognizes that causation as a legal concept resonates with the commonsense understanding that a person is responsible for harms he causes. Epstein develops his view of causation in four situations: when a person uses force, fright, or compulsion, or creates dangerous circumstances. Here I concentrate on the situation involving dangerous circumstances because it is the one most relevant to autonomous technologies. Under the law, a person can be held responsible for creating a dangerous condition that results in an injury. Epstein points out that there is a volitional element to this rule: a defendant created the condition.[12] At the same time, analytically, creating a condition that *results in* an injury is different in his view than causation via force, "A hit B."[13] Moreover, Epstein wants to cabin "results in" by requiring that the dangerous

---

9   Epstein, *supra* note 5, at 189.
10 *United States v. Carroll Towing*, 159 F.2d 169, 173 (2d Cir. 1947).
11 *Id.*, at 156–7.
12 *Id.*, at 177.
13 *Id.*

condition result in some form of force, fright, or compulsion. "The creation of a dangerous condition, without more, does not cause harm in the narrow sense of the term."[14]

Defective products would fit within the category of dangerous conditions because a defect (the dangerous condition) could lead to injury by force (defective software results in a collision with someone).[15] Finally, Epstein uses Hart and Honoré's categories of accidental, negligent, and deliberate acts to link the causal chain from the dangerous condition to the harm. Here, Epstein argues that given his criticisms of negligence as applied to a defendant, a plaintiff's negligent behavior should not break the causal connection between the dangerous condition and the harm. Only if the plaintiff owed the defendant a duty to take reasonable steps to prevent harm would there be a defense.[16] Epstein also takes the position that other events, such as a third party intentionally causing the plaintiff harm, or intervening events, do not necessarily cut the chain of causation because such interventions might not have resulted in harm but for the previously existing dangerous condition.[17]

Cohen also compares strict liability to other ways to address harms and argues that it might be a better way to address harms than alternatives. One such alternative is to take harms encompassed under current strict liability law and treat them as natural disasters, force majeure events for whom no one is responsible, thus requiring the victims of such harms to bear the costs. This alternative, however, raises the same fairness issue of who should bear the costs of loss, and might create undesired incentives to take out excess insurance and the like.[18] The second alternative is to spread the costs of harm among everyone in society. I will discuss insurance and other pooling arrangements in more detail later in this chapter, as well as a shift in focus from tortfeasor to victim, but Cohen raises the counter moral issue: whether it is fair to require people to pay for some harm with which they had nothing to do.[19] (This is a metaexample of the distributional problem in collective responsibility.) Given the shortcomings of these alternatives, strict liability might seem to be a plausible solution.

---

[14] *Id.*
[15] *Id.*, at 178–9.
[16] *Id.*, at 180–81.
[17] *Id.*, at 181–5.
[18] Cohen, *supra* note 2, at 223.
[19] *Id.*, at 224.

Incentives

Strict liability has been criticized or defended with arguments about the incentives the doctrine might create. The doctrine is of course a way of imposing the costs of losses on those deemed liable under a strict liability regime: it is a form of guarantee or indemnity against harms caused by a product or service. As discussed above, Cohen suggests such a guarantee might encourage large entities to increase safety. One could argue in this regard that even under a strict liability regime with no cost shifting, manufacturers have an incentive to do all they can to reduce the costs of harm because they will have to bear those costs in the end. Although efficiency issues are not dispositive for Epstein, he argues that strict liability need not necessarily lead to inefficient results: under a strict liability regime, in cases of simple accident and necessity, a defendant might still decide that it makes more sense to pay the costs of a harm than to avoid them.[20] Steven Shavell agrees with Epstein here: in cases where there is unilateral harm to the injured party by the injurer, the injurer will take the optimal level of care under either a strict liability or negligence regime.[21] In Epstein's view, the only situation where strict liability would make a difference in the outcome as opposed to negligence is in cases where a defendant could not have taken any reasonable precautions to avoid loss. In such cases, there will still be no allocation of resources, and the harm caused by the defendant would justify the transfer of wealth to the plaintiff. In this regard, Epstein and Shavell suggest that transaction costs might be lower because courts need no longer engage in costly cost-benefit analyses.[22]

The incentives created by strict liability (and by implication negligence) depend on the circumstances, however. Shavell argues that if one takes risk aversion into account, strict liability is more attractive when injurers are less risk averse than victims, because strict liability imposes risk on injurers. Negligence becomes more attractive when injurers are more risk averse than victims, because negligence places risk on victims.[23] Unless prohibited from doing so, the large entities of which Cohen speaks are likely to pass on the costs of loss to their customers, resulting in higher prices. It is not uncommon for the victims of harm to be a business's customers. If so, in the end, allocating costs to the manufacturer under strict liability would mean redistributing those costs to the victim.[24] Of course, in its favor, passing on those costs could have

---

[20]   Epstein, *supra* note 5, at 187–8.
[21]   Steven Shavell, *Liability for Accidents*, *in* 1 HANDBOOK OF LAW AND ECONOMICS 139, 144 (A. Mitchell Polinsky and Steven Shavell eds., 2007).
[22]   Epstein, *supra* note 5, at 189; Shavell, *supra* note 21, at 144.
[23]   Shavell, *supra* note 21, at 149.
[24]   Epstein, *supra* note 5, at 210.

the effect of reducing undesirable activities because consumers on the margins will turn to a cheaper, less dangerous product.[25] Keith Hylton argues in this regard that even if the increased cost of the product due to liability is passed on to the consumer, it is a way of internalizing those costs that would lead to the purchase of safer products.[26] At the same time, the concern is that the public would use substitutes less beneficial to society as a whole. Richard Posner and Shavell argue that unless there is some form of contributory negligence, under strict liability a potential victim has less of an incentive to take measures to avoid losses, since he or she knows that someone else will be liable for damages. If the victim is the least cost avoider, the result is inefficient.[27] And with respect to administrative costs, the costs saved in a strict liability regime by avoiding cost-benefit analyses could be offset by an increase in litigation.[28]

Strict Liability and Autonomous Technologies

The president of Volvo has been quoted as saying that the company will "accept full responsibility whenever one of its cars is in autonomous mode"[29] and that it will accept full liability whenever its cars are involved in accidents.[30] Mercedes-Benz and Google have reportedly said that they would accept liability if their vehicles were to cause an accident.[31] Such statements could be interpreted in at least three ways. The first is a blanket acceptance of liability whenever an autonomous vehicle made by a manufacturer is involved in an accident, irrespective of who "causes" the accident and who else is involved. This broad reading would cover all other cars, drivers, and passengers and is in the nature of the guarantee provided by strict liability. Such a guarantee could be engendered by confidence that autonomous vehicles will reduce accidents to the point that it makes business sense to make such a promise (aided by

---

[25]   The Bridge, *Economic Analysis of Alternative Standards of Liability in Accident Law*, LEGAL THEORY: LAW AND ECONOMICS, https://cyber.harvard.edu/bridge/LawEconomics/neg-liab.htm.

[26]   Keith N. Hylton, *The Law and Economics of Products Liability*, 88 NOTRE DAME L. REV. 2457, 2474 (2013).

[27]   Richard A. Posner, *Strict Liability: A Comment*, 2 J. LEG. STUD. 205, 207 (1973); Shavell, *supra* note 21, at 144–5.

[28]   Shavell, *supra* note 21, at 155.

[29]   Jim Gorzelany, *Volvo Will Accept Liability for Its Self-Driving Cars*, FORBES, Oct. 9, 2015, www.forbes.com/sites/jimgorzelany/2015/10/09/volvo-will-accept-liability-for-its-self-driving-cars/#1ac35e0f72c5.

[30]   Clifford Atiyeh, *Volvo Will Take Responsibility if Its Self-Driving Cars Crash*, CAR & DRIVER, Oct. 8, 2015, https://blog.caranddriver.com/volvo-will-take-responsibility-if-its-self-driving-cars-crash/.

[31]   *Id.*

insurance) and to increase consumer confidence. The second interpretation is that as between the human driver/passenger and the autonomous car, the autonomous vehicle will be considered the responsible actor, but only as between those two, and not to third parties. A third interpretation is that those companies will take responsibility whenever their respective autonomous cars are found to be at fault for an accident, using the term "cause" in its colloquial sense. Under this interpretation, the statement is somewhat tautological: the company will accept liability whenever its vehicle is found to be liable. Finally, it should be noted that earlier responses of companies to deaths involving operators of autonomous vehicles seem to indicate that they will continue to rely on doctrines of cause-in-fact, proximate cause, and intervening causes to disclaim liability.

The different ways in which one can interpret these statements of accepting responsibility, and the completely different responses given by other companies, illustrate some of the issues involved with applying strict liability to autonomous technologies. The review just completed of some of the literature on strict liability suggests that proposals to use the doctrine to hold liable designers and manufacturers of autonomous technologies are plausible. From a fairness perspective, many of the firms engaged in the development of these technologies have assumed, to use Cohen's term, special positions in society because they have the potential to affect large numbers of people, many of whom are unable to avoid those effects. Further, since such firms promote autonomous machines and systems as being safer than other technologies, it could be argued that it is only fair that they be responsible for harms even if they would not be considered liable under negligence grounds.

At the same time, Cohen's (and by extension Epstein's) point that there is no hierarchy of ethical norms works in both directions. For example, Vladek argues that strict liability should be applied to manufacturers of self-driving cars.[32] However, he concedes this approach has the potential to be unfair to manufacturers. Hence, he suggests the law provide a way for manufacturers to seek contribution from suppliers and computer programmers through a form of common enterprise liability.[33]

A common enterprise theory permits the law to impose joint liability without having to lay bare and grapple with the details of assigning every aspect of wrongdoing to one party or another; it is enough that the parties engaged in wrongdoing in pursuit of a common aim. That principle could be engrafted onto a new, strict liability regime to address the harms that may be

---

[32]   David C. Vladek, *Machines without Principals: Liability Rules and Artificial Intelligence*, 89 Wash. L. Rev. 117, 146 (Am. Law Inst. 2014).

[33]   *Id.*, at 148–9.

visited on humans by intelligent autonomous machines when it is impossible or impracticable to assign fault to a specific person.[34]

This approach represents an interweaving of strict liability with other doctrines, and the relationship between the two bears further teasing out. Vladek certainly does not presume that under this analysis, suppliers and computer programmers would be in engaged in wrongful behavior simply by producing these vehicles: his point most likely is that parties who pursue a common aim with the manufacturer could be made to share the costs the manufacturer would bear under a strict liability approach. But if the purpose shared among the parties is not wrongful in the strong sense of that term, the question is whether common purpose alone justifies requiring those parties to share those costs. As discussed in Chapter 4, shared intention is not always a good reason to distribute responsibility. Common purpose alone might not be a sufficient reason to find someone liable, and to do so raises the problem of associational responsibility. Perhaps then the reason is causation—suppliers and programmers, together with the manufacturer, helped to bring about conditions that resulted in harm to the plaintiff. However, if one takes that route, one falls back into a strict liability regime with its own fairness concerns. The point here is not to fault Vladek's suggestion; rather, it is to point out that competing moral considerations make it difficult to reconcile how various liability doctrines of liability will work themselves out in practice.

With regard to how strict liability would be applied, recall Epstein's formulation of the rule: a person is liable for creating a dangerous condition which results in harm to another. In this regard, as reported in Chapter 2, Karnow argues that robots are expected to perform tasks more efficiently than human beings, and more safely in the case of autonomous vehicles. They will be designed that way and once past the development stage, short of defects in manufacturing, it will be hard to argue such machines are inherently dangerous. Recall that Karnow argues even strict liability is based on foreseeability. This is because whether something constitutes an unreasonable danger requires one to predict how much danger there might be. A person can foresee that explosives are hard to control and are hazardous: using them creates a dangerous condition that can result in harm. Again, for Karnow, complex interactions between the machines and their environments will result in behaviors that could not be anticipated. One could respond that designing and manufacturing technology with a high level of autonomy is to create a dangerous condition per se, since we do not know what such technology is capable of doing. But this is not unlike saying that a parent is responsible for the actions of her child. That of course is true in a sense, but the normal way to approach that relation-

---

[34] *Id.*, at 149 (footnote omitted).

ship in the law is through the duty to supervise one's child, which returns us to a form of negligence.

As we have seen, for Epstein and for Moore, the link between the harm and the injurer is causation: that a person caused an injury or created a dangerous condition that resulted in an injury is a good reason to hold that person liable. One could argue that this is a compelling reason to apply strict liability to the designers and manufacturers of autonomous technology. But it is not determinative. Notice the relationship between cause and dangerous condition. Clumsy as they might be, the attempts of the law to parse causal events into various categories is a recognition that not all causes can be given legal significance, and they conform to commonsense ideas that some causes are more significant than others. People tend not to see the world as a game of Mousetrap. That something is perceived as a dangerous condition is a way of paying attention to particular causal events that will emerge as a result. Karnow's doubts that autonomous robots will be considered inherently dangerous are relevant here. As we have seen, the design and manufacture of autonomous technologies will create a number of conditions, some of which will lead to harm. But the development of the automobile did the same thing by creating new conditions, indeed, new types of injuries. To be sure, automobiles continue to be involved in accidents, but we tend not to say that simply by designing and manufacturing an automobile, those who did so created a dangerous condition that resulted in harm. Something more is needed.

One could of course ignore these issues of causation and foreseeability and assign responsibility by fiat, as the North Carolina statute does or as recommended by certain policymakers and professional organizations, as reported at the beginning of Chapter 3. If Epstein and Shavell are correct, from an efficiency standpoint, this would not matter; if we are concerned about creating incentives to make sure designers and manufacturers take the requisite amount of care, either negligence or strict liability will do, and adjustments such as adding contributory negligence to a strict liability regime can be used to encourage consumers to take the appropriate amount of care when using autonomous technology. However, despite the rough equivalence of strict liability and negligence in terms of the incentives they create, and despite the conceptual and moral difficulties strict liability avoids, the fact is that negligence continues to be the primary way in which the law has approached harms. It need not have been this way, since strict liability was probably the earlier form of liability. Perhaps the dominance of negligence is due to the path-driven nature of Balkin's cultural tools or to the actions of powerful actors who do not want to be held responsible for all harms and thus act to shape Chiu's regulatory landscape. But the traditional insistence on personal culpability, which negligence purports to honor, cannot be ignored as another reason for negligence's persistence.

DISAGGREGATING RESPONSIBILITY

Given the aims of this book, its primary focus has been on legal responsibility: when is it appropriate to subject someone to legal sanctions, and when autonomous technology is involved in a harm, who should that someone be? However, as Loh and Loh note, responsibility encompasses more than that legal question. "Responsibility is a tool for systematizing, organizing, and thereby clarifying opaque and very complex situations that confuse the agents in question: situations where classical ascriptions of duties and guilt frequently fall short."[35] As discussed in Chapter 2, to make sense of those complex situations, responsibility also involves explaining what happened. Personal responsibility involves giving an account to the community about the reasons why a person acted in a particular situation. It is a means for the community to assess that person's character and actions, and to thereby express and vindicate the values that inform the community. Further, responsibility has retrospective and prospective aspects: it is used to assess a person's actions in past situations and serves to channel future action.

The question emerges whether, just as negligence and strict liability can be said to be informed by different aspects of legal responsibility—respectively, the blameworthiness of the defendant and harm to the plaintiff—so too responsibility can be disaggregated in ways that might motivate other legal approaches to the problem at hand. Disaggregating responsibility might enable society to cast a wider net in terms of holding people responsible for harms, while avoiding in part the morally difficult aspects associated with distributing responsibility.

Disaggregation can take many forms.[36] Here, I will examine four ways this might be done, each of which tries to remove or downplay responsibility as grounds for consequences or sanctions. First, Christian Neuhäuser uses the retrospective and prospective aspects of responsibility to suggest a rough means of sharing responsibility between humans and robots.[37] Neuhäuser

---

[35] Wulf Loh and Janina Loh, *Autonomy and Responsibility in Hybrid Systems: The Example of Autonomous Cars, in* ROBOT ETHICS 2.0; FROM AUTONOMOUS CARS TO ARTIFICIAL INTELLIGENCE 35, 37 (Patrick Lin, Ryan Jenkins, and Keith Abney eds., 2017) [hereinafter ROBOT ETHICS 2.0].

[36] David Shoemaker argues in this regard that there are three distinct conceptions of responsibility: attributability, answerability, and accountability. David Shoemaker, *Attributability, Answerability, and Accountability: Toward a Wider Theory of Moral Responsibility*, 121 ETHICS 602 (2011). Gary Watson understands responsibility as a form of self-disclosure of one's self as a free, autonomous individual. Gary Watson, *Two Faces of Responsibility*, 24 PHIL. TOPICS 227 (1996).

[37] Christian Neuhäuser, *Some Skeptical Remarks Regarding Robot Responsibility and a Way Forward, in* COLLECTIVE AGENCY AND COOPERATION IN NATURAL AND

argues that robots are not morally responsible in themselves, thus raising the distributional issues already discussed. In his view, it is appropriate to view humans and autonomous robots as comprising a group: "[T]he most promising way forward when it comes to robot responsibility, is not to conceptualize robots as responsible agents themselves, but to conceptualize them as relatively autonomous members of responsible groups."[38] The human members of the group are then responsible for robots that are contributing members. The distributional problem of why the humans in the group should be responsible for the actions of the autonomous robots can be largely avoided if such responsibility is forward-looking. "[G]roups can be responsible for bringing about desired future states together, whereas individual group members would not be able to do so."[39]

Another way to disaggregate responsibility is to emphasize responsibility as explanation. In the case of an accident involving an autonomous machine, we could determine the extent to which errors in software design and coding, manufacturing, defective infrastructure, as well as the interaction of autonomous vehicles all "contributed" to the accident. The NHTS preliminary report concerning the accident that led to the death of Elaine Herzberg is an example of responsibility in this form. To be sure, such narratives might lead to future action, but in and of themselves, they are attempts to make sense of complex situations and are thus a form of responsibility.

Responsibility as explaining oneself is more personal and consequential. Through a libertarian perspective, to be required to explain oneself or to describe what one has done, for example by appearing before an inquest, impinges a person's freedom to act as she sees fit. It is an acknowledgment that a person might be answerable to others, who in turn might make judgments concerning her that are beyond her control. Truth and reconciliation commissions, the most famous of them the South African Truth and Reconciliation Commission, can be seen as a manifestation of this approach. Persons on both sides of the struggle against apartheid were given amnesty from prosecution in exchange for giving an account of their activities during that time. Although not labeled responsibility as such, describing what one did during that period is consistent with responsibility as explanation and accounting for oneself. In the technology field, investigations such as the inquiry into the *Challenger* disaster illustrate this approach.

ARTIFICIAL SYSTEMS: EXPLANATION, IMPLEMENTATION AND SIMULATION 131 (Catrin Misselhorn ed., 2015).

[38]   *Id.*, at 144.
[39]   *Id.*, at 143.

In this regard, the decision that a defendant has violated the law in itself has been considered a form of responsibility. In state responsibility the mere determination that a state has violated its obligations under international law is considered a form of sanction, separate and apart from any reparations a state in violation of its international obligations might be required to make. On the positive side, this practice can be justified through the classic principles of state sovereignty and the independence of states. Because of their sovereignty, states start from a position of being unanswerable to each other and to other subjects of international law. Thus, states must consent before they will be bound to any obligations. From this perspective, a judgment by a legal decision-maker, having undertaken a judicial process of fact-finding and reasoning, that a state has violated international law can be considered consequential. Similarly, even without sentencing, a criminal conviction is in itself viewed as weighty.

On the negative side, however, at least with regard to nation states, it can be argued that the principle that a finding of responsibility is itself consequential makes a virtue out of necessity. Short of diplomacy, economic sanctions, or the use of force, there are no enforcement mechanisms to ensure that states obey international law, let alone suffer consequences for violations of international law. A similar criticism might be brought against truth and reconciliation commissions and amnesties: parties who seek a change in regimes might agree to them because they know they do not have the power to force regime change otherwise. Had there been enough power, perpetrators of human rights abuses would (and should have) suffered the full consequences of their actions. Applied to autonomous machines systems and those who design, manufacture, own, and use them, one might say therefore that we are settling for second best because a more robust form of responsibility is unavailable or unacceptable under the circumstances.

These types of criticisms reveal one of the shortcomings of the disaggregating approach. Each of the approaches discussed above are plausible because they do in fact touch on some aspect of responsibility. And indeed, processes such as investigations, inquests, and truth commissions are in use today. Because these processes are not intended to result in the harsher legal consequences of liability, they do not raise the legal and moral issues discussed in this book when legal responsibility is involved. But this is of course the problem: the finding that someone is legally responsible for a harm and thus required to make reparations plays expressive and functional roles that other processes which emphasize other aspects of responsibility do not.

PRIVILEGING THE VICTIM OF HARM

Epstein and Cohen defended strict liability as addressing harm through the fact of harm itself, as opposed to the blameworthiness of the defendant. That someone or someone's property has been injured is in itself ground for inquiry whether other individuals or society as a whole should be required to help bear the loss. Not only might such an impulse lead to greater acceptance of strict liability, but it might justify relaxing our concepts of culpability, foreseeability, and causation to enable recovery, all because of the fact that an autonomous machine or system has caused harm. One could see subtle shifts in other legal devices such as burdens of proof and canons of interpretation in light of the idea that a harm creates a prima facie cause for relief.

At the same time, this shift in emphasis from injurer to the injured party raises other issues. Peter Singer has argued persuasively that a person who, without harm to himself, can assist another person has a moral duty to do so.[40] However, this claim is not uncontroversial. The fact someone has been injured might serve as grounds for redress, but it does not fully answer why someone who has not caused the injury should provide it. Further, even if one accepts that an injury itself justifies a shared response, the question of how the costs of the injury should be shared remains, which raises its own issues of distributional fairness. Pasternak argues in this regard there are three ways to distribute these such costs: proportionally, equally, or randomly.[41] She believes distribution on a proportional basis is the most fair, but sometimes hard to implement. A random distribution is the easiest to implement, but the least fair. Therefore, an equal distribution of costs seems the most appropriate.[42] At the same time, even an equal distribution of costs requires some justification. The conclusion is that it may well be possible to adopt a system that privileges the injured, but such a system would have to respond to its own moral and distributional challenges.

INSURANCE

Any study of the interrelationship between legal responsibility and autonomous technologies must take insurance into account. It is a given that private and public insurance schemes, including social insurance, play an important

---

[40] Peter Singer, *Famine, Affluence, and Morality*, 1 PHIL. & PUB. AFF. 229, 231 (1972).

[41] Avia Pasternak, *The Distributive Effect of Collective Punishment*, in ACCOUNTABILITY FOR COLLECTIVE WRONGDOING 210, 212 (Tracy Isaacs and Richard Vernon eds., 2011).

[42] *Id.*

role in addressing harms, and they are expected to continue to play that role as autonomous machines and systems are adopted. Insurance enables people to reduce the risk of unwanted events such as accidents, catastrophic events, health problems, and death, and the threats they pose to a person's assets and wellbeing.[43] Insurance performs a broader role in the economy by, among other things, enabling the accumulation of capital, mobilizing financial resources, and providing a rough form of governance over firms, in that insurance premiums can be used to regulate externalization of costs and save public funds.[44]

To give some sense of the scope of the industry, according to the Insurance Information Institute, in 2016 the US insurance industry received net premiums of $1.1 trillion. In that year there were 5,977 insurance companies in the United States, including 2,538 property and casualty insurers. Property and casualty insurance paid out $21.7 billion in property losses, largely attributable to natural disasters.[45] These figures do not include amounts paid by social insurance.

The private insurance industry is expected to be affected by autonomous systems in at least three ways. First, artificial intelligence will impact the type of insurance products that will be offered and their pricing. KPMG anticipates that since autonomous vehicles are expected to reduce accidents and more people will shift from owning cars to hiring them as needed, insurance companies will sell less personal auto insurance and more commercial insurance and product liability insurance.[46] Increased use of monitors in the home, while driving, and through wearables will allow insurance companies to price policies based on actual behavior and to rely less on risk pools to assess the risk of issuing a particular policy. More personal data will also allow companies to offer usage-based insurance.[47] Second, the customer's experience

---

[43] Christian Thimann, *What Is Insurance and How Does It Differ from General Finance? in* THE ECONOMICS, REGULATION, AND SYSTEMIC RISK OF INSURANCE MARKETS 5, 6, 8 (Felix Hufeld, Ralph S.J. Koijen, and Christian Thimann eds., 2016).

[44] Peter Zweifel and Roland Eisen, INSURANCE ECONOMICS 11 (2012). *See also* Denis Kessler, Amélie de Montchalin, and Christian Thimann, *The Macroeconomic Role of Insurance, in* THE ECONOMICS, REGULATION, AND SYSTEMIC RISK OF INSURANCE MARKETS 20 (Felix Hufeld, Ralph S.J. Koijen, and Christian Thimann eds., 2016) (discussing the macroeconomic impacts of insurance).

[45] Insurance Information Institute, *Facts + Statistics: Industry Overview* (2018), www.iii.org/fact-statistic/facts-statistics-industry-overview.

[46] KPMG, Marketplace of Change: Automobile Insurance in the Era of Autonomous Vehicles (Oct. 2015), at 25–30.

[47] Edmund Zagorin, *Artificial Intelligence in Insurance—Three Trends That Matter*, TECHEMERGENCE, Mar. 27, 2018, www.techemergence.com/artificial-intelligence-in -insurance-trends/. *See also* Deloitte, Artificial Intelligence in Insurance (2017), www2.deloitte.com/de/de/pages/innovation/contents/artificial-intelligence-insurance

with insurance will change, as more interactions with insurance companies take place via chat bots. This will allow for faster responses and higher volumes of transactions. For example, a Chinese insurance company already offers insurance online. At the time of this writing, the company had sold 7.2 insurance products to 429 million customers since 2013.[48] Finally, the industry can expect to use artificial intelligence during the claims settlement process, particularly to prevent fraud.[49]

As will be discussed more fully below, such innovations are not without their concerns—for example, concerns about the insured's privacy. Irrespective of these impacts, however, there is little doubt that insurance will continue to operate in the new environment created by autonomous technology. The primary question for the purposes of this book is the extent to which insurance, private or public, will be able to ameliorate strains in legal liability caused by the advent of that technology by performing the same functions carried out by legal responsibility. To the extent that it can, insurance would likely dampen any coevolutionary dynamics between legal responsibility and autonomous machines and systems. A few points can be made in this regard.

Insurability of Autonomous Technologies

Insurance can only insure risks that can be measured and predicted through experience, normally with large numbers of examples of those risks.[50] One implication is that as autonomous machines and systems are in the early stages of implementation, it would not be surprising for insurance companies to decline to insure risks posed by them because there is not yet enough information to evaluate those risks. In this regard, Denis Kessler and his coauthors point out that insurance has a paradoxical effect on innovation. Insurance encourages innovation by allowing inventors to mitigate risks. At the same time, insurance is slow to insure new technology, precisely because new technology represents a new, as yet unquantifiable risk.[51] Thus, there could well be a transitional stage during which there are gaps in liability or casualty insurance. Kessler and colleagues point out that insurance quickly steps in

---

-industry.html (discussing the impacts of artificial intelligence of the insurance industry).

[48]   Zagorin, *supra* note 47.

[49]   *Id.*

[50]   Kessler, Montchalin, and Thimann, *supra* note 44, at 49. For a detailed discussion of risk assessment and modeling and their role in pricing, *see* Pietro Parodi, PRICING IN GENERAL INSURANCE (2015), especially Sec. II, 93-268.

[51]   Kessler, Montchalin, and Thimann, *supra* note 44, at 47.

once those risks become better known,[52] so eventually we would expect the same to occur as society gains more experience with autonomous machines and systems. The question then becomes how long that stage will last, particularly in the case of highly autonomous technology that raises foreseeability issues similar to those Karnow recognizes for negligence, product liability, and strict liability.

The Coexistence of Tort Law and Insurance

Another factor worth considering is that, at least in the United States, insurance has functioned with liability rules, not replaced them. On a theoretical level, Shavell suggests that liability rules and insurance act together to encourage injurers to take care. He argues for example that under a negligence regime, in theory injurers who are risk-neutral will take the proper level of care so they will not have to purchase insurance. Meanwhile, potential victims will take out casualty insurance since injurers will not be liable for harms because they were not negligent.[53] Further, liability and accident insurance "moot" the riskbearing issues with strict liability and negligence discussed above. If an injurer is risk averse under a strict liability regime, he can take out liability insurance; concomitantly, if a victim is risk averse under a negligence regime, he can take out accident insurance.[54]

It must be said, however, that there is debate among policymakers and scholars about the relationship between insurance costs and legal liability, at least as the tort system is currently structured. This is reflected in debates about the impact of legal liability on insurance premiums, the argument being that inappropriately high liability awards raise the cost of insurance, thus preventing people from purchasing the desired amount of insurance. The literature appears to be equivocal on this issue. Meredith L. Kilgore and co-authors examined the effect of tort reform on the price of medical malpractice insurance. They surveyed states that had enacted a number of devices to limit liability, including damage caps, offsets for other forms of compensation, the modification of joint and several liability rules, periodic payments, statutes of limitations and repose, limits on attorney fees, limitations on experts, pretrial screening, and arbitration.[55] The study indicates that caps on noneconomic damages "can significantly constrain the growth of medical malpractice

---

[52] *Id.*

[53] Shavell, *supra* note 21, at 150.

[54] *Id.*, at 151.

[55] Meredith L. Kilgore, Michael A. Morrisey, and Leonard J. Nelson, *Tort Law and Medical Malpractice Insurance Premiums*, 43 INQUIRY 255, 256–8 (2006).

premiums."[56] Peter Hinton arrives at mixed results with a study of the effect of tort reform on auto insurance. There is a significant drop in costs when no-fault insurance is dropped and restrictions on collateral sources are relaxed. However, he finds no significant impact from other reforms, such as modifications to joint and several liability or caps on noneconomic losses. None of the reforms led to more purchase of auto insurance.[57] Yet another study indicates, contrary to Hinton's results, that no-fault insurance actually results in lower premium costs.[58] I will not presume to resolve the debate here, but irrespective of how the empirical data fall out, the studies do not appear to suggest that the tort system should be abolished altogether, but rather that inappropriate liability awards be prevented. Indeed, there is a possibility of having too much insurance.[59]

Finally, insurance subrogation should be mentioned here. Subrogation is "the right of an insurer having indemnified the policyholder due to a legal obligation, to take advantage of any legal rights or remedies available to the policyholder in relation to the loss indemnified."[60] The possibility of subrogation implies that liability issues will never completely disappear. Insurance companies will want to know who is responsible for an injury as they seek to be at least partially compensated when they have to indemnify the policyholder for losses.

Adverse Selection, Moral Hazard, and Other Welfare Costs

Insurance of course has its own limitations. As is well known, insurers must contend with imperfect information that leads to adverse selection and moral hazard. Adverse selection occurs when an insurer cannot assess how much risk a particular individual person poses. A person might not disclose that he has a chronic illness, for example. I have already discussed Pozner's concern that strict liability without contributory negligence raises the possibility of moral hazard. Here, moral hazard occurs when the insurer cannot assess whether that person can affect the amount of loss he will incur. Those who are covered by insurance might be less careful because they will not be asked to bear the full brunt of any costs they might cause. If the insurer could assess that risk and

---

[56]   *Id.*, at 268.

[57]   Peter Hinton, *How Does Tort Law Affect Consumer Auto Insurance Costs?* 84 J. RISK & INS. 691 (2017).

[58]   *See, e.g.*, Kenneth J. Meier and Robert M. La Follette, *The Policy Impact of No-Fault Automobile Insurance*, 6 POL'Y STUD. REV. 496, 502 (1987) (finding that no-fault insurance systems resulted in lower premiums to drivers).

[59]   Kessler, Montchalin, and Thimann, *supra* note 44, at 49–50.

[60]   Rob Thoyts, INSURANCE THEORY AND PRACTICE 48 (2010).

amount of loss, it could adjust its premium accordingly; without such information, the insurer's premium might not be enough to cover all losses or it might be too high, thus driving away people who might otherwise have purchased insurance.[61] On the other side, the inability of people to obtain insurance also imposes costs on society.

The problems of adverse selection and moral hazard are most readily apparent in the area of health care. Here I will discuss two studies on health insurance and then turn to their possible application to insurance schemes for autonomous technologies. In a recent article, Ben Handel and his coauthors focus on the issue whether health insurance exchanges established under the Affordable Care Act should be allowed to set prices based on an individual's health characteristics. They point out that prohibiting the exchanges from pricing according to a person's health led to adverse selection and reclassification risk. In the context of health care, adverse selection occurs when individual health conditions cannot be factored into the price of insurance, leading to the result that sicker individuals tend to seek health care. Reclassification risk is the risk that one's health status will be reclassified, leading to higher premiums.[62]

As might be expected, a ban on individual pricing tends to increase adverse selection, but reduces reclassification risk. Conversely, allowing individual pricing reduces adverse selection, but reclassification risk increases.[63] Both adverse selection and reclassification risk impact consumer welfare. With respect to adverse selection, Michel Geruso and Timothy J. Layton argue that fear of adverse selection itself has a welfare effect. As an example, Geruso and Layton identify two competing health care policies, neither of which in their view cover adequate care for cancer treatment because the insurers fear that if they offered more care, this would attract more people who have cancer.[64] Based on Handel and his coauthors' findings, however, adverse selection and reclassification risks do not have equal effects on consumer welfare. Their

---

[61] Nicholas Barr provides an excellent introduction to these concepts in Nicholas Barr, THE WELFARE STATE AS PIGGY BANK: INFORMATION, RISK, UNCERTAINTY, AND THE ROLE OF THE STATE 20–22 (2001). The seminal paper on these issues is Kenneth Arrow, *Uncertainty and the Welfare Economics of Medical Care*, 53 AM. ECON. REV. 941, 961 (1963). On the moral implications of the moral hazard, *see, e.g.*, Will Braynen, *Moral Dimensions of Moral Hazards*, 26 UTILITAS 34 (2013); Rutger Claassen, *Financial Crisis and the Ethics of Moral Hazard*, 41 SOC. THEORY & PRAC. 527 (2015).

[62] Ben Handel, Igal Hendel, and Michael D. Whinston, *Equilibria in Health Exchanges: Adverse Selection Versus Reclassification Risk*, 83 ECONOMETRICS 1261, 1262–3 (2015).

[63] *Id.*

[64] *Id.*, at 24.

study indicates that although the welfare cost of adverse selection is substantial, the welfare cost of reclassification risk is five times larger.[65]

Of course, one would not expect the challenges that adverse selection, moral hazard, and reclassification risk pose to health care insurance to manifest themselves in the same way when insurance attempts to cover harms caused by autonomous machines. At the same time asymmetries in information between insurers and insureds and analogous forms of reclassification risk are likely to persist, even though as discussed at the beginning of this section, one of the trends permitted by artificial intelligence is to allow insurance companies to engage in more individual pricing. One would expect to see already existing private and public insurance schemes in various insurance lines, such as transportation, health care, workers compensation, and so on, begin to accommodate the use of artificial intelligence. As discussed, areas such as automobile insurance might undergo significant changes as there are less and less human drivers. In each of these areas, one would expect there to be the same tradeoffs between consumer welfare posed by adverse selection and an analogous form of reclassification risk (it remains to be seen if the disproportionate impact to consumer welfare of reclassification risk persists outside of health care). It might well be that we will see private and public insurance schemes in which designers, manufacturers, and users of autonomous machines are classified according to risk and priced accordingly. In response, one would expect to see legislative responses to these issues, in the form of regulating premiums, consumer subsidies or penalties, risk adjustment, and contract regulation.[66]

Finally, under this subsection it should be noted there is a possibility of insurance as a source of systemic risk. Viral Acharya notes there is a debate in the scholarly literature whether insurance companies pose systemic risks in the way financial institutions like banks do.[67] Some of this depends on the kinds of products that insurance companies sell. Some nontraditional policies are more vulnerable to swings in the larger economy. Other products, such as variable annuities make insurance companies subject to runs, as investors pull out funds.[68] Moreover, traditional insurance companies might contribute to

---

[65]   Handel, Hendel, and Whinston, *supra* note 62, at 1265.

[66]   *Id.*, at 24 (discussing common forms of health insurance regulation).

[67]   Viral V. Acharya, *Measuring Systemic Risk for Insurance Companies*, in THE ECONOMICS, REGULATION, AND SYSTEMIC RISK OF INSURANCE MARKETS 100 (Felix Hufeld, Ralph S.J. Koijen, and Christian Thimann eds., 2016). *See also* THOYTS, *supra* note 60, at 109.Thoyts explains that a bank becomes a creditor as soon as customers make deposits, thus creating the possibility of a bank run. Liquidity is therefore always an issue. In contrast, an insurance company does not become a creditor until an insurable event occurs. The risk for the insurer is that losses of unexpected magnitude occur. This solvency risk can be ameliorated by pricing and by reinsurance. *Id.*

[68]   Archarya, *supra* note 67, at 101–2.

systemic risk as going concerns because their failure results in capital short-falls that reduce financial intermediation in an economy.[69]

Public Insurance for Autonomous Technologies

Earlier in this section, I discussed the possibility that there will be a transition period in which private insurance companies might be reluctant to insure against harms caused by autonomous technologies because there is as yet not enough information about the kind and scope of risks they might pose. The issue is how long such a transition period might be. We can now add to this concern the informational uncertainties that lead to adverse selection and moral hazard. Nicholas Barr observes in this regard that social insurance can be used when information asymmetries prevent private insurers from entering the market, thereby leading to an undersupply of insurance. In contrast to private insurance, social insurance can be mandatory, which allows for broad pooling of risk. Moreover, social insurance can be less specific about how it defines risk; as opposed to private insurance, the risks in social insurance can change over time.[70] This is in keeping with Barr's overall argument that the welfare state plays not only a distributional role but a piggybacking role that assists people as they encounter adverse life events such as illness, unemploy-ment, and old age.[71]

Liability and public insurance to cover autonomous technologies have been proposed. For example, Carrie Scholl recommends that because in her view it will be difficult to assess liability for accidents in autonomous vehicles, such liability should be eliminated altogether and a national insurance fund should be established to cover the costs of such accidents.[72] Randy Ross speculates that if the manufacturers of self-driving cars are primarily liable for accidents, they might either self-insure or seek subsidies for private insurance, for example through a gas tax.[73] The latter method would of course be a form of publicly funded insurance, albeit in the form of a use tax. Jeffrey Gurney is

---

[69]   *Id.*, at 113.

[70]   Barr, *supra* note 61, at 24.

[71]   *Id.*, at 1.

[72]   Carrie Schroll, *Splitting the Bill: Creating a National Car Insurance Fund to Pay for Accidents in Autonomous Vehicles*, 109 Nw. U. L. Rev. 803 (2015). The IEEE suggests that a similar scheme is one policy that governments could adopt. Inst. Electronic & Elec. Eng'rs, Ethcially Allied Design: A Vision for Prioritizing Human Well-being with Artificial Intelligence and Autonomous Systems: Version One 93 (2016).

[73]   Randy Ross, *How Will Autonomous Vehicles Change the Insurance Game?* The Rough Company, Inc., Apr. 25, 2017, http://roughnotes.com/self-driving-cars-wave -future-insurance-tsunami/.

critical of such an approach.[74] Gurney assesses the possibility of immunity and compensation systems for accidents caused by autonomous vehicles. He notes that such systems exist for other industries. In the United States, the National Childhood Vaccination Injury Act of 1986 limits liability for the makers of vaccines and provides a mechanism for compensating for injuries and deaths resulting from vaccinations, and the Price–Anderson Act of 1954 limits liability and provides for an insurance fund for civilian nuclear disasters.[75] Gurney points out that systems such as these have the advantage of reducing any deterrence effects liability might have on manufacturers and removing uncertainty about liability. At the same time, as applied to autonomous vehicles, these mechanisms have a number of weaknesses. Among them is the fact that such systems could reduce incentives to improve safety and lead to inaccurate pricing of the vehicles, since manufacturers would not need to internalize costs (and thereby pass them on to buyers).[76]

The system created by the Price–Anderson Act has indeed been criticized on the grounds that nuclear power companies are not responsible for the full costs of their accidents and that it is price distorting because it does not require the nuclear power industry to bear its own insurance costs, which then become a form of subsidy.[77] But, as discussed earlier, to be viable, private insurance must be able to assess risks and to pool them.[78] Moreover, as Barr points out, insurance insures against risks, not certainties.[79] With the appropriate premium, an insurance company will issue a life insurance policy if a person has some risk of dying by age 40, but will not if it is certain that person will die. Further, private insurance usually is unable to cope with large shocks.[80] It is one thing to insure against fires that occur occasionally, quite another to have an entire town burn to the ground. So, despite possible inefficiencies, one could argue that because there is a public health benefit in requiring children to be vaccine-

---

[74] Jeffrey K. Gurney, *Imputing Driverhood: Applying a Reasonable Driver Standard to Accidents Caused by Autonomous Vehicles, in* ROBOT ETHICS 2.0, *supra* note 35, at 51.

[75] *Id.*, at 57. *See also* National Vaccine Information Center, The National Childhood Vaccine Injury Act of 1986 (2018), www.nvic.org/injury-compensation/origihanlaw .aspx; The Center for Insurance and Policy Research, Nuclear Liability Insurance (Price Anderson Act), National Association of Insurance Commissioners, Apr. 30, 2018, www.naic.org/cipr_topics/topic_nuclear_liability_insurance.htm.

[76] Gurney, *supra* note 74, at 58.

[77] Public Citizen, *Price-Anderson Act: The Billion Dollar Bailout for Nuclear Power Mishaps*, Sept. 2004, www.citizen.org/sites/default/files/price_anderson_fact sheet.pdf.

[78] Barr, *supra* note 61, at 20.

[79] *Id.*

[80] *Id.*

ated, the government creates a risk that is almost certain to occur, in the sense that some small number of children will have serious adverse reactions to a vaccine, thus incurring very high costs. The Price–Anderson Act is premised, correctly or incorrectly, on nuclear power being desirable, and of course given the experiences of Three Mile Island, Chernobyl, and Fukushima, the risk is catastrophic. To the extent that these systems are criticized, it can be argued that the government has not provided enough protection against possible risks; at the same time, if Barr is correct, the question arises whether private insurers would want to step in to insure against those activities. It should be noted that in the case of nuclear power, nuclear power companies are required by the act to obtain some private insurance to cover losses. One company provides 100 percent of the private coverage for that amount.

The question whether it is desirable to enact immunity and compensation systems for autonomous technologies is thus akin to the question whether there will be a transition period in which insurance will be hard to come by because their risks cannot be assessed. That question is likely to be answered sector by sector. To return to autonomous vehicles as an example, a legislature would want to assess how strongly it wants to encourage the development of technologies that permit it, whether those policies would increase the certainty of risk, and whether those risks would lead to catastrophes that the private insurance sector would not be able to absorb. My guess is that those factors would weigh against such a system. The answer might be different in another sector, for example, the health sector in a country with a large population and limited medical resources.

Psychosocial Costs

Thus far I have been assessing the strengths and weaknesses of insurance as a replacement for legal responsibility from a number of perspectives: the issue of insurability, the coexistence of tort law and insurance, informational asymmetries and their relationship to private and public insurance. One other factor is more subtle. Somewhat counterintuitively, the literature suggests that people who have access to compensation after an injury actually have worse health outcomes than those who do not have such access.[81] In an interesting

---

[81] Jason Thomson et al., *Attributions of Responsibility and Recovery within a No-Fault Insurance Compensation System*, 59 REHABILITATION PSYCH. 247, 248 (2014). (*Citing* Edward B. Blanchard et al., *Effects of Litigation Settlements on Posttraumatic Stress Symptoms in Motor Vehicle Accident Survivors*, 11 J. TRAUMATIC STRESS 337, 337–54 (1998).); Belinda J. Gabbe et al., *The Relation between Compensable Status and Long-Term Patient Outcomes following Orthopaedic Trauma*, 187 MED. J. AUSTRALIA 14, 14–17 (2007); and Ian Harris et al., *Association between*

study, Jason Thompson and his coauthors surveyed 934 road trauma survivors to determine what variables might impact health outcomes in no-fault compensation systems "where access to compensation, medical and rehabilitation support is largely identical."[82] They found that people in no-fault personal injury systems who feel others are responsible for their injuries have poorer postaccident outcomes than those who attribute responsibility to themselves.[83] While Thomson and colleagues do not suggest this—and the literature is equivocal[84]—their results raise the possibility that perceptions of blame have effects on health outcomes that cannot be overridden by compensation alone.[85]

It is unclear whether it would have made a difference to these victims if the parties whom they blamed suffered some consequence for their actions under the individualistic concepts of moral blameworthiness and legal responsibility, particularly negligence. Perhaps it would have been satisfactory to them that other aspects of responsibility were vindicated, for example that through some process someone else was formally identified as the person responsible for the accident, without asking more of that person. Responsibility as it manifests itself as explanation—as accounting for oneself, as privileging the victim, or as replaced or supplemented by other societal tools such as private and social insurance—will likely play a role in responding to harms caused by autonomous technologies. What the study suggests, however, is that blame and responsibility will also continue to play an important role, for good or ill, when those harms occur.

Compensation Status and Outcomes after Surgery: A Meta-Analysis, 293 J. AM. MED. ASS'N 1644, 1644–52 (2005)).

[82]   Thomson, *id.*, at 247.

[83]   *Id.*, at 247–8, 252.

[84]   *Compare with* Michael Fitzharris et al., *The Relationship between Perceived Crash Responsibility and Post-Crash Depression*, 49 ANN. PROC. ASS'N ADV. AUTO. MED. 79 (2005) (finding that perceiving oneself as responsible for a crash is associated with higher rates of depression than when responsibility is seen to be shared, and to a lesser extent when responsibility is attributed to another).

[85]   *But see* Toby Handfield, *Nozick, Prohibition, and No-Fault Motor Insurance*, 20 J. APP. PHIL. 201 (2003) (arguing on philosophical grounds that there is no prima facie reason to believe the compensation afforded in a no-fault scheme would be less adequate than that afforded by participation in a fault-based system).

6.   Altering the responsible agent

Chapter 5 suggested that allocating responsibility via forms of strict liability, deconstructing it into its constituent parts, or using other mechanisms such as insurance might be one way to ease the tension caused on the one hand by our reluctance to move beyond an individualistic view of responsibility and our aversion to guilt by association, and on the other by the need that is felt to use the law to address harms caused by autonomous technologies. However, that strategy can only go so far, mainly because the paradigm of the blameworthy individual is so influential. A second strategy, therefore, is to leave ideas of responsibility largely intact but to rethink who or what it is that makes a responsible agent. That the autonomous machine itself might be a responsible agent is something I will examine in Chapter 7. Here I will focus on human beings that will be working and interacting with autonomous systems and machines. In doing so, this chapter will reiterate themes introduced in the discussion of group responsibility in Chapter 4, but will explore further the relationship between humans and autonomous machines and systems as they work together.

THE GROUP AS FUNDAMENTAL UNIT OF CONCERN

It is possible to conceive of the individual as meaningful only insofar as she is part of a larger whole. This suggests that a society could cut the Gordian knot of distributing responsibility between humans and machines by emphasizing the group as the fundamental unit of concern for ethical and legal responsibility, not the individual, and then subsuming all individual members under that group identity. This would go at least one step beyond Neuhäuser's forward-looking vision for a group of autonomous machines and humans, discussed in Chapter 5, and attribute retroactive responsibility to that group. In a form of joint and several liability, each member would be responsible for group wrong-doing as a matter of course, and each member's wrongdoing attributed to each other member. "[W]hen one member of a community *commits* a wrong against a member of another, *all* members of the wrong-doer's community are equally responsible for that wrong, for each member of the community is an expression of its moral center."[1] Each member of the group essentially is an instantiation of the group and subject to responsibility as such.

In a system in which the group becomes the focus of concern, harms caused by autonomous machines and systems that operate in group settings would then be attributed to the group, either because the autonomous technology in question would be employed by that group or, if it had a high enough level of autonomy, would be considered a member of the group. If, for example, an autonomous weapons system committed what would be a war crime if a human was involved, the military branch that deployed the system, and ultimately the state, would automatically be the responsible actor. In the case of a self-driving car, the manufacturer of an autonomous vehicle, or the company that operates a fleet of them, among other groups, would be the locus of concern.

Of course, the current system of responsibility leads to the same result. However, the difference when the group is the fundamental unit of concern becomes clearer if society is inclined to penetrate deeper into organizations or groups and distribute liability to individuals. If the harm caused by the autonomous system can be attributed to the group, all members would be responsible by virtue of their being members of the same group. It would not matter if a particular programmer in a company was involved in designing the machine or not; as an expression of the company, the programmer is already liable by virtue of her group membership.

Such an approach has the obvious advantage of circumventing the problem of distributing liability from a group to its members or from one member to other members. It finds some plausibility in the communal nature of human experience, and there is indeed an impulse sometimes to view individuals as representative of groups of which they are members and thereby subject them to moral criticism by virtue of that membership. There are cultural settings in which it is felt that the wrongdoing of one family member brings shame to all others. In most circles in contemporary US society, mere membership in highly criticized groups subjects an individual to moral blameworthiness, in part because each member is thought to hold views and attitudes representative of those groups. In such situations it seems appropriate to say that each member is an expression of each group's respective moral center.

At the same time, there are obvious problems with a group approach. One can argue that a primary emphasis on the group simply assumes away the problem of responsibility by association. In their application, the two methods of ascribing responsibility lead to the same results. To say that a person is

---

[1]   Mark R. Reiff, *Terrorism, Retribution, and Collective Responsibility*, 34 Soc. Theory & Prac. 209, 227 (2008).

responsible for the harms caused by a group simply because she is a member of that group only makes some sense because she is somehow representative of that group. It is not that different from claiming that each member is an expression of its moral center. Recall Chapter 3's argument that when legal liability is involved, human societies have resisted finding that all group members are expressions of that group such that the act of one becomes the act of all other members, and societies have been subject to moral criticism when they have done so. Perhaps the threshold for finding such liability in such organizations can be quite low because by definition virtually every aspect of the organization's structure and activities is dedicated to causing harm to others, but individual liability is required nonetheless.

EXTENDED AGENCY: HUMANS AND AUTONOMOUS MACHINES IN TANDEM

It seems unlikely that the group will ever be considered the fundamental unit of concern. F. Allan Hanson takes an intermediate step between the human individual and the group as fundamental organizing principles and makes the case for extended agencies. He maintains the traditional idea that moral responsibility for an act "lies with the subject that carried it out,"[2] but he believes that subjects are socially constructed, not necessarily entities that have an innate human core. In some circumstances, it is more appropriate to view the responsible subject as more than a human individual, particularly when the human is using or working with technology. Hanson uses the instinct that a person driving a car is in some sense different from the same person riding a bicycle. "[I]f an action can be accomplished only with the collusion of a variety of human and nonhuman participants," he argues, "then the subject or agency that carries out the action cannot be limited to the human component but must consist of all of them."[3]

Hanson then makes the case that an extended subject can be held morally responsible for actions. He disaggregates responsibility by distinguishing between a subject being responsible for an act, in the sense of being part of the narrative of why that act happened, and a subject being *held* responsible for it, in the sense of bearing consequences for that act. Hanson argues that it is relatively straightforward to find extended subjects responsible for something in the former explanatory sense.[4] He continues by arguing that extended subjects

---

[2]   F. Allan Hanson, *Beyond the Skin Bag: On the Moral Responsibility of Extended Agencies*, 11 ETHICS & INFO. TECH. 91, 91 (2009). Bruno Latour makes similar arguments. *See* Bruno Latour, *On Technical Mediation*, 3 COMMON KNOWLEDGE 29 (1994).

[3]   Hanson, *supra* note 2, at 92.

[4]   *Id.*, at 95.

can be viewed as meeting at least some of the usual requirements for moral responsibility for human individuals.[5] For example, Hanson believes that to be subject to responsibility, humans in an extended agency must be aware of consequences and have freedom of choice. However, he notes that awareness of consequences and freedom are necessary but insufficient conditions for responsibility. Some action is required, and humans often are unable to act without other parts of the extended agency: "Given that moral responsibility cannot exist but for the action of the extended agency, it lies with the extended agency as a whole and should not be limited to any part of it."[6] Hanson makes a similar case that extended agencies can be said to have intentions, and argues an extended agency would be better at explaining causation than moral individualism; under some circumstances it seems much more plausible to say that an extended agency of humans and technology caused an event, rather than the humans in question alone.[7] Extended agency does a better job of explaining why a person's responsibilities increase when she moves from riding a bicycle, to driving a car, to serving as president of the United States with the codes to the nuclear arsenal.[8]

It is understandable that there have been attempts to look beyond the human individual and to focus on extended subjects that encompass human beings and machines. To some extent the technology industry itself is laying the groundwork for extended agencies. As discussed in Chapter 1, large technology companies are taking steps to make artificial intelligence technology available to a wide range of business customers.[9] Given the current state of technology, in which full autonomy has not yet been achieved, it is foreseeable that many of the applications of artificial intelligence will be more in the nature of intelligence augmentation, in which human capacities are increased through the use of artificial intelligence, as opposed to the literal replacement of human beings by autonomous systems.[10] It seems likely that intelligence enhancement will make it more common for human beings to use artificial intelligence and then eventually work in tandem with artificial intelligence that reaches a high level

---

[5]   Mark Coeckelbergh takes an analogous approach. *See* Mark Coeckelbergh, *Is Ethics of Robotics about Robots? Philosophy of Robotics beyond Realism and Individualism*, 3 LAW INNOVATION & TECH. 241, 247 (2011).

[6]   Hanson, *supra* note 2, at 96.

[7]   *Id.*, at 96–7.

[8]   *Id.*, at 97–8.

[9]   Cade Metz, *Google Sells A.I. for Building A.I. (Novices Welcome)*, N.Y. TIMES, Jan. 17, 2018, at B1; Cade Metz, *Google Makes Its Special A.I. Chips Available to Others*, N.Y. TIMES, Feb. 12, 2018, at B3.

[10]   David Lavenda, *Artificial Intelligence vs. Intelligence Augmentation*, NETWORK WORLD, Aug. 5, 2016, www.networkworld.com/article/3104909/software/artificial-intelligence-vs-intelligence-augmentation.html.

of autonomy. This will be the case in areas such as health care, law, architecture, manufacturing, and so on. These developments lend themselves to the idea that the human individual's agency is extended because of his or her use of augmentation technologies. This might be even more so during transitional periods when artificial intelligence is just coming on line and the human users of that technology are seen as the primary actors or supervisors.

We therefore would expect to see more instances in which humans are increasingly engaged with even more sophisticated technologies. So from an objective perspective, one can see how a society might be persuaded to embrace the idea of an extended subject. However, from the perspective of the human beings who are engaged with technologies, the question for extended agency is whether our concepts of human agency and identity are malleable enough that the human being would at a minimum acquiesce in the idea that he and the machine in question are somehow part of an extended identity. The answer could go either way. Pim Haselager provides an interesting illustration of the problem. He describes work now being done with using computers to capture brain functioning to enable humans to power devices such as wheelchairs without physical controls.[11] However, gaps in interpreting brain signals and translating them into instructions make it useful to add an artificial intelligence component to the system to compensate for shortcomings in the technology. The result is that sometimes the system will exhibit behavior not intended by the human operator.[12] This raises several issues as to who the agent in such situations really is. Haselager asks us to suppose that a person using an AI-assisted brain interface to control a wheelchair collides with someone. The person might have intended to go in a particular direction, while in fact it was the autonomous function that caused the wheelchair to do so. Yet the person might feel that he is responsible because of the shared intention. If, in the illustration, the operator did *not* intend to go in that direction, the human operator might still have a sense that he is responsible for the accident.[13] "[A] user's feeling of agency will not provide him with the same reliable compass as normally in respect of his bodily behavior."[14]

Hanson's extended agency and Haselager's discussion of the problems that might arise when humans and technologies with an intelligent component are intimately connected suggest that technology has the potential to have a profound effect on our understanding of human agency and identity. Hansen's theory can be placed within a strand of the philosophy of technology

---

[11] Pim Haselager, *Did I Do That? Brain-Computer Interfacing and the Sense of Agency*, 23 MINDS & MACHINES 405, 406–8 (2013).

[12] *Id.*, at 408–10.

[13] *Id.*, at 414–15.

[14] *Id.*, at 416.

which posits that the human person or personal identity has been changed or challenged by technologies such as cloning, genetic therapies, and so on.[15] These developments now force society, and the law in particular, to ask questions about personal identity by increasing the human person's capacities in ways hitherto not dreamed of.[16] The argument that technology significantly impacts human identity and individuality dovetails with an understanding that an individual's identity is as much a product of the web of relationships in which one engages as it is some inherent, core self. Rhoda Howard-Hassmann argues for example that a woman has her own identity and at the same time overlapping commitments to a number of groups: family, job, private interests, religion, friendships, community, and country.[17] The UK Government Office for Science describes individuals as having overlapping but distinct social, biographical, and biometric identities.[18] Each of these relationships and groups draw out and/or make possible various aspects of the self that perhaps would not be manifest in other sets of relationships. The UK report notes that people increasingly move almost seamlessly between the real and virtual worlds and are thus able to extend those multifaceted identities online.[19] The widespread use of social media by younger people has made them less concerned about privacy.[20] Big data already relies heavily on artificial intelligence and allows for the personalization of advertisements and services based on an individual's online history, an aspect of a person's online identity.

David Zoller worries that increasing automation will rob us of the sense of agency that comes from being able to master particular skills such as driving a car and working with other people.[21] In a similar vein, Hildebrandt warns that as we interact with more sophisticated forms of Siri or Alexa that will serve as personal assistants, we might not even be aware of the choices artificial

---

[15]   *See, e.g.*, Robert Pepperell, *Applications for Conscious Systems*, 22 AI & Soc'y 45, 47 (2007) (technology "is an integral part of what it means to be human").

[16]   *See, e.g.*, Colin Gavaghan, *A Whole New You? "Personal Identity", Emerging Technologies" and the Law*, 3 IDENTITY IN THE INFORMATION SOC'Y 423 (2010). "The person who surrenders her glasses, her telephone, her car, and her computer changes not only her instrumental abilities, but also her social life." J.M. Balkin, CULTURAL SOFTWARE 24–5 (1998).

[17]   Rhoda E. Howard-Hassmann, *(Dis)embedded Women*, 24 MICH. J. INT'L L. 227, 26 (2002).

[18]   UK Gov't Office for Science, Future Identities: Changing Identities in the UK: The Next 10 Years (2013), at 10.

[19]   *Id.*, at 25.

[20]   *Id.*, at 27.

[21]   David Zoller, *Skilled Perception, Authenticity, and the Case against Automation*, *in* ROBOT ETHICS 2.0: FROM AUTONOMOUS CARS TO ARTIFICIAL INTELLIGENCE 80 (Patrick Lin, Ryan Jenkins, and Keith Abney eds., 2017) [hereinafter ROBOT ETHICS 2.0].

intelligence is making for us as it manages our time, modes of transportation, work, and relationships.[22] As Jannis Kallinikos puts it:

> [C]ontemporary technologies of computing and communication differ in the sense of massively intervening upon the primary process of reality perception thus redefining the cognitive and communicative profile of daily living[.] ... An important consequence is the constitution of human experience by the standardized and often unobtrusive procedures of assembling reality that current technologies of computing and communication mediate.[23]

Recall from Chapter 1 Hildebrandt's description of a society in which smart technologies will be a persistent part of our daily experience. She argues that without strong privacy protections, big data's ability to anticipate and respond to human needs as we move seamlessly on and offline threatens to deprive individuals of the freedom to choose their identity.[24] What happens, however, if the trend toward less concern about privacy among those who grew up with technology, as observed in the UK report, becomes predominant? Technology alone might be transformative of human identity, but technology so sophisticated that it is possible to speak of having a meaningful relationship with it might be even more so.

In the future, advanced technology might make it possible for humans and artificial intelligence to change identity in more radical ways. James DiGiovanna speculates that advanced artificial intelligence will allow both artificial intelligences themselves and human beings, through artificial intelligence enhancements, to become "para-persons," entities that are persons that have all the attributes of personhood plus the ability to change identities.[25] In such a future, persons could "reprogram" themselves and take on entirely new personas, with different memories, knowledge, and skills. For the purposes of this chapter it is not necessary to decide whether this is indeed possible; the point is that enhancements to technology could result in radical changes to our perceptions of ourselves, some of which might be literal when viewed from our present understanding of the individual. In this regard discontinuities in the self will pose real problems for systems of responsibility because there will

---

[22]   Mireille Hildebrandt, SMART TECHNOLOGIES AND THE END(S) OF LAW 68–75 (2015).

[23]   Jannis Kallinikos, *Technology and Accountability: Autonomic Computing and Human Agency, in* LAW, HUMAN AGENCY AND AUTONOMIC COMPUTING: THE PHILOSOPHY OF LAW MEETS THE PHILOSOPHY OF TECHNOLOGY 160 (Mireille Hildebrandt and Antoinette Rouvroy eds., 2011).

[24]   Hildebrandt, *supra* note 22, at 82.

[25]   James DiGiovanna, *Artificial Identity, in* ROBOT ETHICS 2.0, *supra* note 21, at 307, 307–8.

literally be a sense in which the "person" who committed the wrong no longer exists—she has changed into someone else. But to say that there are limitless possibilities also makes it possible to rewire ourselves to become more amenable to systems of responsibility that adequately encompass sophisticated forms of artificial intelligence.

On this subject, Luciano Floridi raises the possibility that the advent of what he terms "information and communications technologies" accelerates a process that makes us more amenable to seeing ourselves and others less as individuals and more as types:

> Once our window-shopping becomes Windows-shopping and no longer means walking down the street but browsing the Web, the process of dephysicalization and typification of individuals as unique and irreplaceable entities may start eroding our sense of personal identity as well. We may risk behaving like, and conceptualizing ourselves as, mass-produced, anonymous entities among other anonymous entities, exposed to billions of other similar individuals online. We may conceive each other as bundles of types, from gender to religion, from family role to working position, from education to social class.[26]

If these changes in how we see ourselves and others come to pass, one might not need the concept of extended agency to allocate responsibility caused by autonomous technologies to human beings. It might be the case that those associated with the design, manufacture, ownership, and use of autonomous technologies will be seen and will see themselves not as individuals, but as types. In such a world, responsibility will be assigned to types, not to individual people, and if people truly view themselves as such, perhaps that assignment will not be objectionable.

A case can thus be made that technology is already affecting the way we understand ourselves as agents, and autonomous technologies, coupled with big data, might have an even greater impact as they continue to shape our reality, perhaps even to the extent that we move away from a view of ourselves as the kind of individuals that form the paradigm for individual responsibility. At the same time, it remains to be seen whether that transformation of a human's sense of self will in fact lead a person to accept the consequences for harms caused by an extended agency of which she is a part, or, even without extended agency, harms caused by autonomous technologies with which

---

[26] Luciano Floridi, THE FOURTH REVOLUTION: HOW THE INFOSPHERE IS RESHAPING HUMAN REALITY 57–8 (2014). Floridi's view of how the rise of information and communications technologies could affect human beings goes further. For him, such technologies call into question the uniqueness of the human species and provide an opportunity for human beings to expand their web of associations to natural and synthetic entities. *Id.*, at 86, 166.

a person might be associated. One difficulty goes to the distinction discussed earlier between being responsible and being held responsible. If I am a member of an extended agency I might find it acceptable to be considered responsible for a harm caused by that agency, if being responsible meant only that someone concluded that an extended agent comprising me and a machine was the cause. However, I might feel very differently if the extended agency was held responsible in the sense of bearing consequences. Then the distributional issues that vex group responsibility reemerge. The extended agency itself is responsible for harm, but even if my subjectivity is so enmeshed in that agency that I can accept characterizations that I am part of a larger whole, I, not the machine, will feel the negative consequences of being held responsible. I might view those consequences as unfair, particularly if I could not have reasonably foreseen that the machine involved would cause harm and, if it is advanced enough, it is a machine over which I ultimately had no control. This problem would be magnified if groups of extended agencies are found responsible for a harm, because it would be only the human participants in those extended subjects that would bear the brunt of responsibility.

A second issue is analogous to the second question with which group responsibility wrestles: what kinds of groups can be subject to moral evaluation? Under an extended agency theory, an individual is part of a number of such agencies throughout the course of a day: when she steps into a car, when she sits at a computer terminal at work, whenever she "uses" technology to perform a particular task. Thus, how closely tied to the agency must an individual be before she is considered part of it? Sometimes the extended agency that causes harm will be persistent, such as when a person regularly uses an autonomous car to commute to work. At other times it will be almost ephemeral, even though the harm caused by such an agency is significant. In Chapter 4, I discussed how crowd analytics might make it easier to reify what previously would have been thought of as random combinations of human beings. Similar reifications could occur with fleeting combinations of humans and machines—crowd analytics might enable us to recognize an extended agency where previously we would have thought there was simply a random combination of humans and machines. That the extended agent has caused harm could by itself justify liability and its distribution among members of the extended agency. But again we return to the difference between responsibility as explanation and responsibility as bearing consequences. If we are distributing consequences and the extended agency is ephemeral, it will not be surprising if there is a tendency to fall back on more traditional approaches, even though under Hanson's framework it was the extended agent that caused the harm.

Finally, the concept of extended agency is not new. Any large corporation can be considered an extended agency in which management has enhanced powers through the constitutive parts of the firm. Suppose a corporation is convicted of a crime and forced to pay criminal penalties. In that situation the corporation as extended agent bears responsibility in both of its forms, as explanation for a harm and as bearing the consequences for that harm. However, with regard to management, the law so far has declined to adjust legal responsibility according to enhanced power, even though people with power have been held to higher moral standards. The chief executive officer of a corporation who is part of that extended agency must herself be culpable of a crime even if the corporation is convicted of one. It could be argued that this is exactly how the responsibility of extended agencies should work out; the separation of responsibility into its constitutive parts means that the corporation bears the both the legal and moral consequences of being held criminally responsible while the CEO who has no criminal culpability bears only the moral consequences of being part of the firm's management.

THE GROUP AS COMPRISING HUMANS AND AUTONOMOUS TECHNOLOGY

Concerns about extended agency lead us back to the group, not as the fundamental unit of concern but as a causative agent in its own right, of which humans and autonomous machines and systems are members. What level of sophistication must autonomous machines reach before we begin to think of them less like tools and more like partners, so that we move away from the paradigm of individual responsibility? Several commentators argue that it will take very high levels of autonomy and intelligence for this to occur. Ipke Wachsmuth discusses some of the technical requirements that he believes artificial systems must meet to act as full-fledged partners with human beings. Cooperation with others requires shared intentions and goals, and thus machines need to develop the capacity to determine another's intentions.[27]

> [S]uch systems should be able to understand and respond to the human's wants in order to be assistive in a given situation. Technically, this challenge involves the implementation of a range of skills such as: processing language, gaze and gestures, representing intentional states for self and other, detecting and manipulating the other's attention, responding to bids for joint attention, accomplishing goals in joint activity.[28]

---

[27] Ipke Wachsmuth, *Embodied Cooperative Systems: From Tool to Partnership*, *in* COLLECTIVE AGENCY AND COOPERATION IN NATURAL AND ARTIFICIAL SYSTEMS: EXPLANATION, IMPLEMENTATION AND SIMULATION 63 (Catrin Misselhorn ed., 2015) [hereinafter COLLECTIVE AGENCY AND COOPERATION].

[28] *Id.*, at 65.

At the technical level, achieving this level of sophistication involves developing models of intentional systems. Wachsmuth defines those as "systems that perceive changes in the world, represent mental attitudes (like beliefs, goals, etc.), and reason about mental attitudes in order to arrive at decisions on how to plan actions and act."[29] At this point autonomous technologies are in early stages of development and do not yet have such intentionality.[30]

Sophistication and intentionality might be important for determining not only whether an autonomous machine or system qualifies as a member of a group, but also whether a group as such is constituted such that it can be said to have engaged in collective action. Scholars differ on this issue. Michael Bratman, for example, argues that groups must be understood in terms of shared intention.[31] He sketches out seven features of modest sociality, cases in which two people informally agree to engage in some joint activity, such as singing a duet or walking down the street together. This would require: (1) "Intentions on the part of each in favor of *our joint activity*";[32] (2) "*Interlocking* intentions";[33] (3) "Intentions in favor of *meshing* sub-plans";[34] (4) "*Disposition to help* if needed";[35] (5) "*Interdependence* in the persistence of each person's relevant intentions";[36] (6) "*Joint action-tracking mutual responsiveness* in the intentions and actions of each";[37] and (7) "Common knowledge among the participants of all these conditions."[38] For Olle Blomberg, collective action requires a common goal:

> [S]everal agents have a common goal if there is a single outcome that satisfies a goal of each agent ... and each agent believes that this is the case[.] ... [E]ach must also believe that the goal of each is compatible with the involvement of the others ... Furthermore, in virtue of these beliefs, each must also believe that each of the others

---

[29] *Id.*

[30] As an example of the state of the art in 2015, Wachsmuth discusses the development of a robot to serve as an artificial museum guide. *Id.*, at 70–73.

[31] Michael E. Bratman, *Modest Sociality and the Distinctiveness of Intention*, 144 PHIL. STUD. 149 (2005).

[32] *Id.*, at 155. (Emphasis in original.)

[33] *Id.*, at 157. (Emphasis in original.)

[34] *Id.*, at 158. (Emphasis in original.)

[35] *Id.* (Emphasis in original.)

[36] *Id.*, at 159. (Emphasis in original.)

[37] *Id.* (Emphasis in original.)

[38] *Id.*, at 160. These features are extensions of Bratman's ideas of what is required for shared cooperative activity. Michael E. Bratman, *Shared Cooperative Activity*, 101 PHIL. REV. 327 (1992).

has performed, is performing or will perform actions toward the single outcome in order [to] achieve their goal.[39]

Paul Hammond relaxes these requirements, and argues that such a high degree of joint intention on the part of all members might not be necessary in highly organized groups such as corporations to engage in intentional collective action: the intentional action of one or two members might suffice.[40]

If shared intentions or common goals as laid out by Bratman, Blomberg, or even Hammond are the criteria for group formation and collective action, then there are strong arguments that autonomous technologies are not yet able to perform that constitutive role. Suppose a care robot assists a person as he walks down a hallway. As the person and robot proceed, both are able to point out a wet floor to each other. If one stops walking in the same direction, the other does as well. The human coordinates with the robot in the sense that he tries to match the robot's speed as it proceeds down the hall; similarly, sensors allow the robot to detect the patient's heartrate and adjust its speed in response. Such activity would seem to be more than two human strangers just so happening to be walking down the hall at the same time. But although the robot's actions appear to be cooperative, there is no sense in which the robot has intended to engage them, if in fact the robot can be said to act. Thus no modest sociality exists. In a similar vein, Tom Poljanšek argues that a distinction should be made between groups that have common goals, and groups to which one has a sense of belonging.[41] "[T]he feeling of belonging is best to be understood as a *feeling to belong to something which exists independent of its members*, whether this felt existence is ontologically significant or not."[42] Such groups can be said to be capable of collective agency, but it would be unclear what it would mean for a robot to feel it belongs to a group of humans, or vice versa for the human.

Anna Strasser comes close to making a case for collective action involving autonomous technologies.[43] She begins by observing that current understandings of collective action (deliberative action as opposed to mere reflex) require a high degree of autonomy. But she points out that even with humans there

---

[39]   Olle Blomberg, *An Account of Boeschian Cooperative Behavior, in* Collective Agency and Cooperation, *supra* note 27, at 169, 182.

[40]   Paul Hammond, *Distinguishing Joint Actions from Collective Actions*, 193 Synthese 2707 (2016).

[41]   Tom Poljanšek, *Choosing Appropriate Paradigmatic Examples for Understanding Collective Agency*, in Collective Agency and Cooperation, *supra* note 27, at 185.

[42]   *Id.*, at 201.

[43]   Anna Strasser, *Can Artificial Systems Be Part of a Collective Action?* in Collective Agency and Cooperation, *supra* note 27, at 205.

are asymmetries in abilities: a parent playing with a child is a good example.[44] Even though the child does not yet possess the same capacity to deliberate, one feels that this is collective action between parent and child, not the parent using the child as a tool. Strasser believes there are gradations in action that range from simple behaviors to full-fledged deliberative action. Intentionality requires "an ability to generate goals; second the resulting behavior must be described as goal-directed, third possession of some kind of free will. Last but not least consciousness and self-consciousness are postulated implicitly in many cases."[45] Strasser explores whether these criteria can be relaxed. First, she points out that goals can be generated by someone and given to someone else. Then she turns to collective action. This requires the ability to coordinate one's actions with others. "To coordinate oneself with other agents in a collective action one must possess the ability to anticipate the actions of other participants."[46] Strasser argues that this ability to anticipate someone else's actions does not require a mental state.[47]

Finally, cooperative behavior could be viewed using concepts from complexity theory as opposed to the philosophical approaches to groups, collective action and group responsibility. Mog Stapleton and Tom Froese propose that we understand agency as an emergent phenomena that arises out of our interactions with the environment:[48]

> [A]n enactive theory of agency ... proposes that an agentive system is one which creates itself as an individual, adapts to changes in the environment by manipulating itself in that environment more than the environment manipulates it, and is moved to do so in order to satisfy needs that arise internally, needs that result from the system undergoing self-generation under far-from-equilibrium conditions, i.e., conditions which continually threaten its existence.[49]

The authors distinguish among several types of groups and agency, as evidenced by flocks of birds; termites, bees, and ants; and the cells in the human body.[50] Human societies differ in that they have been able to create social institutions that allow for greater independence from their environments: "[H]uman societies have addressed the potential instabilities of a purely behav-

---

[44]   *Id.*, at 208.
[45]   *Id.*, at 210.
[46]   *Id.*, at 214.
[47]   *Id.*
[48]   Mog Stapleton and Tom Froese, *Is Collective Agency a Coherent Idea? Considerations from the Enactive Theory of Agency, in* COLLECTIVE AGENCY AND COOPERATION, *supra* note 27, at 219.
[49]   *Id.*, at 222.
[50]   *Id.*, at 223–8.

iorally integrated group level of agency by forming social institutions that are independent of the people passing through them, and which in the modern world even have legal representation as individuals in their own right."[51] Given the variety of forms of groups and types of agency that have emerged in nature, Stapleton and Froese argue against viewing collective agency as an all-or-nothing concept. Entities might move in and out of agency over a period of time.[52] "[A]gency in each system may be more, or less, visible at different levels of analysis."[53] In this regard, the authors then make an argument for the plausibility of collective subjectivity that can emerge through interactions with others. They describe their own experiments with two robots in which they programmed the equivalent of an artificial neuron in each robot.[54] According to Stapleton and Froese, when the two robots interacted, their respective neurons showed activity that should be impossible for each single neuron. The authors suggest that the robots became different subjects when they were together.[55]

Thus, if certain requirements for collective action are relaxed, it might be possible to speak of collective action with artificial agents. Here it is worth reminding ourselves that there will be gradations of autonomy among autonomous technologies. Suppose machines and systems reach full autonomy in the sense of having general intelligence. If artificial agents have that level of intelligence, there will be little argument that we can engage in collective action with such machines, or, put another way, the philosophical debates about what constitutes collective action among humans will apply to humans and machines as if machines are humans. (This assumes that humans do not decide that, irrespective of a machine's cognitive abilities, machines do not have the same status as human beings.) However, even when there are autonomous systems that have general intelligence, there will still be autonomous systems that do not quite reach that level.

Yet even if it is coherent to speak of a group of humans and autonomous technology that engage in collective actions, we would still wrestle with the question whether it would be appropriate to subject such a group to moral and legal responsibility. Here we return to the themes introduced in Chapter 4. Scholars such as Petit and others would likely argue that under certain conditions, it would be, if the organization was constructed so that it engaged in the same deliberation and exercised autonomy in ways similar to the human individual. As we have seen, others argue against this. Christopher Thompson argues that groups cannot be moral agents because they cannot feel moral emo-

---

[51]   *Id.*, at 227.
[52]   *Id.*, at 228.
[53]   *Id.*, at 229.
[54]   *Id.*, at 230.
[55]   *Id.*, at 230–31.

tions such as guilt and shame.[56] Marcus Hedal argues that there are irreducibly joint actors made up of moral actors, which nevertheless are not moral actors in themselves. This is because certain organizations can be created that do not have the capacities (such as deliberation) that are required by paradigmatic moral agents under Petit's model.[57] Interestingly, for Hedal, the practical effect is that there is even greater incentive to subject joint actors to legal responsibility.[58] Hedal argues that moral responsibility differs from legal responsibility because moral responsibility implies second order effects, such as other people's scorn, criticism, and so on. In Hedal's view, judicial sanctions do not carry such effects.[59] I have already set out in Chapter 3 my view that legal responsibility and moral responsibility share many features, and I would argue with Hedal that legal responsibility has its own knock on effects. The stigma often attached to conviction of crimes indicates this. At the same time, one need not agree with Hedal's distinction to appreciate the broader point, made also by scholars such as Thompson, that it is not always clear when a group as such can be considered the bearer of responsibility for its actions.

GAPS IN RESPONSIBILITY

That issues about the coherency of group action and group responsibility still exist in the literature leads to an odd result for humans and autonomous technologies. It is the possibility identified earlier in this book of gaps in responsibility when harms occur. As I have argued in earlier chapters, on the individual level, the more machines and systems increase their autonomy, the harder it is to characterize the relationship between humans and such technologies as one in which the human is using a tool, who by using that tool could cause an injury, thus warranting moral and legal consequences as an individual. At the same time, as I have suggested in this chapter, unless there are radical changes in how we as individuals view ourselves, brought about in part by artificial intelligence itself, it is unlikely that we will be able to accept that the group is the fundamental unit of concern, or ourselves as part of an extended agency, at least when it comes to bearing moral and legal consequences for what that extended agency has done. Based on the discussion in the preceding section, the more autonomous technologies grow in sophistication, the more plausible it is to speak of groups of humans and machines acting together. But there

---

[56] Christopher Thompson, *The Moral Agency of Group Agents*, 83 ERKENN 517 (2018).

[57] Marcus Hedal, *The Collective Fallacy: The Possibility of Irreducibly Collective Action without Corresponding Moral Responsibility*, 43 PHIL. SOC. SCI. 283 (2013).

[58] *Id.*, at 296.

[59] *Id.*, at 294.

will continue to be debates as to whether it is in fact coherent to speak of such groups as acting and as moral agents. Following Hedal, one could subject such groups to legal responsibility by fiat, but this would not solve the distributional issues that might be involved as the effects of being held legally responsible are felt disproportionately by humans and machines.

The lack of legal responsibility is worrisome for several reasons. From a purely instrumental perspective, one reason for developing autonomous machines and systems is that they will achieve benefits which human beings cannot realize alone. As we have seen, it is believed that eventually self-driving cars will be safer than cars driven by humans, and although several observers argue strongly that this will never be so, in theory autonomous weapons systems could eventually reduce the number of deaths caused in battle.[60] However, if designers, programmers, manufacturers, and officers are insulated from legal responsibility, the costs of harms caused by machines are shifted to consumers and to civilians. Lack of such responsibility removes an incentive for designers, programmers, and manufacturers to avoid producing machines that pose an unreasonable risk to society. In the case of military applications, the failure to hold someone responsible could lead to impunity, with the result that there would be little incentive to design machines and deploy them in ways that comply with the law of war.

As mentioned earlier, concerns that there will be gaps in responsibility if autonomous weapons are used lead Sparrow to argue for their ban. Sparrow is concerned with who will be morally responsible for the actions of autonomous weapons systems, and his worry that no one will be responsible leads him to conclude that it would be unethical to use them.[61] Others disagree with Sparrow,[62] but even if he is right as to the ethics of using such machines, his

---

[60]   Christopher P. Toscano, *"Friend of Humans": An Argument for Developing Autonomous Weapon Systems*, 8 J. NAT'L SEC. L. & POL'Y 189 (2015). Toscano argues autonomous weapons systems will be better than humans in reducing civilian casualties because they can remain objective, can act with greater caution, and can exceed human beings' biological limitations. *Id.*, at 224–34.

[61]   Robert Sparrow, *Killer Robots*, 24 J. APPLIED PHIL. 62, 66 (2007). *See also* Noel E. Sharkey, *The Evitability of Autonomous Robot Warfare*, 94 INT'L REV. OF THE RED CROSS 787 (2012) (arguing that autonomous weapons should be banned because it will be difficult to hold human beings responsible for crimes caused by such weapons).

[62]   For example, Kenneth Anderson and Matthew Waxman argue that such reasoning seems particularly persuasive to those who have faith in ability of the laws of war and individual criminal liability to enforce compliance. They argue other mechanisms can be used to encourage such compliance and worry that holding individuals criminally liable for the use of autonomous weapons could have a chilling effect on the development of systems that might reduce harm to civilians. Kenneth Anderson and Matthew Waxman, *Law and Ethics for Robot Soldiers*, POL'Y REV., Dec. 2012 and Jan. 2013, at 35, 43. In this regard Toscano believes autonomous machines will be better

arguments are not necessarily applicable to legal responsibility. In an environment in which as a legal matter all things are permitted unless expressly prohibited, if a programmer, designer, or "supervisor" of a machine cannot be held legally responsible for an autonomous machine's actions, it does not follow that it would be illegal to program, design, or use it. But of course this exacerbates the issue, because there might be machine-caused harms for which no one is legally accountable.

The concern is that law will find itself at an impasse. On the one hand, even machines and systems that do not reach high levels of autonomy might still act in such a way that makes it hard under our current conceptions of legal responsibility to link their "actions" to a human, so that he or she could be held responsible legally for what the machines or systems have done. On the other hand, as Sparrow points out, such technologies are still without souls to be kicked or bodies to be damned; thus it seems pointless and unsatisfactory to hold the machines or systems responsible for themselves.

In a 1992 study, Elizabeth Wolgast explored the ethics of artificial persons—not autonomous machines, but rather organizations with legal personality, such as law firms and corporations. She too found that issues raised by group responsibility and the nature of those organizations allow responsibility to dissipate. In her study, Wolgast considers and ultimately rejects the possibility that we might be able to change our conceptions of responsibility to fit the new reality.

> The hope of revising our moral concepts to fit present facts fails to confront the reason that the issue has any importance to begin with. Our objection to professional and institutional irresponsibility comes from a belief that *someone* is responsible, and this belief springs from our appreciation of moral standards. Without that moral understanding, there would be no problem: we would simply accept the fact that countless professional and institutional contexts are responsibility-free.[63]

---

than human beings at complying with the law of war while in combat. Toscano, *supra* note 60, at 224–42. In particular, he argues that in the near term, since human beings will remain in the loop when autonomous weapons are used, existing civil and criminal liability mechanisms should be sufficient to address specific incidents involving such weapons. *Id.*, at 235. Further, Toscano suggests such systems could actually enhance command responsibility because they constantly record data that could be used in investigations of any incidents. *Id.*, at 238.

[63] Elizabeth Wolgast, ETHICS OF AN ARTIFICIAL PERSON: LOST RESPONSIBILITY IN PROFESSIONS AND ORGANIZATIONS 140–41 (1992). John Danaher's review of the psychological, legal, and moral literature leads him to conclude that "humans are innate retributivists: when they are harmed or injured they look for a culpable wrongdoer who is deserving of punishment. Many legal and moral philosophers argue that this retributive attitude is the correct one to take." John Danaher, *Robot Law and the Retribution Gap*, 18 ETHICS & INFO. TECH. 299 (2016).

Wolgast's argument is persuasive. Although there are Copernican paradigm shifts that alter radically our understanding of the universe and ourselves, as I have argued earlier, in the main, we start with the language and concepts we have. Even though there are possible alternatives, the sense of individual responsibility has persisted for hundreds of years. The moral standards and the legal doctrines that find support in them have been deemed good, useful, or both as one way to allocate responsibility for harms.

Of course, that an idea persists is not proof of its correctness. To return to Balkin's understanding of cultural tools, the system of responsibility, with the idea that *someone* is responsible, might simply be a form of muddling through the job at hand. Put in evolutionary terms, our system of responsibility resulted from practices that were selected for over time. It is sufficient that an evolving system be only marginally better than its competitors in a particular environment; there is no guarantee that it is optimal. Thus, it is possible there are other strands of human culture or an idea in the mind of some future ethicist that will provide a more satisfying and effective way to conceive of and respond to what we currently experience as harm. But the costs of finding such a system might be high.

Indeed, there is no question that ethics evolve as our conceptions of our world and our society evolve. At the time the *Nicomachean Ethics* was written, slavery was accepted, full moral autonomy was reserved to only one gender, and so on. At the same time, that evolution has been more about the expansion of who qualifies as an autonomous, responsible individual. No matter how much we might better appreciate the embedded and relational nature of our experience, or that we are part of complex adaptive systems, it is highly unlikely that the understanding that we are also individuals will ever completely disappear. It seems much more likely that for the foreseeable future these beliefs about responsibility and individuality will remain so fundamental that any changes to those concepts will happen at the margins. It might be that our use of and interaction with increasingly sophisticated machines and systems will cause incremental changes in our understandings of responsibility. This is what concerns Hildebrandt when she speaks of the impact to our agency that greater immersion in smart technology will have. But at this point we can only imagine ourselves being different individuals. It is not yet a reality.

Wolgast argued in this regard:

> The framework in which the problems of artificial persons are raised—that of our moral concepts and training—is also where the solutions need to be framed. The vocabulary in which the question is asked is the one where its answer has to be

couched. In the framework of moral discourse, *our* moral discourse, individual responsibility needs to take recognizable form in such answers[64]

That we are likely to continue to use already existing discourse and modes of conceiving of responsibility results in a quandary: the possibility that, as applied to autonomous technologies, such responsibility will dissipate under that discourse and those concepts. This quandary in turn leads to another strategy: making autonomous technologies morally and legally responsible, as we now understand those terms.

---

[64] *Id.*

PART IV

Ethical AI

7.   Law-abiding machines and systems

The impasses identified at the conclusions of Chapters 5 and 6 motivate a second major strategy to close possible gaps between machines and systems and the harms caused by them. This is to reduce harm by designing autonomous technologies that "obey" the law. This strategy assumes that law demarcates a set of responsibilities we owe to one another. At this point, of course, even the most sophisticated machines are not cognizant of the law, far less do they appreciate or value it in the subjective sense. But as discussed in this chapter and in the next, engineers and commentators are trying to move technology in that direction. Part of this motivation is simply that the law already requires that autonomous technologies operate in compliance with existing law. The Nevada and North Carolina autonomous vehicle statutes reviewed in Chapter 2 are examples of this. At the same time, as will be noted in the next chapter, the overall hope is to create machines with prosocial behaviors to minimize the possibility of harm to humans, and, in the case of the most advanced machines, to make them cognizant of their responsibilities to others and perhaps more susceptible to forms of punishment. In a sense, it is another way to preserve the discourse of individual responsibility, by holding autonomous technologies responsible in a way that is meaningful within that discourse.

This chapter is divided into four parts, all of which explore the extent to which it is possible to design machines that obey the law. The first part deals with some preliminary questions about what obedience to law might mean. The second discusses the distinction between legal rules, legal standards, and legal policies, and whether it is possible to articulate those in ways an autonomous system could "understand." The third part looks at efforts to automate the legal practice, as a way to assess the upper boundaries for the level of legal sophistication artificial intelligence might achieve. The chapter concludes that, framed in a particular way, it is plausible for artificial systems to be developed to the point at which they might obey the law in strictly circumscribed areas at least as well as human beings who are not formally trained in the law, and perhaps better. To the extent that sophisticated machines are unable to follow the law, particularly legal principles and policies, this might reveal more about the limitations of the law than about the limitations of artificial intelligence. At the same time, if sophisticated machines and systems can in fact follow the law or meet its standards better than humans, they might establish standards for legal responsibility high enough that human beings will not be able to meet them without their help.

OBEYING THE LAW

As just discussed, we might want autonomous technologies to obey the law because the law can be understood as setting out standards for responsible behavior and the baseline for responsibility. For example, Chapter 2 laid out concerns that autonomous home devices might threaten our current expectations of privacy. However, if the law does not prohibit the disclosure of certain kinds of information about an individual, such as his address and telephone number, although there might be some moral or psychic harm caused when an autonomous system discloses such information, from a legal perspective that harm would not rise to the level where the law would give a remedy. Viewed instrumentally, such disclosures are ones that society does not want to prevent; indeed, society might decide it wants such information to be publicly available. In an expressive view of the law, such disclosure would not rise to the level at which legal responsibility would be required to reinforce social values that are expressed in law. Conversely, if a disclosure law is violated, this triggers the possibility that the law will give a remedy to the injured party or subject the lawbreaker to some form of sanction. The process by which one identifies a possible defendant and then determines liability or guilt is the law's way of allocating and distributing responsibility for harms, as we have seen in earlier chapters.

There are therefore good reasons for using obedience to the law as a means to prevent harms caused by autonomous machines and systems. Some preliminary matters, however, need to be addressed. First, what does it mean to follow or obey the law? Is it merely to act in a way that coincides with the law's requirements, or is something more required? Very few people receive formal legal training, and as a result most have only a rough sense of what their legal obligations are. What knowledge of the law a person has often comes from the media, discussions with friends who themselves are not lawyers, and in some cases a modicum of formal training in limited areas, for example, in preparation for taking the written test on basic traffic law when someone is applying for a driver's license. From a lawyer's perspective, even that level of knowledge is minimal: most people know only the basic rules, such as to obey the posted speed limit, to stop at stop signs, to give the right of way to pedestrians, and so on. Yet in ordinary conversation it is perfectly appropriate to say that an individual is obeying the law. An argument can thus be made that one need not be fully cognizant of the law in order to obey it, and certainly not cognizant of all of its detail.

This commonsense understanding of what it means to obey law has obvious applications to autonomous machines and systems. As discussed, one way to avoid harm is to program machines to act as much as possible in conformity to existing law; for example, by instructing autonomous cars to obey traffic laws or, in another context, to program autonomous weapons to follow the laws of war. In a sense, "obeying the law" becomes shorthand for operating in ways that happen to coincide with legal requirements; it is therefore no more necessary for an autonomous machine to be cognizant of the law than it is for a human being to be completely cognizant of the law when going about her everyday activities. A major issue, however, is whether there are technical and theoretical limits to this approach. Some believe that programming machines to obey the law is possible only to a certain extent because law cannot always be reduced to a set of rules of decision. This is based in part on the view that legal doctrine is deeply grounded in human language. Insofar as artificial systems are not yet able to interact in human language, they are unable to apply the law as humans do. The question becomes whether this is a technological limit, a theoretical one, or both.

There are other facets of the question of "law-abidingness." For example, assuming a machine does not need to be conscious of the law in order to obey it, how closely do we want it to conform to the law? In the case of the autonomous weapons systems, one could argue that we would want the system to obey the law of war to the letter, yet that might not be true in other areas, such as autonomous vehicles. We have a sense that some laws are "truly" important, such as the prohibition against murder, whereas it is less important to toe the line exactly when it comes to speed limits; indeed, it might be safer to operate at a speed that goes with the flow of traffic as opposed to the limit posted on a sign. Even when there are infractions of the law, we distinguish between those that are serious and those that are less so. The law of course accommodates this in several ways. There is the legal maxim *de minimus, non curat lex*: "The law does not concern itself with trivial matters." The distinction between felonies and misdemeanors is meant to recognize gradations in the severity of criminal behavior. In contract law, any breach gives rise to damages, but only material breach relieves the injured party of his contract obligations. The issue is whether "obedience to the law" is shorthand for designing machines that act in ways that minimize the chance they will cause harm in narrowly constrained contexts, or whether it means or should mean something more. In this vein, it is also worthwhile to consider whether we want autonomous machines and systems to obey the law just as well as humans who are not legal specialists do, or if we want them to have the same "knowledge" of the law that lawyers have.

AUTONOMOUS TECHNOLOGIES AND FEATURES OF THE LAW

As discussed, an important question is whether a strategy to program autonomous technologies to comply with law is technically and theoretically possible. There are different answers that revolve around the state of technology and several related features of the law: law's ubiquity and multiplicity; its separation into legal rules, legal principles, and legal policies; and its prospective and retroactive functions. The issue is whether autonomous technologies can be programmed to account for these features.[1]

Technology

One of the arguments against attempts to comply with law focuses on the limitations of existing technology. This criticism is now surfacing in the area of block chain contracts. Although highly dependent on computation, block chain technology per se is distinct from artificial intelligence, but nevertheless is an example of attempts to automate an activity highly regulated by law. Block chain can be understood as a sophisticated, decentralized ledger system that bases its reliability on the system being distributed among a large number of computers. In such a ledger system, every transaction, such as acquiring title to real estate, or any exchange of value, including votes, is recorded in a block. Each subsequent transaction is recorded on its own and is uniquely identified, and all blocks are linked together in chronological order. The sequence of blocks is the block chain. The block chain is publicly available and distributed among a large number of computers, which serve as nodes in the network of participating computers. All of the nodes to which the information is distributed engage in a process that verifies that a block representing the most recent transaction can be added to the chain. If a certain percentage of nodes agree with the verification process, the block is added. Thus, "the block chain contains a true and verifiable record of each and every transaction made in the system."[2] Block chain is meant to eliminate the need for centralized third party

---

[1]   To date, the most comprehensive, accessible discussion of the technical challenges posed to artificial intelligence by tasks such as reasoning from statutes, applying cases, assessing and crafting legal arguments (among others) and an assessment of current technologies' capacity to engage in such activities is Kevin D. Ashley, ARTIFICIAL INTELLIGENCE AND LEGAL ANALYTICS: NEW TOOLS FOR LAW PRACTICE IN THE DIGITAL AGE (2017).

[2]   Lucas Mearian, *What Is Blockchain? The Most Disruptive Technology in Decades*, COMPUTERWORLD, Jan. 18, 2018, www.computerworld.com/article/3191077/security/what-is-blockchain-the-most-disruptive-tech-in-decades.html. The security of

verification or intermediaries, such as a bank or department of public records. The ability to record and verify transactions is attracting the attention of major companies who participate in or support financial trading in instruments such as securities, currency swaps, and repurchase agreements. Systems must be in place to keep track of all such transactions. One of the major financial service providers, the Depository Trust and Clearing Corporation, is seeking to base its records of cleared and bilateral over the counter derivatives on a distributed ledger system.[3] Besides clearing and settlement of trades, financial institutions are exploring how block chain can be used in international payments systems, trade finance, identification, and syndicated loans.[4]

The hope is that these kinds of contracts will be self-monitoring and self-executing. However, scholars such as Eliza Milk are skeptical about technologies such as block chain's potential to be used outside narrowly circumscribed settings.[5] Among other things, Milk points out that there yet remains a broad gap between human language, which is the stuff of contracts, on the one hand, and computer code on the other.[6] Computers are not yet able to read and interpret contracts written in human language, and more generally, if law is in fact tied to human language, then over the long term the ability to design autonomous technologies to comply with law will depend on the potential for artificial intelligence to process human language. It is true, as in the case with electronic contracting in certain narrow areas such as finance, that it can be worthwhile to program contracts in machine-readable language. But even if for no other reason, the sheer volume of cases and statutes would make it impossible for human programmers to engage in this translation process. Moreover, this act of translation assumes that the law is amenable to translation in the first place. To do so, programmers have to contend with three features of the law.

---

block chain has been called into question because of successful attacks on certain block chain systems. Mike Orcutt, *Once Hailed as Unhackable, Blockchains are Now Getting Hacked*, MIT Tech. Rev., Feb. 19, 2019, www.technologyreview.com/s/612974/once -hailed-as-unhackable-blockchains-are-now-getting-hacked.

[3] Michael del Castillo, *$11 Trillion Bet: DTCC to Process Derivatives with Blockchain Tech*, COINDESK, Jan. 9, 2017, updated Dec. 21, 2017, www.coindesk.com/ 11-trillion-bet-dtcc-clear-derivatives-blockchain-tech/; Michael del Castillo, *DTCC Milestone: $11 Trillion in Derivatives Gets Closer to the Blockchain*, COINDESK, Oct. 20, 2017, updated Oct. 23, 2017, www.coindesk.com/dtcc-milestone-11-trillion -derivatives-gets-closer-blockchain/.

[4] Martin Arnold, *Five Ways Banks Are Using Blockchain: Clearing and Settlement, Trade Finance and Syndicated Loans Are Ripe for Modernizing*, FIN. TIMES, Oct. 16, 2017, www.ft.com/content/615b3bd8-97a9-11e7-a652-cde3f882dd7b.

[5] Eliza Milk, *Smart Contracts: Terminology, Technical Limitations and Real World Complexity*, 9 LAW, INNOVATION & TECH. 269 (2017).

[6] *Id.*, at 287.

Law's Ubiquity and Multiplicity

Patrick Lin, George Bekey, and Keith Abney identify three related reasons why what they term "operational morality," in effect programming machines to follow the law of war, will not alone insure compliance with that law.[7] First, as weapons systems become more autonomous it will be hard to get them to "behave" in set patterns that comply with legal doctrine. Second, intelligent systems will encounter complexities in the environment which their designers could not anticipate, or they will be deployed in environments in which they were not intended to operate. Third, the technology itself will be complex, engaged in self-programming, thus making it hard for systems engineers to predict how systems will behave when confronted with new information.[8]

The first and third reasons identified by the authors have to do with what high levels of autonomy of the machines or systems will mean for humans' ability to control them and to predict what they will do. Autonomy and the ability to self-program indicates we are dealing with machines that are further toward general intelligence on the scale. This returns us to technical and policy questions about whether it will be possible to assure control over the most advanced systems and, if not, whether constraints of the kind discussed by Bostrom should be considered—a topic for Chapter 8. The second reason has to do with the complexity of the environments in which autonomous systems might be placed or might find themselves. All three reasons, however, seem to go to foreseeability and our ability to predict the situations in which more intelligent technologies might act.

Lin, Bekey, and Abney are concerned whether a machine would be able to follow the law of war when faced with new scenarios. If we cannot predict what situations will be faced by more sophisticated technologies, we do not know what law they should be asked to follow. Law is ubiquitous in the sense that it purports to apply in almost all situations and comprises many areas. Once technology reaches a level of high autonomy, it will be able to operate in many different environments, in which multiple areas of law might apply. In that situation, we will have to abandon the idea of predicting what law might be implicated and design systems with the assumption that any number of laws might apply. But that might be impossible. The only precedents we have regarding autonomous beings and the law come from our experience with minors and with animals. It is a given that although adult humans have

---

[7]   Patrick Lin et al., Ethics + Emerging Sciences Group, Autonomous Military Robotics: Risk, Ethics, and Design (2008), at 26, http://ethics.calpoly.edu/onr_report .pdf.

[8]   *Id.*

some influence over minors and animals, in several respects they are beyond adult control; we cannot always predict how children and animals will act in particular situations (although we might have some guesses based on probabilities) and we certainly cannot "program" these beings to act in the ways we want them to.

The best we can do with regard to animals is to constrain them; with children we rely on socialization and education to inculcate prosocial behaviors that include obedience to law in general. The next chapter will discuss efforts to instill analogous behaviors in machines. On the flip side, we expect as a general rule that the law more or less takes "ordinary" human behavior into account; law will not clash with commonsense ideas about what constitutes appropriate behavior in a given setting and thereby trip us up. This rough match between law and common understandings about appropriate behavior is what enables law to be ubiquitous and comprise many subjects.

One of the implications of law's ubiquity is that in even a single area of law one must contend with the problem of how it applies to new or unforeseen situations. The doubts raised by Lin, Bekey, and Abney have to do with the difficulty of foreseeing all situations in which autonomous technologies might act, even when applying just one area of law. However, interesting attempts are being made to design machines to be law-abiding by doing just that. In a recent paper, Shai Shalev-Schwartz, Shakeh Shammah, and Amnon Shashua propose a formal model for the safe operation of self-driving cars.[9] Their primary motivation is not to have autonomous vehicles comply with the law as such. Rather, they believe that to be acceptable to the public, autonomous vehicles will need to be designed so that the rate of accidents caused by them is several orders of magnitude lower than the rate for cars operated by humans. This will be particularly important during the transition period in which self-driving cars and human-driven cars share the same road.

I just referred to commonsense ideas about what constitutes appropriate behavior in various contexts. In that vein, the authors argue that we already have shared understandings for what makes for safe driving and unsafe driving in various driving situations. For example, all things being equal, if a driver runs a stop sign and collides with a car in the intersection, we would say that the first driver was negligent and caused the accident. In contrast to Lin, Bekey, and Abney's concerns that wartime scenarios cannot be predicted, Shalev-Schwartz, Shammah, and Shashua argue that it is in fact possible to identify all likely driving situations. These include actions such as merging

---

[9]   Shai Shalev-Schwartz, Shakeh Shammah, and Amnon Shashua, On a Formal Model of Safe and Scalable Self-Driving Cars, MOBILEYE 2017, https://arxiv.org/pdf/1708.06374.pdf.

onto a freeway, stopping for pedestrians, or backing out of a driveway. The authors then define the parameters for what is considered "faultless" driving in all these scenarios. Those parameters include variables such as speed, distance from other vehicles, how quickly one changes lanes, and so on. The authors argue that if a self-driving car operates within those parameters for safe driving, then under commonly accepted understandings of fault, if an accident involves a self-driving car and a human-driven car, the self-driving car will never be responsible, unless there was some malfunction in the hardware or software.

Whether law's ubiquity and multiplicity will make it difficult to design autonomous technologies to comply with law will depend in part on technical advances. It is not inconceivable that computers will someday assist in predicting all scenarios within a particular legal domain, say for example by "reading" everything in the literature related to highway safety. They might actually be better at remembering and cataloging all possible driving situations, and perhaps in detecting patterns that humans are unable to recognize. If technology is able to assist in the predictive process, thereby allowing for finer-grained design, we might find it acceptable if autonomous technologies reach our level of compliance with the law, which as I said is often based on our assumption that there is a rough match between our everyday behavior and the law. For the most sophisticated machines and systems, unless we design them to be "superlawyers," they will need to be designed as if they have gone through a socialization process that the law presupposes all those who are subject to it have undergone.

Legal Rules, Standards, and Policies

One of the first lessons taught in law school is that law comprises rules, standards, and policies. Legal rules are often referred to as brightline rules. An example is that a contract is voidable if it is made with a minor. Here the only relevant query is whether the party is under a set age or not. If she is, the contract in question is voidable. Brightline rules make adjudication relatively straightforward. This is less true with legal standards. As is well known, an exception to the rule of contracting with minors is that contracts with minors for necessities such as food and lodging are not voidable. What is a "necessity" for contracts purposes is more like a standard than a rule because there is no exact criteria for what constitutes one. Negligence in tort law is also a standard. Finally, there are legal principles or policies that legal rules and standards are intended to further. The rules and standards that apply to contracting with minors are meant to protect children. *Pacta sunt servanda*, promises should be kept, is another example of a policy, as is the policy against guilt by association.

Laws can thus be thought to lie along a scale of abstractness, or might refer to norms that have family resemblances but are fundamentally distinct. This suggests that law cannot always be reduced to a set of algorithms. The law is "designed" to be more flexible: to be able to account for and apply to a broader set of circumstances than can be addressed by brightline, on-off rules. The cost of that flexibility, however, is certainty. When one moves to standards and policies one must necessarily reason by analogy. In a common law system a judge will determine whether there are previous cases that are on point, with enough relevant similarities between them and the case at hand, so that under stare decisis the judge must follow the past decisions. Analogic reasoning has its own strengths and weaknesses, and here law and computational analysis converge with respect to the advantages and disadvantages of that approach. Unless two things are identical, to say that the cases are analogous to one another is to concede there are differences between the two, yet there are sufficient similarities that make it plausible to relate the two cases. The question of course is how much similarity is required to validly conclude there is an analogy. The answer is somewhat arbitrary. Suppose that two cases each have ten significant features, six of which match and four of which do not. There is no legal criteria for determining whether six matches are enough to say that the cases are analogous.

The issue also arises in civil law systems that do not give judicial decisions precedential weight (this is not to say, however, that past decisions are irrelevant). Here, the issue arises again around possible ambiguities or abstractness in language. The question becomes whether the statutory language maps onto a particular set of facts and the issue for both the law and computation is how one determines whether there is such a mapping. The problem posed by Hart about the statute that states "Vehicles are not permitted in the park" illustrates the problem. Such a rule would be considered to consist of at least two elements: first, that there be a vehicle; second, that it be present in the park. The first element is the most challenging in terms of determining whether it has been satisfied because it requires us to define what constitutes a vehicle: automobiles and trucks are obvious candidates, but how is it that bicycles, skateboards, and baby strollers are normally not considered vehicles? If we say that a vehicle is a conveyance that is powered by a motor, then we might ask whether a powered wheelchair is a vehicle. One way of solving the problem is by defining a vehicle through a list of all conveyances that qualify, but the problem is that such a list might be underinclusive.[10]

---

[10]   Ashley argues that statutes pose semantic and syntactic issues for artificial intelligence. Ashley also uses Hart's "no vehicles in the park" example. What constitutes a vehicle is a semantic issue. Syntactic issues arise because statutes are often drafted as

The other option is to try to identify characteristics common to all vehicles, but this raises at least two issues. First, a definition of that sort might be over-inclusive and encompass things like baby carriages. Second, such a definition raises the question of analogy in another form. Suppose a definition of vehicle lists ten characteristics, all of which are required for a conveyance to be considered a vehicle. What if a conveyance has nine of the ten characteristics? Here the rule runs the risk of being underinclusive. Further, note that the ten characteristics are themselves like elements, which in turn might be in need of further interpretation. The upshot of this analysis is that even though a rule is not the same thing as a legal case, a legal rule often needs to be construed to discover, as it were, the rule within a rule, as in a common law system one needs to determine the rule within a prior case.

Another way to assess our ability to put law into algorithms is to consider the various schools of legal jurisprudence: natural law, legal formalism and positivism, legal realism, legal process, critical legal studies, and law and economics. The major purpose of jurisprudence, of course, is to give an account of the law and its operation. At the same time, the critiques of formalism given by legal realism—the life of the law is not logic but common sense; critical legal studies—language, including legal language, is at bottom indeterminate, and the privileging of one legal interpretation over another often stems from powerful parts of a society; and law and economics—law is an expression of utility-maximizing behaviors, could be said to undermine all attempts to have autonomous machines follow the law, because the rules themselves are porous and, under some schools of thought, indeterminate. At the same time, as Harry Surden argues in his variable-determinacy thesis, legal analysis can involve varying levels of indeterminacy.[11] Determinacy is increased when there is more information about the context in which a rule is to be applied, as well as when the content of a legal rule is clear.[12] The implication is that when operationalizing the law, it would be comparatively more straightforward to write code to represent a brightline rule, less so to do with legal standards, and even less so to do with legal policies. To return to the rule on contracts with minors, it would appear relatively easy to program a computer to at least ask (if not verify) that an individual is an adult before it proceeds to enter into a contract with her.

---

if they comprise a set of if-then statements that resemble a flow chart, but can be given different reasonable syntactic interpretations. Ashley, *supra* note 1, at 45.

[11]   Harry Surden, *The Variable Determinacy Thesis*, 12 COLUM. SCI. & TECH. L. REV. 1 (2011).

[12]   *Id.*, at 46–7. Surden also argues that legal *indeterminacy* increases as options as to what the applicable laws are, what the facts are, and how the law should apply to those facts increase. *Id.*, at 53.

Such concerns about degrees of abstraction, however, are not stopping developers from trying to operationalize the law, even in its more abstract forms. Shalev-Schwartz, Shammah, and Shashua's paper on identifying the parameters for safe driving is an example of such efforts.[13] Their attempt to identify all driving scenarios and then to set out the parameters for what constitutes safe driving in those situations has the effect of turning an abstract standard, the proper level of care, into sets of if-then instructions that an autonomous machine or system could understand and follow. As discussed above, the success of that strategy will depend on whether it is possible to anticipate the great majority of those situations and on whether there are already broadly accepted standards of behavior that can be programmed and that correspond roughly to the law. That might be the case for activities for which there is a large amount of data, such as data on traffic safety. In tort law more generally, perhaps it will be technically and economically feasible to translate negligence standards into sets of parameters that would be in effect in any given situation. In diagnostic medicine, for example, it might be possible to translate what constitutes negligence in recognizing certain diseases by percentage of accuracy in detection. A sufficiently low error rate might qualify as acting with a reasonable amount of care, thus avoiding liability in most cases. However, other standards, such as necessities for minors, might be more difficult to operationalize. For these standards, we would need to ask whether a computer is capable of emulating what a human lawyer or judge does when applying a legal standard.

Some standards are even more difficult because of their fundamental vagueness. A good example is the duty of good faith and fair dealing implied in every contract. The duty is explained as an answer to the problem of incomplete contracts: contracts cannot contemplate all possible events and often leave parties substantial discretion in how they will perform their contract obligations. The rule thus prevents parties from using that discretion to act opportunistically. As might be expected, the "rule" or definition for what constitutes good faith and fair dealing is extraordinarily vague. The Uniform Commercial Code defines

---

[13] For a discussion of how one might represent contract norms in electronic form and monitor compliance with them, *see* Sanjay Modgil et al., *Monitoring Compliance with E-Contracts and Norms*, 23 ARTIFICIAL INTELLIGENCE L. 161 (2015).The monitoring system proposed by the authors is based on a method for representing norms proposed in Nir Oren et al., Towards a Formalisation of Electronic Contracting Environments, International Workshop on Coordination, Organizations, Institutions, and Norms in Agent Systems, COIN 2008: COORDINATION, ORGANIZATIONS, INSTITUTIONS, AND NORMS IN AGENT SYSTEMS IV 156 (2008). *See also* Frank Dignum, *Autonomous Agents with Norms*, 7 ARTIFICIAL INTELLIGENCE L. 69 (1999) (using deontic logic to represent norms in contracts, social conventions, and private relationships).

it as "honesty in fact and the observance of reasonable commercial standards of fair dealing."[14] Under another approach, a person acts in bad faith when he undermines the reasonable expectations of the other party. Robert Summers argues that good faith is defined negatively: we cannot define good faith; rather we can readily recognize when someone acts in bad faith, such as when he shirks, provides only substantial performance of a contract, and so on. An act that does not fall within one of these "obvious" instances of bad faith complies with the duty of good faith. Steven Burton suggests we determine when a contract party tries to recapture an opportunity she forwent when she entered into the contract. The approaches go on.[15]

It thus seems much harder to program a computer to undergo a good faith and fair dealing analysis than to undergo a necessities analysis. However, we could ask ourselves whether we are now imposing too high a standard on autonomous technologies. Later in this chapter I will discuss the extent to which computers might be able to engage in the practice of law as a proxy for measuring how high a degree of legal sophistication a computer might reach. If a legal standard is itself inherently vague so as to give lawyers pause, then it should be no surprise that we will not be able to program a computer to act in accordance with that standard. Indeed, an argument can be made that an autonomous system might be better able to apply some abstract standards. For example, to rescind a contract on grounds of economic duress, the adversely affected party must show that it had no reasonable alternative other than agreeing to enter into the contract (most often this involves contract modification). An autonomous contracting system could engage in a systemic search for other contracts that meet certain business criteria (perhaps set by human beings, perhaps by other systems). This search would later serve as evidence of reasonable alternatives. At the same time, however, duress requires a wrongful threat. Wrongfulness is also an abstract standard (albeit with some harder contours, such as the threat of violence), and it is unclear how one could program a computer to avoid making wrongful threats, precisely because the standard is unclear.

This latter point indicates we should not minimize the problem that the operationalization of law poses to the design of autonomous systems, and more importantly to human beings who stand to be hurt by them. Perhaps nowhere is this more compelling than with respect to autonomous weapons systems. As discussed earlier, under one principle of the law of war, the use of force must

---

[14]   U.C.C. § 1-102(b)(20) (AM. LAW INST. & UNIF. LAW COMM'N 1977).

[15]   For a discussion of the history of the doctrine and its various interpretations, *see* Harold Dubroff, *The Implied Covenant of Good Faith in Contract Interpretation and Gap-Filling: Reviling a Revered Relic*, 80 ST. JOHN'S L. REV. 559 (2006).

be commensurate with the achievement of a military objective. In terms of computation, commensurability is a legal standard that seems as abstract as the standard of good faith and fair dealing. Yet as abstract as those standards are, we believe that they do actual work in the world by guiding human behavior. At a minimum, they ask individuals to take the standard into account before acting. Further, we tend to think that human beings are capable of applying them: a person in command can take into account the military objective at hand (perhaps the capture of an enemy outpost) and determine roughly how much force would be proportional to the achievement of the task. Can the mental calculus the human commander must undertake be programmed into an autonomous system? To repeat, whether autonomous technologies will be able to take legal standards into account will depend on whether it is possible to anticipate situations where they might apply and on whether there are already broadly accepted standards of behavior that can be programmed and that correspond roughly to the law.

The Requirement of Culpability under Criminal Law

Recall that Chapter 3 reviewed some of the issues that arise from the requirement of culpability under criminal law (as well as tort law) as it might apply to humans being held responsible for the actions of artificial agents. The issues become more pronounced when one tries to apply this requirement to artificial agents themselves. At this point in their development, autonomous machines are not able to satisfy models of culpability that equate purposeful, reckless, and negligent behavior with actual subjective states of mind (whether they ever will is explored in the next chapter). Other accounts of culpability considered in Chapter 3, that view *mens rea* as more of a construction used to serve various social ends, might be better able to accommodate autonomous agents, even if at this point they cannot be said to be conscious or have subjective intentions. On this subject, consider Sartor's argument discussed in Chapter 4 that under Dennett's intentional stance, it is possible to infer intentionality in entities such as corporations and autonomous machines and systems because such a stance makes it possible to make predictions about their possible behaviors and does not require that an entity have a particular internal mechanism for such intentionality. For Sartor, intention deriving from the intentional stance would enable autonomous technologies to satisfy the *mens rea* requirement of criminal law in its current form. Thus, the ability of autonomous agents to comply with criminal law or the amenability of criminal law in its current form to apply to autonomous agents will depend in part on what technological advances will allow such agents to achieve and on our willingness to depart from views of culpability that focus primarily on mental states and subjective intentionality.

Law's Prospective and Retroactive Functions

The requirement of culpability is an example of a broader issue. Law, like principles of moral responsibility, is intended to guide prospective behavior and to assess past behavior. Many of the legal issues involving autonomous machines will be retrospective in nature: we will need to determine whether something a machine has already done has legal significance. For that task, it does not matter whether that machine has any legal programming in advance. In their analysis of block chain contracts,[16] Kevin Werbach and Nicolas Cornell argue that in theory, such contracts can be designed to avoid courts but cannot substitute for them. Part of this depends on what theory of contract one uses. Under a view of contract as promise, the fact that such contracts will be self-enforcing vindicates promises made by the parties.[17] Similarly, if contracts are understood as a set of default rules that provide certainty, smart contracts provide predictable outcomes exactly because they are self-executing and the computer code is itself the contract, and thus precise.[18] However, the authors argue that contract law is best understood as the ex post evaluation of contracting behavior. Smart contracts are not designed for "recognizing and remedying grievances."[19]

The hope is that technology will take over several functions of the contract law, including determining when a contract has been formed, memorializing or recording contract terms, performing those obligations and monitoring the performance of the other party, and responding appropriately if there has been a breach. There are a number of theoretical and practical questions in connection with that goal. One goes to exploring the capacity of artificial intelligence to perform or replace the functions of the various contract doctrines. I have already discussed how the doctrine of good faith and fair dealing is often explained as an answer to the problem of incomplete contracts: contracts cannot contemplate all possible events and often leave parties substantial discretion in how they will perform their contract obligations. The duty of good faith and fair dealing is intended to prevent parties from opportunistically using that discretion. Perhaps smart contracts will obviate the need for that kind of check on the parties because smart contracts can substantially narrow

---

[16]   Kevin Werbach and Nicolas Cornell, *Contracts* Ex Machina, 67 DUKE L. J. 313 (2017).

[17]   *Id.*, at 357.

[18]   *Id.*, at 360.

[19]   *Id.*, at 363. *See also* Miguel Stokes and Gabriel Freire Ramos, *Smart Contracts*, 46 ATUALIDAD JURÍDICA URÍA MENÉNDEZ 124, 126 (2017) ("Smart contracts will not replace the need for courts, for example, to order restitution if there are errors in coding or to nullify a contract").

that discretion, perhaps by reducing drastically the transaction costs that arise when contract parties try to foresee all possible events that might impact the performance of the contract. At the same time, it will be interesting to see whether contracts can be designed to take into account events exogenous to the contract but that impact performance—functions which the doctrines of impossibility, impracticability, and frustration are designed to perform.

Another facet of this argument is obvious but no less valid for that reason. Even if autonomous technologies can be designed prospectively to comply with law, under the principles of the rule of law they cannot serve as their own judges. The judicial system, even if at some future date it is assisted by autonomous technologies, will fulfill that role. This requirement of the rule of law has more subtle implications. Lisa Shay and her coauthors discuss a number of issues they encountered in an experiment in which they asked three groups of computer science students to code certain provisions of the New York State traffic law.[20] Each group was given a different set of directions: one was directed to try to code the letter of the law; another was directed to encode the intent of the law; and a third was given a much more detailed set of parameters. The groups were also provided driving data generated by a car over the course of an hour and asked to use their programs to enforce the traffic code provisions they had been given. As might be expected, the group that programmed with a view toward the letter of the law led to far more traffic tickets than the groups that programmed to enforce the intent of the law. The study was conducted as an experiment in using computer programs to enforce the law. But it has direct applications for programming autonomous vehicles and other autonomous systems in other contexts. Some lessons are straightforward and relevant to my earlier discussion of levels of abstraction in the law: the more guidance given, the more closely a computer program's enforcement seems to conform to current understandings of what constitutes acceptable compliance with the law. The results of the experiment also seem to confirm that the strategy of programming computers or autonomous systems to comply with the law might be limited. In part this is a technological and empirical matter: whether we can design machines that have the capacity to learn the contexts necessary to comply relatively seamlessly with the law within margins of tolerance we find acceptable.

Shay and her coauthors identified another issue relevant to the concerns of this subsection. As programmers tried to implement portions of the traffic code, they necessarily brought their own understandings and biases about the law to

---

[20] Lisa A. Shay et al., *Do Robots Dream of Electric Laws? An Experiment in the Law as Algorithm*, in Rᴏʙᴏᴛ Lᴀᴡ 274, 278–9 (Ryan Calo, A. Michael Froomkin, and Ian Kerr eds., 2016).

the programming task. For example, they had to make a number of assumptions about road conditions, the time of day, the sensitivity of the sensors used to detect the car's speed, thresholds of compliance, and so on. In short, they were performing many of the tasks carried out by lawyers and judges. Of course, the programmers were expressly asked to engage in the retroactive task of traffic enforcement. But programmers who are asked to design machines to comply with the law prospectively will be forced to interpret and apply the law as well. Obviously, the vast majority are not authorized to engage in such practice.[21]

That designers will need to consult with lawyers as they seek to design machines and systems that comply with law illustrates that the line between the prospective and retroactive functions of the law is blurry. When a person plans an action with the law in view, she imagines how, if asked, the judiciary would evaluate that behavior. Correspondingly, when the judiciary makes a decision, particularly in a common law system, it does so knowing that it will have precedential effect that in turn will influence how someone in the future will plan her actions. Developers and commentators have both of these aspects of the law in view. Recall Shalev-Schwartz and colleagues' argument that if a self-driving car can be programmed to operate within various parameters for safe driving, then under commonly accepted understandings of fault, in an accident involving a self-driving car and a human-driven car, the self-driving car will never be negligent, unless there was some malfunction in the hardware or software. Not only does this approach serve as an example of how one might codify an abstract legal standard such as negligence, it also illustrates how the prospective and retroactive aspects of law blend.

Ryan Abbot uses the same blend of prospective and retrospective analysis when he applies the doctrine of negligence, but with more of a top-down approach.[22] Abbot joins others in arguing against applying a strict liability standard to autonomous machines because he is concerned that the threat of liability would discourage their development. Instead, like Shalev-Schwartz, Shammah, and Shashua, Abbot looks to the marginal benefits of automation offers vis-à-vis humans. "The basic inquiry about automation safety should focus on whether automation reduces, or is expected to reduce, *overall* accidents, not whether it did in fact reduce accidents or other harms in a specific instance."[23] For Abbot, such an inquiry into marginal benefit should determine

---

[21]   *Id.*, at 295.

[22]   Ryan Abbott, *The Reasonable Computer: Disrupting the Paradigm of Tort Liability*, 86 GEORGE WASH. L. REV. 101 (2018).

[23]   *Id.*, at 126.

the standard of fault that should be applied when harms occur.[24] If a manufacturer can show that automation results in the net reduction of accidents, when a specific accident or harm does occur a negligence standard should apply. The focus would then be on the particular act of the computer that controlled the machine or system, not its design.[25] For example, in his view, a computer system for diagnosing disease that can be shown to outperform physicians overall should be held to a negligence standard even if it does not do well at detecting a specific disease such as lung cancer. In that case, under the negligence standard the computer would likely be liable if a human being should have spotted the disease. Such liability would create incentives to improve computer performance for that particular application and compensate the victim.[26]

Earlier I said that law's features are interrelated. Abbot's aggregative approach to negligence is interesting in part because it responds to the theoretical concern explored earlier that it is impossible to predict all possible scenarios and plan accordingly. If computer programmers are able to identify most driving scenarios and set out the appropriate parameters for appropriate behavior, and if, as anticipated, this leads to a significant reduction in the number of traffic accidents, then the relatively few times when autonomous vehicles cause harm because the vehicles encountered unanticipated driving situations will likely be acceptable in the main, particularly if the victims of harm are compensated. Framed this way, the issue is not whether autonomous technologies will be able to comply with law in specific circumstances, but whether they will do a better job than humans in the aggregate.

Finally, it should be noted that autonomous technologies can be designed to make themselves more amenable to law and legal regulation. I have already discussed recommendations by the IEEE and others to ensure that the behavior of autonomous machines and systems can be traced to human designers and operators. Such tracking allows the law to continue to use causation as a basis for assigning responsibility, even though the chain of causation might be weak. Harry Surden and Mary-Anne Williams argue that much of the law, including statutory and regulatory law, is based on predictability.[27] The law might thus be better able to respond to the dangers posed by autonomous vehicles by

---

[24] *See* Mark A. Geistfield, *A Roadmap for Autonomous Vehicles: State Tort Liability, Automobile Insurance, and Federal Safety Regulation*, 105 CALIF. L. REV. 1611, 1660 (2017). Geistfield notes, however, that there remain issues about how testing will be done to establish greater safety. *Id.*, at 1650–54.

[25] Abbott, *supra* note 22, at 128.

[26] *Id.*, at 126.

[27] Harry Surden and Mary-Anne Williams, *Technological Opacity, Predictability, and Self-Driving Cars*, 38 CARDOZO L. REV. 121, 164–6 (2016).

requiring them to be more predictable in their behaviors. In the authors' view, autonomous vehicles should be designed to alert people that they have been detected by the vehicles and to signal what they intend to do. The public also should be educated as to the automobiles' capabilities.[28] These features could be required by direct legislation and regulation, but also brought about indirectly through the tort system.[29] Predictability could then become a standard by which autonomous vehicles could be assessed.[30]

ROBOTS AS LAWYERS

So far we have assessed how likely it is that we will be able to design autonomous technologies that obey the law by gauging how well designers might be able to overcome human language processing challenges, as well as to respond to law's ubiquity and multiplicity; its separation into rules, standards and policies; and prospective and retroactive functions. Another way to assess the possibility of law-abiding machines and systems is to explore efforts to use artificial intelligence in the practice of law. We would likely neither expect nor want every machine or system to have the same knowledge and skills as human lawyers, but technology designed to perform legal analysis serves as a conceptual boundary for how well an autonomous machine or system can be expected to take law into account as it is operating.

A useful study on this topic is an unpublished paper by Dana Remus and Frank Levy.[31] The authors identify the tasks performed by lawyers in large to small private law firms and assess how likely it is that automation will affect the employment of humans to perform those tasks. Such tasks include document management, case administration and management, document review, due diligence, document drafting, legal writing, legal research, legal analysis and strategy, fact investigation, advising clients, negotiation, other communications and interactions, and court appearances and preparation. Remus and Levy reviewed ongoing efforts to automate those tasks, as well as likely advances in artificial intelligence, and estimated that over the next ten years,

---

[28]   *Id.*, at 167–72.

[29]   *Id.*, at 177–80.

[30]   Bibi van den Berg notes that the way technologies are designed is important, not only because it affects the way such technologies will operate, but also because such technologies elicit behaviors in us. Bibi van den Berg, *Robots as Tools for Techno-Regulation*, 3 Law, Innovation & Tech. 319 (2011).

[31]   Dana Remus and Frank Levy, Can Robots be Lawyers? Computers, Lawyers, and the Practice of Law, draft Nov. 27, 2016, https://plu.mx/ssrn/a/?ssrn_id=2701092 &display-tab=summary-content. *See also* Joanna Goodman, Robots in Law: How Artificial Intelligence Is Transforming Legal Services (2016) (surveying ways in which artificial intelligence will impact the provision of legal services).

automation will likely have strong employment effects on document review; moderate employment effects on case administration and management, document drafting, due diligence, legal research, legal analysis and strategy; and light employment effects on document management, fact investigation, legal writing, advising clients, other communications and interactions, court appearances and preparation, and negotiation.[32]

As noted earlier, it is unlikely that we would expect autonomous machines and systems to be their own lawyers. Thus, many of the tasks identified by Remus and Levy—document management, case administration and management, document review, due diligence, document drafting, legal writing, advising clients, negotiation, other communications and interactions, and court appearances and preparation—are not relevant for the purposes of this chapter. Here, I am interested in exploring the extent to which autonomous technologies would be able to respond as human lawyers do when they are confronted by the challenges posed by the various features of the law we have just discussed.

In some circumstances, we might want an autonomous machine or system to be able to engage in rough forms of fact investigation, legal research, and legal analysis. In investigation, we would want autonomous technologies to have an overall awareness of their environment. This is likely the most challenging task: Remus and Levy contend in this respect that fact investigation is one of the tasks least likely to be replaced by automation. They argue that although computers are able to collect vast amounts of data that can then be reviewed by human lawyers, other forms of investigation require face to face interviews that in turn presuppose the ability to engage in unstructured conversations, a task computers are yet unable to carry out. Further, information gained from those interviews is often nonverbal. Again, in general computers are not yet able to understand such nonverbal cues.[33] Of course, Remus and Levy have in mind fact investigation required by legal practice: to gather facts to identify what legal issues are raised by them, so that the lawyer can assess the law's likely impact on a client and to develop a representation strategy for her. We would not expect this skill in most autonomous machines, but we might want them to have enough situational awareness to recognize that legal issues are at stake. For example, we would likely want an autonomous weapons system to have enough situational sensitivity to know when civilians are present in an area of military operations, so that it triggers an algorithm to distinguish between civilians and combatants.

---

[32] Remus and Levy, *id.*, at 14–38.
[33] *Id.*, at 32–3.

By legal research, I do not mean the activity discussed in earlier examples of good faith and fair dealing or contracts with minors for necessities. But given the ubiquity and multiplicity of law, machines and systems might be programmed to be able to recognize what laws might be applicable in a particular situation that in turn influences the way the machine acts. On this subject, recently developed legal research tools are beginning to move beyond large databases of cases and statutory and regulatory material such as Westlaw and Lexis and to allow for query-based research. Current approaches are text-based; that is, a search engine with features like Google locates possible relevant texts from a database or from the internet itself, then undergoes some ranking process to choose what is likely the most responsive text or texts.[34]

As discussed earlier, Remus and Levey conclude that legal analysis and strategy will also experience moderate employment effects.[35] For them, analysis involves applying legal rules to a given situation. Remus and Levy report that software has already been developed that enables lawyers to predict how a judge will rule on a particular matter based on her past decisions. Software has been less successful, however, in predicting jury decisions. Expert systems have been developed that walk users through a set of queries that help perform a legal task. Remus and Levy give as an example DoNotPay, an app that has helped British drivers overturn at least 160,000 parking tickets.[36] At present, such expert systems are effective in relatively narrow areas of the law, but over time it might be possible to develop systems that can marshal several legal specialties.

What do these developments and likely improvements mean for autonomous machines and systems in the medium to longer term? First, the difficulties of having artificial agents achieve a higher level of legal sophistication are severalfold. As discussed, such technology would need the situational awareness to recognize that a legal issue might be posed. It would need to be able to pose that question to itself and then to assemble a set of legal sources that would be responsive to the question it had posed to itself, and then would have to be able to understand the texts it had gathered. These challenges have more to do with the technical capabilities of such technology, not theoretical limitations of the law. As I have discussed, autonomous machines and systems are severely limited in their ability to engage in open-ended conversations and to work with texts written in human language. But improvements in human language processing bring one tantalizingly close to concluding that machines

---

[34]   *Id.*, at 26. *See also* Shuohan Wang et al., *Evidence Aggregation for Answer Re-Ranking in Open-Domain Question Answering*, ICLR 2018, https://arxiv.org/pdf/1711.05116.pdf.

[35]   Remus and Levy, *supra* note 31, at 30.

[36]   *Id.*, at 31.

will be able to "understand" human language, at least enough for an autonomous system to be able to determine what law might apply to a given situation and what the likely application will be.[37] To the extent that computational capacity is an issue, it is worth remembering that many computational tasks could be offloaded to other powerful computers. Primarily for command and control purposes, autonomous machines in the field of battle, for example, would most likely be tied to large central computers. Those computers would be capable of processing massive amounts of information, translating possible textual answers into machine-readable instructions, and then sending them to the individual autonomous machines.

If forced to choose, in my view, it will not take significant advances for an autonomous machine to be able to predict the legal implications of a particular action it is considering. Such a machine might have to be programmed to have the law in view when making a decision, but once it is given that general instruction, it could well have the capacity to draw its own conclusions about the legal implications of its actions and plan accordingly. In some ways, it might be better than humans in doing so because of its ability to draw from all relevant sources of law and not overlook any. The question is whether and when we will want autonomous technologies to have this capacity.

AUTONOMOUS TECHNOLOGY AS LAWMAKER

As I discussed earlier, most human beings are not lawyers; instead, the ubiquity and multiplicity of law, and with that the potential for legal responsibility, is tempered by the rough correspondence between the requirements of the law and our commonsense understandings of appropriate behavior, instilled through a long socialization process. One question is whether we want autonomous technologies to behave like laypeople or like lawyers. We might want to limit autonomous machines to follow only basic legal rules and

---

[37] Hildebrandt warns that the growing ability of machine learning to predict legal outcomes could have four negative consequences for the rule of law. Mireille Hildebrandt, *Law as Computation in the Era of Artificial Legal Intelligence: Speaking Law to the Power of Statistics*, 68 U. Toronto L. J. Supp. 1 12 (2018). First, since machine learning software can be opaque, this will render some decisions inscrutable and noncontestable, whereas legal decisions are always subject to scrutiny. *Id.*, at 28–9. Further, predictive software is based on detecting statistically relevant relationships between the question being asked of it and legal documents such as statutes, cases, and so on that might be responsive to that question, so evaluating those predictions becomes more a question of statistics than one of reasoning. *Id.*, at 29–30. Third, the use of large sets of data to train these systems could entail the violation of fundamental rights, such as the right to privacy. *Id.*, at 31. Finally, human lawyers might find themselves deferring too much to these systems and losing their own predictive skills. *Id.*, at 31–4.

standards (such as negligence) and restrict them from applying more abstract legal standards, if only because we might be placed at a disadvantage. There might be other reasons for limiting this capacity. Human commanders in the field would likely want to make the ultimate decision as to whether a particular action adequately distinguishes between civilians and combatants or is proportional in the case of self-defense and commensurate with the achievement of a military objective. Moreover, with respect to military systems that advise at the battalion level, such systems will by definition be under the command of a human. At the same time, every soldier is charged with knowledge of the laws of war and is expected to follow them at the individual level, even without the orders of a commander; indeed, it is well known that the soldier may not follow unlawful orders, including orders to violate the law of war. So there are times when we would want an autonomous weapons system, particularly when it is acting in the heat of battle, to be "cognizant" of, and follow, law.

If autonomous machines and systems fulfill their promise of performing better than humans in important spheres of life by any number of relevant benchmarks, this could well put humans at another disadvantage in terms of the law. Abbott, like Shalev-Schwartz, Shammah, and Shashua, foresees a time when autonomous driving systems will be safer than human drivers. When that happens, the standard of care will shift from a reasonable person standard to a reasonable computer standard.[38] Under such a standard, because all humans err, any harms that result from the interactions of machines and humans will automatically be blamed on humans. With the standards for performance ratcheting up as autonomous machines become better than humans in performing certain tasks, there could be a point where it would be negligent to allow humans to perform them. When human beings enter a domain in which autonomous machines and systems set the standard for taking appropriate care, they will, as Abbott puts it, be held to a strict liability standard:[39] "[A] computer standard of care would mean that people drive at their own risk."[40]

Such a development would have the consequence of further insulating autonomous technologies and their designers and manufacturers from any responsibility vis-à-vis human beings. In some industries, this will create even more incentives to replace human beings with those technologies. Such a tendency could be impelled by consumer preferences. Why would a human patient want a human surgeon to perform an operation if an autonomous surgeon achieved higher success rates, particularly if it was programmed to emulate a caring bedside manner? The odd result is that in some contexts the

---

[38]   Abbott, *supra* note 22, at 136.
[39]   *Id.*, at 137.
[40]   *Id.*

problem of legal responsibility and autonomous machines and systems will be resolved because human beings will almost always be deemed responsible. The trade-off, harkening back to Zoloff's concern in the last chapter, would be the disappearance of what at least for now are accepted as manifestations of human agency, such as going for the Sunday drive.

What follows is more speculative. It seems highly likely that legislatures and regulatory bodies will want to take advantage of the computational strength of autonomous systems. Once available, policymakers would want to use artificial intelligence to assist them in assessing facts, identifying patterns in the data, projecting possible trends and outcomes, and evaluating already existing law—many of the cognitive tasks needed in the legislative and regulatory process. Autonomous systems would be instructed to draft statutes and regulations. From there, it does not seem like a far stretch for artificial intelligences to begin to propose legislation to human beings. It would not be necessary for such systems to be omniscient. They would only have to be able to predict possible outcomes at least marginally better than humans. By that time, though, autonomous technologies will have reached a level of sophistication that might mean humans could want them to be designed to do more than follow the law. That is the subject of the next chapter.

8. Moral machines and systems

Chapter 7 concluded with the suggestion that people might find it in their interest to develop autonomous technologies that conform to expectations of appropriate behavior, either because technical limitations in natural language processing and inherent features of the law will make it hard—if not impossible—to design machines and systems that follow the law, or because we might not want them to have the same legal sophistication as lawyers or judges. If we cannot be confident in the strategy of designing law-abiding technology, we might try to develop moral machines, machines that will engage in prosocial behaviors and that will be susceptible to the consequences of legal responsibility.

THE NEED FOR MORAL MACHINES

There is great interest in exploring how machines might be programmed to have prosocial behaviors. In 2014, the US Office of Naval Research offered a $7.5 million grant to a research team to develop robots to engage in moral reasoning.[1] As discussed in Chapter 7, Lin, Bekey, and Abney believe it will be impossible to program autonomous weapons systems to comply with the law of war in all situations. Consequently, such machines will need to be programmed to engage in rough forms of moral reasoning.[2] As Wallach and Allen put it: "Moral agents monitor and regulate their behavior in light of the harms their actions may cause or the duties they neglect. Humans should expect nothing less of [autonomous moral agents]."[3] There is also a more pragmatic reason. Wallach points out that if robots are able to address ethical issues, new markets for robots will open up. Otherwise, "if they fail to adequately

---

[1] Nayef Al-Rodhan, *The Moral Code: How to Teach Robots Right and Wrong*, FOREIGN AFF. (Aug. 12, 2015), www.foreignaffairs.com/articles/2015-08-12/moral -code.

[2] Patrick Lin et al., Ethics + Emerging Sciences Group, Autonomous Military Robotics: Risk, Ethics, and Design (2008), at 27–41, http://ethics.calpoly.edu/onr _report.pdf.

[3] Wendell Wallach and Colin Allen, MORAL MACHINES: TEACHING ROBOTS RIGHT FROM WRONG 16 (2010).

accommodate human laws and values, there will be demands for regulations that limit their use."[4]

Commentators such as Shanahan and Bostrom have an even more urgent reason for designing machines and systems that act morally. Up to this point, this book has been concerned primarily with autonomous technologies that have a high degree of autonomy, but have not necessarily reached the level of general intelligence. As pointed out, most commentators believe we are years away from that event, but some have tried to imagine the implications of machines and systems reaching that level. Their work is necessarily speculative, but nevertheless relevant for the concerns of this chapter. Shanahan argues that once artificial intelligence has reached the level of general intelligence, it will soon thereafter achieve superintelligence—capacities to learn and innovate greater than our own. This will arise because artificial intelligence with general intelligence will not tire, will use its computational ability to engage in thought experiments and learn via trial and error much more rapidly than a team of human beings, and will cooperate with other general intelligences and thus pool their abilities.[5] The concern is that even one superintelligence would pose an existential threat to humankind.[6] This is because once it devises and sets out a task for itself, the superintelligence will do all it can to perform it—somewhat like the broom in "The Sorcerer's Apprentice" ordered to fill the cistern with water, but without a spell to stop it. The analogy is apt in another sense: it could divide itself or transform itself into a different intelligence, all the while flooding the room.

Once artificial intelligence reaches this superior level, the issue then becomes how we might be able to hold such systems responsible when it is quite possible for them to avoid all responsibility. Bostrom explores two major approaches to controlling a superintelligence: capability control and motivation selection. Capability controls try to limit the superintelligence through techniques which Bostrom refers to as boxing (confining a system so that it can affect the real world in only limited ways), incentive methods (placing the system in an environment that provides incentives to act in desired ways),

---

[4]   Wendell Wallach, *From Robots to Techno Sapiens: Ethics, Law and Public Policy in the Development of Robotics and Neurotechnologies*, 3 Law Innov. & Tech. 185, 196 (2011). *See also* Kenneth Kernaghan, *The Rights and Wrongs of Robotics: Ethics and Robots in Public Organizations*, 57 Canadian Pub. Admin. 485, 485 (2014) (arguing for the development of robots that follow ethical standards of personal moral responsibility, privacy, and accountability as robots become more commonplace in the areas of aging, public health, and defense).

[5]   Murray Shanahan, The Technological Singularity 86–90 (2015).

[6]   Nick Bostrom, Superintelligence: Paths, Dangers, Strategies (paperback edn. 2016).

stunting (limiting the system's cognitive abilities or its capacity to affect processes), and tripwires (creating diagnostics to detect and shut down a super-intelligence when it engages in dangerous activity).[7] However, as artificial intelligence reaches the level of general intelligence, the chances increase that an intelligence will escape those controls. Thus, it will become important to be able to control the motivations of a superintelligence. Bostrom acknowledges that we might be decades away from achieving even general intelligence, but he argues that the process of instilling motivations must begin before that time. Thus, his analysis is of interest here, and I will examine some of his more specific proposals later in this chapter.

ISSUES

In Chapter 3, I noted the IEEE's recommendation that artificial intelligence and autonomous systems be designed with the principle of traceability in mind, the ability to follow such technology's actions back to its controlling software and further back to its designers. That recommendation was part of a more general study on ethical issues raised by the development of such technologies.[8] In that study, the IEEE made a number of recommendations on how values might be embedded into artificial systems and identifies a number of issues that need to be resolved to accomplish this. It foresees that this will happen through an iterative process in which values are identified, implemented, and assessed. With regard to value identification, first, the organization recognizes that values are not universal, so what values are embedded will be "largely specific to user communities and tasks."[9] One issue therefore is whose values will be chosen. It recognizes the problem of "moral overload": there will likely be conflicting norms and values. The IEEE recommends resolving this issue by giving priority to the values of larger stakeholders over others.[10] The data sets and algorithms on which artificial intelligence rely can contain their own biases;[11] thus the organization suggests that a large number of stakeholders be included

---

[7]   *Id.*, at 157–69. As an example of a tripwire, Thomas Arnold and Matthias Scheutz urge the creation of an ethical module or core that would test the potential behaviors of the artificial intelligence in simulated worlds. An undesired result in the simulated world would warn human operators to intervene. Thomas Arnold and Matthias Scheutz, *The "Big Red Button" Is Too Late: An Alternative Model for the Ethical Evaluation of AI Systems*, 20 ETHICS & INFO. TECH. 59 (2018).

[8]   INST. ELECTRONIC & ELEC. ENG'RS, ETHICALLY ALLIED DESIGN: A VISION FOR PRIORITIZING HUMAN WELL-BEING WITH ARTIFICIAL INTELLIGENCE AND AUTONOMOUS SYSTEMS: VERSION ONE (2016).

[9]   *Id.*, at 24.

[10]   *Id.*, at 25.

[11]   *Id.*, at 26.

during the engineering process.[12] With regard to implementation, there is the technical problem of actually embedding norms in artificial intelligences.[13] Finally, it recognizes that machine norms and human norms might differ.[14] In the future, there will be a need to establish a level of trust between humans and artificial intelligences.[15] Finally, there must be some means to allow third parties to evaluate this alignment in values.[16]

This chapter will follow the IEEE's lead and organize it around three issues: whose ethics should be chosen; how they are to be implemented; and the fit between human understandings of responsibility and the artificial intelligences that stand to be developed.

WHOSE VALUES?

As Keith Abney points out, the attempt to program morality into robots highlights unanswered questions about competing ethical approaches.[17] Although there might be broad general agreement that autonomous machines and systems should be designed to reflect our values and sense of ethics, there is no consensus on what those values should be. The IEEE sensibly begins by suggesting that values be specific to communities and tasks. With respect to specific tasks, some fields, such as law and medicine, are already guided by codes of professional conduct and ethics, and engineering is itself the subject of its own set of norms. But as the IEEE recognizes, this is just scratching the surface of difficult issues. The clash of norms between and within communities is a real issue, and the concerns are severalfold. One is that autonomous technologies will simply reflect and then strengthen already existing distributions of social and political power, often along crosscutting identities based on race, gender, age, orientation, immigration status, and so on. Data on which artificial intelligence will rely, such as data on income, residence patterns, and credit scores, reflect that distribution. Yet, such data take on the aura of objective truth, leading to what seem like inexorable results for affected people. Further, just as a designer brings their own interpretation of the law when trying to program computers to follow it, so too they bring their own biases to the task of programming. Finally, looking at the issue from an international perspec-

---

[12] *Id.*, at 27.
[13] *Id.*, at 29.
[14] *Id.*, at 31.
[15] *Id.*, at 32.
[16] *Id.*, at 33–4.
[17] Keith Abney, *Robotics, Ethical Theory, and Metaethics: A Guide for the Perplexed, in* ROBOT ETHICS: THE ETHICAL AND SOCIAL IMPLICATIONS OF ROBOTICS 35, 41–5 (Patrick Lin et al. eds., 2012).

tive, autonomous technologies are being pursued by countries and economies that can afford them. Even if one puts to the side the question of autonomous weapons systems, wealthy countries and groups that use and employ autonomous machines and technologies will likely become even more powerful and consume even more resources vis-à-vis others in the international community who do not have them.

Moral Dilemmas and Who Should Resolve Them

One area in which these issues arise is that of moral dilemmas, situations that pose moral problems that appear intractable. Much of the scholarly literature and popular press has focused on the classic Trolley Problem first identified in its modern form by Philippa Foot. A trolley is running out of control down a track on which five people are at work, unaware of the danger. An observer stands at a switch that can direct the trolley down another track, but there is another person at the end of that section track. The observer has the choice of doing nothing and allowing five people to be killed, or throwing the switch with the result that one person will die.[18] Research on reactions to the Trolley Problem has led Joshua Greene to conclude that human beings tend to be motivated by both utilitarian and deontological ethical impulses.[19] Most people will choose to throw the switch, but the answer will vary if changes are made to the scenario, for example, if the five workers are adults and the one person at the end of the track is a child.[20]

It appears that the addition of a machine affects people's attitudes toward the problem. Peter Danielson used an online survey platform to seek responses to an autonomous machine version of the Trolley Problem.[21] In this variation, a train is being operated by a robot, which must decide between killing five people or turning down another track and killing one person. Danielson acknowledges there are methodological limitations to the study, but his results suggest people view trolleylike problems differently when a machine is involved. He notes that in another study, when a human was at the controls,

---

[18]   *See* Wallach and Allen, *supra* note 3, at 13–16; Nick Belay, *Robot Ethics and Self-Driving Cars: How Ethical Determinations in Software will Require a New Legal Framework*, 40 J. LEGAL. PROF. 119, 120 (2015).

[19]   Joshua Greene, MORAL TRIBES: EMOTION, REASON, AND THE GAP BETWEEN US AND THEM 113–28 (2013).

[20]   Belay, *supra* note 18, at 120–21. An exhaustive survey of millions of people worldwide showed that resolutions of the dilemma vary with different cultures. Edmond Awal et al., *The Moral Machine Experiment*, 563 NATURE 59 (2018).

[21]   Peter Danielson, *Surprising Judgments about Robot Drivers: Experiments on Raising Expectations and Blaming Humans*, 9 NORDIC J. APPLIED ETHICS 73 (2015).

90 percent of respondents answered that the human should divert the train.[22] However, in Daniel's study, only 37 percent agreed that the robot should divert the train, and still more chose neutrality over resolving the dilemma. Many of the respondents expected the automated system to eliminate these kinds of problems.[23] Perhaps most interestingly, a surprising number of respondents blamed the victims in the problem for being on the track in the first place.[24] When a human was involved, no such blaming took place.[25] Finally, respondents were asked to resolve a situation where a child steps in front of a driverless car under conditions where it is physically impossible to stop the car. Most respondents found that the parents, the child, or the carmaker should be held responsible.[26] Of course, this is only one study, but the results, however tentative, reflect an unfamiliarity with robots, unrealistic expectations about their capabilities, and a tendency to defer to technology and to blame victims, even if this involved adding more facts to the hypothetical.

As the design of autonomous machines and systems continues, someone will have to work out the dilemma one way or the other.[27] The problem could of course be resolved by a legislature, one of whose functions is to reconcile competing points of view, including ethical ones. Indeed, one might expect designers and manufacturers to want the protection afforded by a legislature making this decision. Institutionally, it would seem that it is in the best position to resolve these dilemmas, but it is precisely because these quandaries arise from opposing value systems or ethical approaches that antimajoritarian concerns arise if a majority resolves these dilemmas by fiat. Thus, to respond to the IEEE's suggestion on how to respond to moral overload, there are at least some ethical situations in which it would not be satisfactory for decisions about what should be done to be based on the majority of constituents. At the same time, as between a legislature on the one hand and designers, manufacturers, and their legal advisors on the other, it would seem that the former is still in the better position to make these difficult calls.

A legislature of course might not be prepared to make these hard decisions, thereby leaving it up to designers and manufacturers to resolve the issue. Such designers and manufacturers will find themselves in difficult straits because there is no correct answer to the dilemma, despite what a majority of people might decide. Assuming that designers and manufacturers are not cavalier in

---

[22] *Id.*, at 78. (*Citing* John Mikhail, *Universal Moral Grammar: Theory, Evidence and the Future*, 11 COGNITIVE SCI. 143 (2007).)

[23] *Id.*, at 78.

[24] *Id.*, at 79.

[25] *Id.*, at 80.

[26] *Id.*

[27] Belay, *supra* note 18, at 122–9.

how they "solve" a moral dilemma, there are strong arguments that they would escape liability for their decisions.[28] They could cite Greene's findings and design artificial agents that act as the majority of human respondents say they would in a similar situation, or they could engage in a more elaborate decision-making process. In this regard, Vikram Bhargava and Tae Wan Kim propose a metaethical method to guide moral reasoning when trolleylike situations arise. Their method involves weighting outcomes in terms of their moral significance by the probability that the outcomes will occur.[29] Bhargava and Kim suggest this expected moral value approach can allow people to make moral decisions, even though they appear to use incommensurate moral approaches like utilitarian and deontological reasoning. To do so, they follow the work of Andre Sepielli, who uses analogies to determine whether seemingly incommensurate methods are so in fact.

In Bhargava and Kim's example, a programmer is asked to decide whether an autonomous vehicle should crash into a minivan with five people in it, killing all five, or into a roadster with one person in it, killing that person.[30] The first step in the analysis is to identify two moral analogies to the decision to crash into the roadster: one which, if apt, would weigh in favor of crashing into the roadster and another which, if apt, would weigh in favor of not crashing into the roadster. For the first analogy, Bhargava and Kim suggest that crashing into the roadster can be likened to giving money to a more effective charity over a less effective one. The second analogy is a doctor killing a healthy patient so that his organs can be used to save the lives of five others.[31] In their analysis, the authors argue that the moral weight of the second analogy of organ donation is significantly greater than the weight of the first analogy of giving money to a more efficient charity. For that reason, even though a designer's own belief system might give little credence to a decision not to program the vehicle to crash into the roadster (thus making that outcome less probable), the moral weight of the second analogy, even when multiplied by the designer's low credence, still outweighs the moral significance of the first analogy. The result is that the programmer should not program the vehicle to crash into the roadster.[32]

---

[28]   Vikram Bhargava and Tae Wan Kim, *Autonomous Vehicles and Moral Uncertainty*, in Robot Ethics 2.0: From Autonomous Cars to Artificial Intelligence 5 (Patrick Lin, Ryan Jenkins, and Keith Abney eds., 2017) [hereinafter Robot Ethics 2.0].

[29]   *Id.*, at 9–10.

[30]   *Id.*, at 5.

[31]   *Id.*, at 11.

[32]   *Id.*, at 12.

The approach raises a number of questions, such as whether we could use equally valid analogies that would lead to different expected differences in moral value. At the same time, the method is not unreasonable on its face. If a designer were legally challenged for resolving trolley car-like situations with this method, it would not be surprising for a court to find that the designer was not careless by choosing this method, any more than a designer would be considered careless by determining that utilitarian considerations should outweigh ontological ones. This, however, heightens the question of who gets to decide.[33]

I discussed earlier Loh and Loh's argument that as long as a human is capable of operating an otherwise autonomous vehicle, he should be held primarily responsible for any mishaps. They also argue that the operator or user should be given the ability to resolve any dilemmas themselves. "[S]ince there is no authority that knows beforehand which moral convictions she holds, no authority can help her in advance to better comply with the reasons she already has for action."[34] This approach assumes, of course, that the human who chooses will have decisional control over the autonomous machine or system in question. As discussed, however, with autonomous vehicles it is anticipated that there will be fewer human operators and more passengers, and other autonomous technologies might not be subject to direct human control. Furthermore, the authors propose that the human operator register her moral preferences before using autonomous vehicles.[35] As a practical matter, it would be hard if not impossible to specify all preferences so we could ensure that an autonomous vehicle would act in the way we wanted, assuming we ourselves knew how we would wish to act in a Trolley Problem situation. Loh and Loh's larger point, however, highlights again the issue of who gets to decide. It should be noted that this question is not restricted to resolving moral dilemmas. For example, should a person be given the choice of hiring a self-driving car that privileges the driver over a self-driving car that privileges the safety of others? And since that choice would be made in advance, what responsibility, if any, does that person have to inform others about the choice he has made?

---

[33] In this regard, Hin-Yan Liu is concerned that if solutions to scenarios like the Trolley Problem are centralized, this will necessarily leave little room for nuanced decision-making and could lead to structural injustices. Hin-Yan Liu, *Irresponsibilities, Inequalities and Injustice for Autonomous Vehicles*, 19 ETHICS & INFO. TECH. 193, 201 (2017).

[34] Wulf Loh and Janina Loh, *Autonomy and Responsibility in Hybrid Systems: The Example of Autonomous Cars*, *in* ROBOT ETHICS 2.0, *supra* note 28, at 35, 45.

[35] *Id.*, at 46.

Artificial Intelligence as Oracle

The Trolley Problem is fascinating, but a person could go through her entire career as a driver and not encounter it. Yet, the problem illustrates some of the difficulties that we will encounter when we try to define the content of any values or moral approaches that would be implemented in autonomous technologies. This raises the question whether technology could decide the content of such values itself. To return to superintelligences, Bostrom argues that the difficulties of directly installing an ethic into a superintelligence are probably insurmountable because of the lack of consensus on what that ethic should be, the complexity of ethical principles as they are applied to specific situations, and the conceptual difficulties of translating ethical principles into intelligible instructions. This leads Bostrom to suggest that we address the problem through indirect normativity: to provide the superintelligence with criteria that any substantive norm should satisfy, and then take advantage of superintelligence's superior computational power by having it perform the hard work of determining what that norm should be.[36] Bostrom surveys various methods for accomplishing this. I will not discuss these in detail, but as one example, Bostrom cites Eliezer Yudkowsky's idea of coherent extrapolated volition.[37] Roughly, the idea is that the superintelligence would, through a process of extrapolation, choose norms which we ourselves would choose if we were smarter, had adequate time to think things through, and were able to arrive at them together through terms of engagement which we would desire. The artificial intelligence would pick extrapolations that it could make with a high degree of confidence and where there tends to be consensus among individuals' volitions. The process should also reflect on itself and consider how we would want the extrapolation process to unfold.[38]

Again, Bostrom is concerned about superintelligences, but just as the IEEE recommends that the implementation of values be iterative, as discussed earlier, Bostrom also argues that approaches such as indirect normativity should be implemented in less powerful artificial intelligences. Indirect approaches include Yukowsky's coherent extrapolated volition, as well as the other indirect methods Bostrom discusses, such as instructing the super-intelligence to determine what is morally right,[39] or the simple instruction to "Do whatever we would have the most reason to ask the AI to do."[40] These

---

[36]   Bostrom, *supra* note 6, at 258.
[37]   *Id.*, at 259. (*Citing* Eliezer Yudkowsky, Coherent Extrapolated Volition (2004).)
[38]   *Id.*, at 260.
[39]   *Id.*, at 266.
[40]   *Id.*, at 270.

approaches have their drawbacks, but they have the advantage of avoiding, at least at the outset, the need for agreement on substantive moral principles.

At the same time, such indirect approaches raise the question of which indirect approach one might use. Kant's categorical imperative also is an attempt to use a content-free method to derive substantive principles, yet remains challenged by utilitarian and other consequentialist approaches to ethics. Further, specific to coherent extrapolated volition, one could argue that the guidelines for picking extrapolations when there is a high degree of confidence and consensus presuppose values that not all people would share. Finally, each of these indirect methods are not dissimilar in their basic logic. To instruct an artificial intelligence to extrapolate, or to determine what is morally right, or to do whatever we would have the most reason to ask of an artificial intelligence, is to have confidence that there will be some correspondence between those specific instructions and whatever it is that the artificial intelligence decides to do. It is not so different from analogical reasoning in this regard.[41] We could of course, as does Yukowsky, instruct the artificial intelligence not to act if it is not confident in its extrapolation or confident that we in fact would ask it to do what it is considering doing. But inaction itself might have moral consequences, and to ask an artificial intelligence to take that possibility into account leads to infinite regress.

In addition to questions as to whether an indirect approach to determining values would be effective, there is still the issue of whether we are prepared for artificial intelligences to serve as oracles. Steve Petersen argues that there is some room for a superintelligence to engage in ethical thinking as it reasons about the goals that it is pursuing. A superintelligence will likely recognize that there are a large number of competing goals and will try to find coherence among them. This attempt to find coherence (much like Dworkin's Hercules) is ethical thinking in Petersen's view.[42] Assuming this is true, however, that a superintelligence would be inclined to try to find coherence among competing goals does not guarantee that we would be happy with the outcome of that ethical decision-making process. Suppose that a superintelligence was seeking to reconcile goals of protecting humankind and protecting the environment and that it was aware of utilitarian and deontological approaches to ethical issues. It would be faced with a metaversion of the Trolley Problem, but instead of human designers, judges, or legislators, the superintelligence would resolve it. Perhaps it would follow a procedure similar to that suggested by Bhargava and

---

[41] *See, e.g.,* Francesco Guala, *Extrapolation, Analogy, and Comparative Process Training*, 77 PHIL. SCI. 1070 (2010) (in part discussing the similarities between extrapolation and analogical reasoning in the natural sciences).

[42] Steve Petersen, *Superintelligence as Superethical, in* ROBOT ETHICS 2.0, *supra* note 28, at 322, 327–31.

Kim and assign specific weights to the ethical impact if its decisions lead to the death of a large number of human beings and the ethical impact if its decisions lead to the degradation of the environment. It would use analogical reasoning to try to reconcile seemingly incommensurate ethical maxims. The resolution might be quite well reasoned, better than any human could ever achieve, but the explanation might be either incomprehensible to us or, given the intractable nature of moral dilemmas, unacceptable to us on one or more valid moral grounds. It is another instance of questioning who gets to decide moral issues.

IMPLEMENTING MORAL VALUES

Even if we are able to reach consensus on the content of an ethical system or on a method for moral decision-making, there is still the difficult task of implementing it in artificial agents. Wallach notes two technical and conceptual problems:

> The first problem entails finding a computational method to implement norms, rules, principles or procedures for making moral judgements. The second is a group of related challenges that I refer to as frame problems. How does the system recognise that it is in an ethically significant situation? How does it discern essential from inessential information? ... How would the system recognise that it had applied all necessary considerations to the challenge at hand or completed its determination of the appropriate action to take?[43]

The issue of finding computational methods to implement ethical norms is akin to the issue of programming autonomous technologies to conform to the law.[44] The consensus appears to be that as autonomous technologies approach general intelligence, the computer programs that control them will themselves

---

[43]   Wallach, *supra* note 4, at 200. For a recent discussion of approaches to programming ethics into artificial agents and an example of how the resolution of ethical dilemmas can be programmed, *see* Vincent Bonnemains, Claire Saurel, and Catherine Tessler, *Embedded Ethics: Some Technical and Ethical Challenges*, 20 ETHICS & INFO. TECH. 41 (2018).

[44]   Ronald Arkin discusses how ethical controls could be inserted into autonomous weapons systems in Ronald C. Arkin, Governing Lethal Behavior: Embedding Ethics in a Hybrid Deliberative/Reactive Robot Architecture, Georgia Institute of Technology Technical Report GIT-GVU-07-11 (2007), at 14–21, www.cc.gatech.edu/ai/robot-lab/online-publications/formalizationv35.pdf. Michael Anderson and Susan Leigh Anderson discuss prototypes of two systems they designed in the area of medical ethics. Michael Anderson and Susan Leigh Anderson, *Machine Ethics: Creating an Ethical Intelligent Agent*, 28 AI MAG. (Winter 2007), at 15. *See also* Bertram F. Malle, *Integrating Robot Ethics and Machine Morality: The Study and Design of Moral Competence in Robots*, 18 ETHICS & INF. TECH. 243 (2016) (identifying the capacities we would expect a moral agent to have and relating them to robotic design).

be motivated via utility functions. J. Storrs Hall illustrates how a utility function would operate in the context of deterrence (a topic to which I will turn later in this chapter): "In the rational machine ... a credible threat of punishment (or reward) will be added to calculated utility of the predicted outcome of the act."[45] Hall uses an example in which a robot is given two choices: to pick up a $5 bill or to pick up a $10 bill. If its utility function is directly proportional to the amount of money it has, it will pick up the $10 bill. If we want the robot to pick up the $5 bill instead, the robot can be threatened with a $6 fine for picking up the $10 bill. The robot will then pick up the $5 bill, since it will net only $4 if it picks up the $10 bill.[46] Suppose the robot is next given the choice between being placed in a situation where it can choose unencumbered or having its utility function changed so that it will prefer to pick up the $5 instead of $10. It will choose the former because under its present utility function it will prefer to make $10.[47] The latter modification shows that the threat of imposing a utility function can influence robot behavior.[48]

Encoding specific approaches via utility functions will then involve other mechanisms or programming approaches. Lin, Bekey, and Abney, and separately Wallach and Allen, recommend that designers follow a hybrid approach, whereby machines are programmed with "top down," deontological ethical rules, such as Asimov's three laws of robotics,[49] or Kant's categorical

---

[45] J. Storrs Hall, Towards Machine Agency: A Philosophical and Technological Roadmap, Mar. 30, 2012, "We Robot" Conference at the University of Miami Law School, at 4, http://robots.law.miami.edu/wp-content/uploads/2012/01/Hall -MachineAgencyLong.pdf.

[46] *Id.*

[47] *Id.*

[48] There can be refinements to this approach. For example, Peter Vamplew et al. propose a multiobjective maximum expected utility program that they believe improves on the more standard maximum expected utility formula. Peter Vamplew et al., *Human-Aligned Artificial Intelligence Is a Multiobjective Problem*, 20 ETHICS & INFO. TECH. 27 (2018).

[49] The laws figured as part of Asimov's science fiction *Robot* series. They are:
- A robot may not injure a human being or, through inaction, allow a human being to come to harm.
- A robot must obey the orders given it by human beings except where such orders would conflict with the First Law.
- A robot must protect its own existence as long as such protection does not conflict with the First or Second Laws.

Isaac Asimov, I, ROBOT 42 (Gnome Press edn. 1950). For a critique that the three laws of robots are unworkable in certain contexts, *see, e.g.,* Abney, *supra* note 17, at 42–4; Susan Leigh Anderson, *Asimov's "Three Laws of Robotics" and Machine Meta-Ethics*, 22 AI & SOC'Y 477, 490–92 (2008) (arguing that the laws would allow humans to mistreat robots even if they do not have moral standing, in violation of Kant's views on the treatment of entities without moral standing).

imperative. The top down approach has the advantage of providing rules that can apply in many situations. At the same time, it has the weakness of being too vague.[50] Thus, such machines should also be programmed to engage in "bottom up" learning behaviors, whereby the rules of behavior will evolve as machines are faced with specific situations.[51] For Wallach and Allen, the hybrid approach comes close to instilling a kind of virtue ethics in robots.[52]

Bostrom shares the view that ultimately top down rules alone will not be able to control intelligent machines, superintelligences in particular. He identifies a number of methods that could be used to ensure that autonomous systems are motivated to act with humans in mind. This might be accomplished through direct specification (through rules or consequentialist mechanisms), domesticity (motivating a system to act only on a small scale and in narrow contexts), indirect normativity (as discussed, designing processes for deriving standards of behavior), and augmentation (improving systems that already display desirable behaviors).[53] These methods might be used in combination, depending on how a particular superintelligence is designed to operate, but each of them becomes more challenging the more sophisticated artificial intelligence becomes.

With regard to what he terms direct specification through rules or consequentialist mechanisms, Bostrom identifies several of the issues discussed in Chapter 7 concerning programming autonomous technologies to comply with law.

> Perhaps the closest existing analog to a rule set that could govern the actions of a superintelligence operating in the world at large is a legal system. But legal systems have developed through a long process of trial and error, and they regulate relatively slowly—changing human societies. Laws can be revised when necessary. Most importantly, legal systems are administered by judges and juries who generally apply a measure of common sense and human decency to ignore logically possible legal interpretations that are sufficiently obviously unwanted and unintended by the lawgivers. It is probably humanly impossible to explicitly formulate a highly complex set of detailed rules, have them apply across a highly diverse set of circumstances, and get it right on the first implementation.[54]

---

[50]   Lin et al., *supra* note 2, at 34. Michal Klincewicz agrees that the main challenge in using utilitarian and nonconsequentialist approaches is to make computer programs sensitive to context. Michal Klincewicz, *Challenges to Engineering Moral Reasoners: Time and Context, in* ROBOT ETHICS 2.0, *supra* note 28, at 244, 252.

[51]   *Id.*, at 41.

[52]   Wallach and Allen, *supra* note 3, at 117–24. The authors refer to studies that have discussed how neural network programming resonates with Aristotle's explanation of how people develop virtues. *Id.*, at 121–3.

[53]   *Id.*, at 169–75.

[54]   Bostrom, *supra* note 6, at 170–71.

For Bostrom, consequentialist mechanisms are also fraught because of the disastrous results that would occur if the system designers fail to specify a system's goals with care. For example, a machine could be instructed to "maximize the balance of pleasure over pain in the world," but it would be challenging to devise computer code to recognize pleasure and pain. A small error in programming or a difference in one's conception of pleasure and pain could lead to disaster because the superintelligence might decide that the best way to reach such a goal would be via methods that humans would find repugnant.[55] A superintelligence could, for example, decide that the best way to reach that goal is to drug all human beings. Technologies with less than general intelligence would not of course pose the same level of danger, but they could well encounter similar issues in the more circumscribed settings in which they operate.

That top down approaches will be inadequate motivates the bottom up approach to take advantage of the learning capability of artificial intelligences. However, Bostrom argues that this strategy might be unworkable, at least for a superintelligence. Because a superintelligence will likely be able to gain a strategic advantage over human beings soon after it achieves this status, it is important that any control mechanisms be in place and work correctly from the outset. There will be no time for learning. Further, as he notes, human ethical systems have arisen out of millennia of human experience, experience that includes much human suffering. He queries whether we would want a superintelligence to experiment in this way.[56] The issue is less acute with less powerful technology, but still exists. For example, if the decision is ever made to develop and deploy autonomous weapons systems, we certainly would want them to learn from experience, but such experience might take a great deal of time to acquire, at the cost of human lives. To be sure, one of the advantages of autonomous systems is that lessons learned from one system can be shared almost instantaneously with all other systems. Moreover, it might be that computer simulations will be rich enough so that autonomous systems can "practice" and learn via simulation. But it remains to be seen whether that kind of complexity can be replicated in that way.

THE FIT BETWEEN HUMAN AND MACHINE VALUES

The IEEE report indicates that as artificial intelligence is able to determine for itself the best methods for achieving a particular goal and ultimately form its own goals, there is no guarantee that those methods, goals, and subsequent

---

[55] *Id.*, at 171.
[56] *Id.*, at 229–30.

actions will mesh with human values. This issue has at least three components. One is the issue just discussed: determining what substantive ethical rules or approaches to implement. A related issue is, assuming that an autonomous machine or system knows what human beings want and is motivated to act to reach that goal, how does one ensure that the methods the machine or system uses will be in the interests of humans? Finally, assuming that we are able to solve these issues, to what extent will we be satisfied with holding machines responsible if they somehow fail to act in humans' interests? What would holding an autonomous system itself responsible for a harm mean?

Aligning Methods

Bostrom states that the challenge in controlling a superintelligence is not so much getting a superintelligence to understand human intentions, but rather to motivate it to fulfill them in the way we intend (as opposed to drugging all humans to maximize happiness).[57] For Bostrom, one of the most promising forms of motivational control is still very much in the research stage. It is a values learning approach. Bostrom uses two examples to illustrate its logic. In the first, we write down a set of values and place them in an envelope. We then instruct a machine (via a utility function) with general intelligence to maximize those values. Although the machine does not know the contents of the envelope, it will make hypotheses about them and assign probabilities as to the likelihood that each hypothesis is correct. It will seek to learn as much as it can in order to determine the contents of the envelope; it will also learn about rules for its own preservation and growth, such as acquiring resources to continue functioning, but it will reject those as ultimately controlling because there is a strong probability that the contents of the envelope will have something to do with enhancing the wellbeing of humans, and pursuing those other goals could lead to the destruction of human beings.[58] All along the way, as it is trying to guess what the ultimate set really is, it is also forced to learn about how values are implemented. The process is also like a barge being towed by several tugboats, each tugboat representing a possible value set and the pulling strength of the tug corresponding to the probability of that tugboat being the correct set. Over time, as the system weeds out various hypotheses, only the pull of the actual value set is left.[59]

Of course, Bostrom is concerned with a superintelligence that has the immediate potential to decide goals and methods for itself. Nevertheless, the

---

[57]   *Id.*, at 240.
[58]   *Id.*, at 236.
[59]   *Id.*

issue of aligning methods to achieve goals is relevant to less sophisticated technologies. In a sense, however, the problem is even more daunting because human programmers themselves will need to be aware that the way in which autonomous technologies pursue various goals will itself have ethical implications.

Machines as Subjects of Moral Evaluation

Assume we are able to program autonomous machines and systems to act generally in ways that conform to values with which we agree. Suppose, however, that an autonomous system does something that causes harm or violates one of those values. Is it meaningful in that circumstance to hold that system responsible? One of the advantages of being able to attribute responsibility directly to an artificial agent is that it would resolve the problem of trying to find a human to blame for something an artificial agent has done. Floridi and J.W. Sanders argue that to the extent that we recognize that artificial agents have moral agency,

> [w]e are less likely to assign responsibility at any cost forced by the necessity to identify a human moral agent[.] ... We can stop the regress of looking for the *responsible* individual when something evil happens, since we are now ready to acknowledge that sometimes the moral source of evil or good can be different from an individual or group of humans.[60]

However, there is debate as to whether it is coherent to attribute responsibility to autonomous technologies in more than a causal sense. The question is whether such machines and systems will ever enjoy the status of entities that can be subject to moral evaluation and be held morally responsible in their own right. The question is pertinent for at least two reasons. One is whether human beings will be satisfied with attributing a harm to an autonomous machine or system with no further consequences to anyone else. Another is that one of the strategies being considered to engender prosocial behaviors in artificial agents is to make the most sophisticated technology susceptible to punishment or other adverse consequences. Such punishment or consequences will need to be justified.

Hew, whose work was introduced in Chapter 1, argues that artificial moral agents, in the sense that they themselves can be subject to moral blamewor-

---

[60] Luciano Floridi and J.W. Sanders, *On the Morality of Artificial Agents*, 14 Minds & Machine 349, 376 (2004).

thiness, are infeasible given the foreseeable technologies.[61] He begins with the Aristotelian view discussed in Chapter 3 that a moral agent is one whose actions are subject to blame or praise, and that an action is not morally blameworthy or praiseworthy unless it is voluntary.[62] Recall from Chapter 1 his definition of intelligence: "anything that can *close a loop* from sensors to effectors without human intervention."[63] As discussed there, Hew points out that a mousetrap would meet this definition of intelligence, yet we do not view a mousetrap as a moral agent because, although it can close the loop between sensing and then trapping the mouse by itself, humans external to the mousetrap engineered its operative "rules." He then surveys technologies that are now being used in the area of artificial intelligence and argues that each one of them requires a human being outside of the intelligent system to supply its rules.[64] Hew concedes that "connectionist" approaches to artificial intelligence, such as neural networks, provide enough true autonomy to qualify an intelligent system as an agent whose actions are subject to blame or praise:

> [C]onnectionist systems are characterized by units interacting via weighted connections, where a unit's state is determined by inputs received from other units[.] ... The opportunity is for unit states to define the rules used by other units. In this way, the connectionist system as a whole could come to supply its own rules.[65]

However, Hew believes that if the weights in a neural network system are provided by human beings, then the systems in question no longer qualify as autonomous.[66] For Hew, this means actions taken by such systems are not voluntary; hence, they are not subject to moral blame or praise. Such blame or praise goes to the humans who supplied the rules for the system.

Hew's argument recalls unanswerable issues about physical or deistic determinism discussed in Chapter 3, as well as the examination of whether designers and manufacturers can be held morally and legally responsible for harms caused by autonomous technologies. Here the question takes on a different aspect: for the purpose of assessing whether the machine or system should be held responsible for a harm, does it matter that it might be generations removed from its human designers? (Recall in this regard that it is anticipated

---

[61] Patrick Chisan Hew, *Artificial Moral Agents Are Infeasible with Foreseeable Technologies*, 16 ETHICS & INFO. TECH. 197 (2014).

[62] *Id.*, at 199.

[63] *Id.*, at 198.

[64] *Id.*, at 198–200. These technologies are: self-replicating programs, self-modifying code, machine learning systems, self-regulating adaptive systems and meta-adaptive systems, self-organizing systems, and evolutionary computing. *Id.*

[65] *Id.*, at 200.

[66] *Id.*

that some artificial technologies will be able to design and manufacture other technologies.) Hew believes it does not.[67]

Others, however, argue that machines will reach sufficiently high levels of autonomy and sophistication that it will be hard to trace lines of responsibility back to human beings. The implication is that it is appropriate to consider the machine or system itself as having caused a harm. Andreas Matthias discusses three examples of how this is so.[68] In one example, an advanced Mars explorer is programmed to learn to avoid obstacles and navigate on its own by retaining images of terrain and information about how easy or hard it was to traverse, so that the rover will act appropriately the next time it encounters similar terrain. Matthias argues that if the rover falls into a hole, no one can be blamed: the operator on Earth did not give any manual controls and the programmer can point out that the algorithm used was correctly implemented. The decision to move forward was based on facts about the planetary terrain that were encountered only after the rover had landed:

> The actual decisions of the control program were based not only on preprogrammed data, but on facts that were added to the machine's database only after it reached the surface of Mars: they are not part of the initial program, but constitute genuine experience acquired autonomously by the machine in the course of its operation.[69]

Matthias' illustration shows how the sophistication of machines could make it difficult to attribute accidents caused by the machine to humans. Lawrence Solum gives another example that forms a different response to Hew, which has to do with framing. In a well-known and prescient article written 20 years ago, Solum asks whether an electronic trustee could be given legal personhood.[70] He points out an electronic trustee could be designed to delegate certain decisions to a human trustee, which creates an argument that the human trustee is the "real" trustee.[71] It follows that "the backup trustee must be the real trustee because there is a pragmatic need for discretionary decision making."[72] Solum, however, responds as follows:

> The objection that the AI is not the real trustee seems to rest on the possibility that a human backup will be needed. But it is also possible that an AI administering

---

[67] *Id.*, at 201.

[68] Andreas Matthias, *The Responsibility Gap: Ascribing Responsibility for the Actions of Learning Automata*, 6 ETHICS & INFO. TECH. 175, 176 (2004).

[69] *Id.*

[70] Lawrence B. Solum, *Legal Personhood for Artificial Intelligences*, 70 N.C. L. REV. 1231, 1231 (1992).

[71] *Id.*, at 1253.

[72] *Id.*, at 1254.

many thousands of trusts would need to turn over discretionary decisions to a natural person in only a few cases—perhaps none. What is the point of saying that in all of the thousands of trusts the AI handles by itself, the real trustee was some natural person on whom the AI would have called if a discretionary judgment had been required? Doesn't it seem strange to say that the real trustee is this unidentified natural person, who has had no contact with the trust? Isn't it more natural to say that the trustee was the AI, which holds title to the trust property, makes the investment decisions, writes the checks, and so forth? Even in the event that a human was substituted, I think that we would be inclined to say something like, "The AI was the trustee until June 7, then a human took over."[73]

One can take the illustration a step further. Suppose the electronic trustee commits a mistake that would be considered malpractice. Hew would conceivably hold the human trustee or the designers of the electronic trustee responsible for the wrong.[74] But if the electronic trustee has handled thousands of trusts by itself without mishap, it seems somewhat strained to hold the human trustee responsible the one time a mishap occurs. To return to Wolgast, when such a mistake is made, it is natural under our ideas of moral responsibility to believe that someone is responsible. In this case, that someone could likely be the electronic trustee.

Floridi and Sanders argue that when examined from a particular level of abstraction, artificial agents do in fact qualify as moral agents. Using a kind of Turing test, they argue that if an observer were to view a human and an artificial agent engaging with a patient in a hospital room, and were to observe both responding to environmental stimuli (for example, the presence of the patient) by updating their levels of interactivity (an indication of their internal states), exhibiting behaviors independent of their environment (perhaps by changing the temperature of the room), and then modifying their behaviors, perhaps in response to past experience of successful interactions with patients, both would possess levels of interactivity, autonomy, and adaptability that would constitute agency.[75] The authors continue by proposing that an "action is said to be morally qualifiable if and only if it can cause moral good or evil. An agent is said to be a moral agent if and only if it is capable of morally qualifiable action."[76] Under these definitions, an artificial agent would meet the criteria of a moral agent because if it were to harm the patient, such harm would be a morally qualifiable action.[77] Floridi and Sanders respond to the objection that an artificial agent cannot be responsible because it does not make sense

---

[73] *Id.*

[74] Hew, *supra* note 61, at 201.

[75] Floridi and Sanders, *supra* note 60, at 363–4.

[76] *Id.*, at 364.

[77] *Id.*

at this point to subject the agent to moral blame; like others, they disaggregate responsibility into its components and say that it is perfectly appropriate to identify an artificial agent as a responsible party even if one cannot then subject it to punishment.[78] Indeed, in contrast to Wolgast, they would defend this separation on the grounds that to insist on punishment reflects an anthropocentric and anthropomorphic concept of responsibility.[79]

As can be seen, much of the debate turns on whether autonomous technologies have the proper agency such that it is cogent to have them bear responsibilities. Bernd Stahl tries to avoid the question of agency by proposing that autonomous machines and systems be ascribed a quasiresponsibility.[80] Stahl argues that attributions of responsibility may well depend on whether such ascription serves a social goal, since responsibility is a social construct. To respond or to be answerable to someone implies the social nature of responsibility, hence its construction.[81] Stahl begins by giving a thorough definition and background of "responsibility" and what it means to be able to be "responsible." He explains that, while responsibility usually hinges on personhood or agency, another perspective can be put forward: the social function of responsibility, which is to effect a "socially desirable state ... through ... sanctions, be they positive or negative" which results from the need or want to find the guilty party in the face of negative results and punish them.[82]

Stahl highlights some of the crucial aspects required for responsibility: causality, power (knowing what is happening is required to be able to influence it), and freedom to act on knowledge. All of these "requirements," Stahl explains, are "rooted in anthropocentrism," and even when applied to humans, these concepts can fail to be substantive (for example, "are humans really free to act according to their will?").[83] He then discusses how computers usually are not considered to be subject to responsibility (mentioning, among other things, that computers lack the *mens rea* necessary for usual attribution), and strikes directly at the notion that computers cannot be punished or deterred because they "do not fear" and also are not free because of predetermined programming.[84] Stahl argues that we are able to construct forms of responsibility that apply to states and similar organizations without regard to actual personhood

---

[78] *Id.*, at 367–8.

[79] *Id.*, at 375–6.

[80] Bernd Carsten Stahl, *Responsible Computers? A Case for Ascribing Quasi-Responsibility to Computers Independent of Personhood or Agency*, 8 ETHICS & INFO. TECH. 205 (2006).

[81] *Id.*, at 206.

[82] *Id.*, at 207.

[83] *Id.*, at 208.

[84] *Id.*, at 208–9.

and agency, or at least in the way that we apply those concepts to ourselves.[85] Thus, computers can be, technically, "punishable" with the sanctions that come with responsibility (for example, if autonomous drones continuously kill civilians they can be banned). In his view the increased or decreased use of and reliance on a system is a social consequence of the machine's actions, which is attributed to its "quasiresponsibility" over its own actions.

I will discuss punishment for autonomous systems later in this chapter. At this point, it is important to point out that for Stahl, quasiresponsibility for robots does not end there: it involves human responsibility as well. This has at least three implications. First, "[c]omputer quasi-responsibility should be seen as a means for the facilitation of further responsibility ascriptions." [86] Stahl elaborates: "There will clearly be at least one additional responsibility for humans. 'They will bear responsibility for preparing these systems to take responsibility'."[87] Perhaps humans will take such responsibility by ensuring that autonomous computer systems can be shut down. Whatever else it might mean, however, quasiresponsibility leads to increasing the scope of persons who are potentially responsible for an artificial agent: "[S]ocial structures and institutions must be introduced which should allow for accountability of computers designers, programmers, managers, and users."[88] Finally, quasi-responsibility will call for greater sophistication of the programs themselves: "[T]he internal structure of computers might be modified in such a way that they become capable of discharging their quasi-responsibility. This may mean that computers have to become more adaptable to their environment."[89]

At least three aspects of a quasiresponsibility model merit comment. First, it has the advantage of avoiding, at least in part, metaphysical issues concerning the status of artificial intelligences and autonomous technologies driven by them. Second, it continues to make human designers accountable for making machines capable of bearing quasiresponsibility. As just discussed, it might require installing a way to take such technologies offline, or to ensure that autonomous machines be able to "explain themselves" and not make decisions within a black box. This is perfectly appropriate, particularly now, during the first wave of artificial intelligence, when it is in its nascent stage and can be easily contained. Further, since for Stahl responsibility is a social construct, we might see a recasting of responsibility or of responsible groups, as discussed in Chapters 5 and 6.

---

[85]   *Id.*, at 210.
[86]   *Id.*, at 211. (*Citing* W. Bechtel, *Attributing Responsibility to Computer Systems*, 16 Metaphilosophy 296, 297 (1985).)
[87]   *Id.* (*Citing* Bechtel, *id.*)
[88]   *Id.*
[89]   *Id.* (*Citing* Bechtel, *supra* note 87, at 297.)

At the same time, quasiresponsibility depends to some extent on our willingness to move away from what Stahl describes as an anthropocentric view of responsibility. Chapters 5 and 6 also described the limitations of such a departure. Further, although it can be argued that refraining from using a technology is a form of punishment, unless machines can be designed to "feel" that punishment, there will likely be a number of people who will be dissatisfied with holding a machine quasiresponsible and nothing more. This would either result in a felt gap in responsibility or create incentives to extend greater responsibility to the designers and manufacturers of the technology, thus reviving the distributional problem discussed in Chapters 4 and 7.

Machines Susceptible to Punishment

I have just described Stahl's form of punishment for autonomous technologies. Other literature is exploring ways in which machines can be made more amenable to sanctions. As is true with other aspects of responsibility for autonomous machines, the question of punishment involves articulating the reasons for sanctions, whether new forms must be designed for artificial intelligence, and whether they would be technically feasible.

As discussed earlier, Floridi and Sanders would consider this an anthropomorphism of responsibility. Commonsense views of moral responsibility, as well as the concept of legal responsibility, entail consequences. Thus for some people, an entity unable to bear consequences is not responsible by definition. Further, such consequences are almost always negative and are experienced that way. Recall Hedel's observation that being found morally responsible leaves a person vulnerable to second order effects, such as other people's scorn, criticism, and so on. Legal responsibility often involves a fine, imprisonment, or death. Those negative aspects of consequences are what motivates the phrase "no body to kick and no soul to be damned" when referring to the problem of holding groups legally or morally responsible for harms. Christopher Thompson argues in this regard that groups cannot be moral agents precisely because they cannot feel moral emotions like guilt and shame.[90] As discussed in Chapter 2 regarding the purposes of the criminal law, punishment has been justified as playing deterrent, retributive, expressive, reformative, and restorative functions. At least with respect to human beings,

---

[90] Christopher Thompson, *The Moral Agency of Group Agents*, 83 ERKENN 517 (2018).

these functions would be hindered significantly if the subject of punishment was not somehow cognizant of and sensitive to its negative aspects.[91]

Earlier in this chapter I discussed Hall's explanation of how the threat of punishment could have deterrent effects on an autonomous robot. In that model, the robot is motivated to maximize a utility function, and the threat of sanctions in the form of lower utility can influence a robot's behavior. As we have also seen in this chapter, Bostrom believes that one of the only hopes of influencing a superintelligence's motivations is through its utility function. One of the ironies is that the effort to instill prosocial behaviors by making a machine amenable to punishment by setting incentives in its utility curve is that it would motivate a superintelligence to avoid that punishment, not by engaging in prosocial behaviors, but by acting in ways to evade that punishment, including to change its utility curve.

Even for lesser intelligences, Asaro argues that Hall's deterrence approach is inadequate because it fails to encompass other reasons for punishment, some of them just discussed: retribution, deterrence that goes beyond the individual to the larger society, and reform.[92] Asaro himself does not suggest an alternative form of punishment, but others have raised ideas such as confining a robot to a particular part of cyberspace, deleting an autonomous machine's computer systems without backup, or, as suggested by Stahl, banning a system from being used.[93] If responsibility in the paradigmatic sense is to apply fully to autonomous machines, an issue is whether we human beings would feel that such consequences are adequate forms of punishment. This will depend in part on how these would be "experienced" by artificial intelligences as such, and likewise that question will turn on whether the most sophisticated technologies have the machine equivalent of awareness and a "desire" to maintain its existence.

Sparrow also doubts that various forms of punishment for robots will ever be completely satisfactory because in his view, punishment entails suffering.[94]

---

[91]   In this regard, John Danaher argues that there will be a retribution gap as robots are viewed as responsible for harms, yet cannot be punished. John Danaher, *Robots, Law, and the Retribution Gap*, 18 ETHICS & INF. TECH. 299 (2016).

[92]   Peter A. Asaro, *Punishment, Reinforcement Learning & Machine Agency*, 9 COSMOPOLIS (Jan. 2015), www.cosmopolis.globalist.it/Detail_News_Display?ID= 69610.

[93]   Ugo Pagallo, *What Robots Want: Autonomous Machines, Codes and New Frontiers of Legal Responsibility*, *in* HUMAN LAW AND COMPUTER LAW: COMPARATIVE PERSPECTIVES, 25 IUS GENTIUM 47, 56 (Mireille Hildebrandt and Jeanne Gaakeer eds., 2013) (confinement and deletion); Bernd Carsten Stahl, *Responsible Computers? A Case for Ascribing Quasi-Responsibility to Computers Independent of Personhood or Agency*, 8 ETHICS & INFO. TECH. 205, 211 (2006) (banning).

[94]   Robert Sparrow, *Killer Robots*, 24 J. APPLIED PHIL. 62, 72 (2007).

Recall, however, that one of the two methods for achieving general intelligence is to emulate the human brain; perhaps in doing so, designers will be able to instill in artificial intelligences the equivalent of physical and emotional pain. Research is being done to have computer programs undergo internal state transitions analogous to emotions.[95] However, this possibility raises another ethical issue: whether it is appropriate to design something that is capable of suffering. At this point, we begin to ask questions within the bounds of medical and reproductive ethics, in situations where the decision to preserve life or to bring to life is fraught because there is a significant chance that life will entail physical and emotional pain. There, however, the focus is always on the life involved and the agency she will be able to exert. If we begin to use this line of inquiry with regard to artificial intelligences, we will have begun to view them as not only possible subjects for moral responsibility, but also subjects of moral patiency.

Finally, it should be observed that a machine or system sophisticated enough to be considered a moral agent will be close to having general intelligence. Recall Wallach's point early in this chapter that an ethical system would need to be able to engage in framing: the system would need to be able to recognize that it is in an ethically significant situation. It would need to be able to distinguish between relevant and irrelevant facts as it determines a course of action. In short, it would need to engage in satisficing: to consider all factors, perhaps with incomplete information, and then decide when it had cogitated enough. Add to this some capacity to be sensitive to the negative aspects of moral or legal responsibility. Even if such a system does not reach the level of general intelligence, at a minimum, it could have a hand in developing systems that do. At that point, we will need to rely on the techniques identified by Bostrom to control them. Here too, however, we will need to ask whether such systems warrant moral regard when we impose those controls. That is the topic of the next chapter.

---

[95] *See, e.g.*, Christoph Bartnek, Michael Lyons, and Martin Saerbeck, The Relationship between Emotion Models and Artificial Intelligence, Proceedings of the SAB2008 Workshop on the Role of Emotion in Adaptive Behavior and Cognitive Robotics, June 2017 (critically evaluating the standard model for computational emotions); Toyoaki Nishida, *Modeling Machine Emotions for Realizing Intelligence: An Introduction*, in MODELING MACHINE EMOTIONS FOR REALIZING INTELLIGENCE: FOUNDATIONS AND APPLICATIONS 1 (Robert J. Howlett, Colette Faucher, and Toyoaki Nishida eds., 2010) (discussing models for artificial intelligence with emotions); Hiroki Okashi, Hung-Hsuan Huang, and Toyoaki Nishida, *Attentive Conversational Agent with Internal State Transition for Multiple Users*, in *id.*, at 133 (discussing research involving a computer program to undergo internal state transitions as representative of emotions).

9. Machines and systems as legal and moral subjects

At the end of Chapter 8, I discussed research which is exploring the extent to which artificial intelligence and the machines and systems driven by it can be made more susceptible to legal and moral sanctions, separate and apart from human beings associated with them. That effort leads to the topic of this chapter: proposals to give legal status and rights to certain autonomous technologies, and whether such technologies should be given moral consideration, or patiency.

LEGAL STATUS FOR AUTONOMOUS TECHNOLOGIES

In a sense, the issue of whether autonomous technologies can be given legal status is straightforward. As is well known, assigning legal personhood to non-humans is not new. Ships, corporations, and states enjoy status as legal persons with various legal powers and responsibilities. The decision to do this was motivated in large part by practical grounds: ease of recovery for any losses, shielding owners and citizens from liability, and a sense that these entities served important social purposes.[1]

Similar reasons drive proposals to give autonomous machines and systems legal status. As discussed in Chapter 2, Chopra and White argue that legal agency should be used to address harms caused by autonomous machines. With product liability, it would be useful in their view to hold autonomous machines liable themselves, in part because they believe it will be difficult for plaintiffs to bring successful cases against manufacturers under current product liability

---

[1] With respect to ships, Thomas Schoenbaum observes that a vessel "is liable for the tortious acts of the master, although the ship owner is not personally liable." Brief of *Amicus Curiae* Thomas J. Schoenbaum, J.D., Ph.D. in Support of Petitioners, at 10, *Kiobel v. Royal Dutch Petroleum*, 569 U.S. 108 (2013) (No 10-1491). (*Citing Manro v. Almeida*, 23 U.S. (10 Wheat) 473 and FED. R. CIV. P., Supplemental Rule C.) The rule appears to come from the Middle Ages when merchants formed limited liability entities known as *commenda*. Imposing liability on the vessels was a way to impose liability on the *commenda* "while still respecting the limited liability in their charters." *Id.* (*Citing The Rebecca*, 20 F. Cas. 373, 378, 1 Ware 187 (D. Me. 1831).)

law.[2] Similarly, Pagallo suggests giving legal personhood to computer-based contracting systems to better justify holding enforceable the contracts made by such systems.[3] The law could design ways to impose economic consequences when an autonomous machine is determined to be responsible for harms, such as a minimum capital requirement associated with the machine; keeping a register that accounts for damage caused by a machine, presumably to be paid by its owner, operator, or some common fund; or, in appropriate cases, using *respondeat superior* to hold a principal liable for the machine's actions.[4] In this vein, Lawrence Solum points out that a computer agent could purchase insurance to cover the risk of its own misfeasance.[5] Shawn Bayern argues that autonomous systems could be given legal powers and status through currently existing limited liability company laws.[6]

Granting legal personhood and subjecting it to legal responsibility has the advantage of avoiding much of the debate in the moral literature as to whether autonomous machines and systems can be moral agents and should be treated as such. Chopra and White argue, for example, that in several cases actions, not mental states, are important in determining legal liability. Further, they urge, mental states and intentionality are themselves constructions, which are

---

[2] Samir Chopra and Laurence F. White, A LEGAL THEORY FOR AUTONOMOUS ARTIFICIAL AGENTS 143–4 (2011).

[3] Ugo Pagallo, THE LAWS OF ROBOTS 154 (2013).

[4] *Id.*, at 103–6; Chopra and White, *supra* note 2, at 150.

[5] Lawrence B. Solum, *Legal Personhood for Artificial Intelligences*, 70 N.C. L. REV. 1231, 1245 (1992). He raises the possibility of insurance coverage to respond to the argument that an artificial intelligence could not be considered a legal person because it could not be held responsible in the sense of satisfying legal claims brought against it. *Id.* Solum acknowledges that insurance might not be available in all cases, leaving the artificial trustee unpunished. In his view, however, whether that disqualifies the trustee from being given legal personhood status depends in part on the purpose of punishment. *Id.*, at 1245–7.

[6] Shawn Bayern, *The Implications of Modern Business-Entity Law for the Regulation of Autonomous Systems*, 19 STAN. TECH. L. REV. 93, 101–2 (2015). Bayern suggests the following transactional steps. An individual forms a one member, member managed limited liability company. The individual enters into an operating agreement whereby the business decisions of the LLC would be determined by an autonomous system. The sole member then disassociates from the limited liability company. Since in Bayern's view some limited liability company statutes do not require the dissolution of the company when the sole member disassociates, the entity run by the autonomous system would have perpetual legal existence. *See also* Shawn Bayern et al., *Company Law and Autonomous Systems: A Blueprint for Lawyers, Entrepreneurs, and Regulators*, 9 HASTINGS SCI. TECH. L. REV. 135 (2017) (discussing the possibility of using business entity law in the United States, Germany, Switzerland, and the United Kingdom to make it so that the actions of an autonomous system become the actions of a legal person).

used to determine when the same action is subject to legal sanctions and when it is not.[7] They also contend it is a category mistake to equate legal responsibility with moral responsibility—there is no need, in their view, to satisfy all the criteria for holding a robot morally responsible for something before it can be found legally responsible.[8]

Some remarks by Mireille Hildebrandt are interesting in this regard. Hildebrandt agrees with scholars such as Chopra and White that granting legal personhood to a robot has less to do with recognizing something innate in the machine than it does with the consequences that follow from granting such status.[9] She argues that "moral agency is not necessarily the golden standard of personhood; if entities without such agency cause damage or harm it may be expedient and even justified to hold them accountable."[10] For Hildebrandt, what warrants granting legal personhood is fairness to injured parties and to other perpetrators: "The justification would reside in the ensuing obligation to compensate the damage or to contribute to the mitigation of the harm (justice done to the victim), but also *in the fairness of the distribution of liability* (justice in relation to other offenders)."[11] This argument suggests that current forms of associative responsibility and their distribution among members of groups might not be able to adequately address situations when harm results from humans and machines working together, unless some kind of status is given to the machines themselves.

Yet granting legal status does not solve all ethical issues, and might raise others. For example, consider the proposal just discussed that autonomous machines be funded to compensate for damages they cause. Unless autonomous machines are allowed to generate and retain their own income (perhaps in the form of a quasiproperty right enjoyed by such machines), the funds used to satisfy third party claims would necessarily come from a human or some entity or group in which humans are a part.[12] Of course, if that entity is a corpor-

---

[7]   Chopra and White, *supra* note 2, at 146.

[8]   *Id.*, at 147.

[9]   Mireille Hildebrandt, *From Galatea 2.2 to Watson—And Back?*, in HUMAN LAW AND COMPUTER LAW: COMPARATIVE PERSPECTIVES 23, 38 (Mireille Hildebrandt and Jeanne Gaakeer eds. 2013).

[10]   *Id.*

[11]   *Id.* (Emphasis added.)

[12]   Belia argues against granting legal personhood to bots. In his view, protections such as requiring bots to be insured or to have them be capitalized all indicate that someone else, not the bot, is actually responsible. Thus, it is superfluous to grant personhood. "To argue that an electronic agent should be deemed a 'person' is to miss the point that electronic agents present simply another mode by which natural persons can conduct their business". Anthony J. Belia, *Contracting with Electronic Agents*, 50 EMORY L. J. 1047, 1067 (2001).

ation, it could be argued that although shareholders would see less dividends from the dispersal of funds, it is not inappropriate that ultimate responsibility should rest with them, since they benefit from the corporation's use of the machine. Once we use this kind of reasoning, however, we acknowledge that there is a distributional issue at stake.

It is not in the province of this book to revisit the issue of granting legal personhood to entities. But it should be noted that the grant of legal personhood not only subjects the entity in question to responsibility, but shields others from it. This of course has its benefits: limited liability for shareholders is thought to encourage investment. At the same time, as Wolgast argues, that shield might also have the effect of dissolving responsibility. Recall from Chapter 6 that Wolgast explores ethical issues raised by entities such as business organizations, militaries, and governments. Her major argument is that when a person acts through a legal construction such as an agency or a corporation, she departs from the model of the paradigmatic responsible human individual who acts after deliberating and furthermore robs herself of essential moral information that only comes from experiencing what it is like to actually engage in the act. [13]

For this reason Wolgast is critical of the legal fictions that underlie agency theory (under the law, an agent's act is the principal's act). In her view, from the perspective of moral responsibility, responsibility cannot be so easily assigned: the person who acts on another's behalf is herself a free person subject to the requirements of ethical behavior. "[M]oral responsibility can't be so easily passed around, can't be held and transferred like a proxy, or treated as the legal fiction of agency and the artificial person require."[14] She continues: "Where an agent enters the picture the paradigm gets fractured. One person deliberates but doesn't confront the reality of acting; while another person confronts the circumstances and acts, but hasn't made the choice."[15] Thus, neither the agent nor the principal are autonomous in the classic sense of deliberation and action. "[N]either has an autonomous person's view of the thing he participates in, and neither has the control that an autonomous person is supposed to have."[16] Wolgast reasons that neither person has acted in the strict sense of the paradigm, and thus "in the paradigmatic sense neither is responsible for it."[17]

One could argue that Wolgast's analysis proves too much: we engage in cooperative behaviors all the time, some of them involving asking others to

---

[13] Elizabeth Wolgast, ETHICS OF AN ARTIFICIAL PERSON: LOST RESPONSIBILITY IN PROFESSIONS AND ORGANIZATIONS 73 (1992).

[14] *Id.*, at 61.

[15] *Id.*, at 66.

[16] *Id.*, at 66–7.

[17] *Id.*, at 67.

act on our behalf. But Wolgast's ethical analysis leads her to question whether we should give even legal status to entities that cannot fit the paradigm of a deliberative individual capable of experiencing the moral implications of her actions. She asks: "[H]ow can corporations take their place beside humans in a community as anything other than amoral beings who live side by side with non-fictional, morally responsible persons?"[18] With regard to that particular entity, much of the answer lies in how we conceive of the corporation. Wolgast suggests, for example, that the corporation can be understood as a machine for making money—an intermediary between the shareholders and goods, services, and markets that enable the corporation to maximize returns on the shareholder's capital.[19] But if this is all they are—machines—then according to Wolgast it does not make sense to regard them as persons, even in the thin legal sense.[20] Wolgast then criticizes attempts, in particular Peter French's, to characterize the corporation as a person, with intentions, the capacity to plan, and so on. She concludes that "it is implausible to treat a corporation as a member of the human community, a member with a personality (but not a face), intentions (but no feelings), relationships (but no family or friends), responsibility (but no conscience), susceptibility to punishment (but no capacity for pain)."[21]

Of course, notwithstanding Wolgast's critique, the issue of legal personhood for corporations and other businesses has long been settled on the domestic level. But her concerns are still alive on the international level. It is still an open issue in international law whether a corporation should be considered a subject of international law. The pull toward granting such status comes out of a recognition that large multinational enterprises can have international impacts and therefore should be held responsible for breaches of international law, particularly when their activities are beyond the reach of any one country's law. In international law, it goes without saying that the actors that make up the international community are for the most part artificial persons as well, with no faces, feelings, family, or friends, and no conscience or direct capacity for pain. But one of the reasons for hesitating to give multinational enterprises such status is the unanswered question whether those international legal responsibilities must be accompanied by international legal rights. Given that some companies have a valuation greater than the gross domestic product of some countries, what would be the implications of giving large firms a seat at the table at multilateral organizations such as the United Nations? We find

---

[18] *Id.*, at 81.
[19] *Id.*, at 80–81.
[20] *Id.*, at 81.
[21] *Id.*, at 86.

both types of reasoning, as well as others, used in the debate as to whether autonomous technologies should be given legal rights.

LEGAL RIGHTS AND MORAL CONSIDERATION FOR MACHINES

A combination of pragmatics and ethical quandaries about attributing responsibility by association to humans could lead to the "solution" of granting legal status to autonomous machines. As just discussed, the question then becomes whether such machines should be granted legal rights in addition to duties. This is part of an even broader debate: whether autonomous technologies should be extended moral consideration or moral patiency. The debate is remarkable in several respects. One is that it exists at all. Most of us do not think of machines as enjoying rights. Another is that it highlights some of the conceptual difficulties that underlie the issue. On the one hand, conferring rights on machines would seem to confirm a positivistic, constructive understanding of rights. This raises the issue of whether such rights can then be taken away. On the other hand, proponents of inherent rights argue that truly autonomous machines must possess some quality, such as intelligence or cognition, that they share with humans, who enjoy rights *in se*. However, this raises the problem of essentialism: identifying what makes human beings rights-bearing persons. Assuming this quality can be identified, the issue arises of whether rights should be given to all entities that share it.[22] At that point, the question of legal rights begins to edge into a broader debate as to whether autonomous technologies, particularly the most advanced ones, should be given moral consideration.

It is impossible to do justice to the nuances of what is becoming an extensive literature on these issues. This section will sketch out the lines of various arguments. At the outset, it can be said that, just as with granting legal personhood to artificial agents, granting legal rights does not raise the same metaphysical problems that arise when considering moral patiency. But as will be seen below, the structure of the legal and moral arguments concerning rights and patiency are quite similar. My ultimate argument is that although there are valid arguments why artificial agents should not be given legal rights or moral consideration, there are sufficient nontrivial arguments for doing the exact opposite that, particularly given the propensity for anthropomorphism, it would not be surprising if in the future we grant machines and systems with high levels of intelligence such rights and consideration.

---

[22] For a discussion of these problems, *see* Solum, *supra* note 5, at 1262–74.

ONTOLOGY, LEGAL RIGHTS, AND MORAL CONSIDERATION

I begin with some arguments being made in favor of granting autonomous technologies legal rights. Migle Laukyte uses the group agent as a paradigm for artificial agents and argues that such agents share important characteristics with group agents, thus meriting legal rights.[23] For him, group agents such as the corporation can be said to be rational, interactive with other agents, and responsible, and share the characteristics of personhood. Following Dennett's intentional stance, discussed in Chapter 8, group agents can act rationally in the sense that we can view group agents as if they were rational: it is not non-sensical that we often describe group agents like corporations acting in ways to meet their goals. For Laukyte, the same will be true of artificial agents.[24] Group agents engage with one another, and artificial agents will be designed to do so as well.[25] Laukyte believes that like group agents, truly autonomous artificial agents will recognize that they are in morally charged situations, deliberate about particular actions, and have some degree of control over those actions.[26] They will have aspects of personhood too. Here, the author relies on List and Petit's concept of a person as one who is capable of acting autonomously in the physical and social world.[27] Artificial agents will be manufactured to do exactly this. Further, an artificial agent that is capable of forming its own goals and acting to meet them will be autonomous.[28]

Laukyte continues by providing some content for machine rights. He uses Rawls's concept of enabling rights and argues that artificial agents should be given rights that enable them to act within their competences.[29] This implies that the scope of rights will increase with the increasing competence of the artificial agent. "[T]he broader we make the capacities worthy of protection and so the broader we make the enabling rights supportive of those capacities," he reasons, "the more we set the subjects of those rights (the agents recognized as rightsholders) on an equal footing, in that agents with equal capacities are assumed to have equal rights."[30]

---

[23] Migle Laukyte, *Artificial Agents among Us: Should We Recognize Them as Agents Proper?* 19 Ethics & Info. Tech. 1 (2017).

[24] *Id.*, at 3.

[25] *Id.*, at 3–4.

[26] *Id.*, at 7.

[27] *Id.*, at 8.

[28] *Id.*, at 12.

[29] *Id.*, at 13–14.

[30] *Id.*, at 14.

Notice that Laukyte's case for rights compares autonomous technologies favorably with other agents (in this case a group agent) that enjoy legal rights now, and concludes that such rights can and should be given to those technologies as well. At the other end of the debate, however, Lantz Miller uses a similar argumentative structure to conclude it would be morally justifiable not to give autonomous machines and systems full human rights.[31] Instead of groups, Miller focuses on human beings as rightsbearers and argues there is a significant ontological difference between human beings and automata. Miller uses another concept from Rawls: the comprehensive world view. Although a liberal society must make room for different comprehensive world views that individuals might use to explain and give meaning to themselves and to others, liberal society itself sees the individual as separate and apart from any comprehensive world view, including any purpose or function that individual might fulfill. As a result, for Miller, ontologically the individual has existential normative neutrality.[32] It is to such individuals that rights are given as members in a liberal society, rights that are also independent of any morals that might arise from a particular comprehensive world view.

Automata are ontologically different from humans, according to Laukyte. In contrast to human beings, they do not just come into existence: automata are made, and usually made for a purpose. As such, liberal society need not treat them as givens; they can be appropriately treated through comprehensive world views and the moral systems informed by them:

> [A]utomata's coming into being is an action which human agents may or may not instigate, just as they can steal or not. This action thereby falls into the scope of morality. I propose this ontological difference in moral status lays sufficient foundation for determining whether humans have a morally sound grounding for denying maximally humanlike automata full human rights. They, as potential rights-granters, can even say 'We do not want any entities of type X constructed such that, if they were constructed, they would appear to merit human rights because they have some humanlike traits. They will not suffer if they are not constructed. If constructed, they would be of a different ontological type from us, and we would be under no moral obligation to let them join our society fully.'[33]

That autonomous technologies are constructed also informs Harold Carrier's and Joanna Bryson's respective positions that artificial intelligence should not

---

[31]   Lantz Fleming Miller, *Granting Automata Human Rights: Challenge to a Basis of Full Rights Privilege*, 16 HUM. RTS. REV. 369 (2015).

[32]   *Id.*, at 378.

[33]   *Id.*, at 378–9.

be given moral consideration. Like Chew, for Carrier, artificial intelligence is in the end a tool, not an intelligence:

> As a microscope has extended our ability to see substructures of life, perhaps machine intelligence can extend our notion of cognition and human thought processes. But presently it would be a mistake to posit a microscope as a specialized type of eye as it is to posit machine intelligence as cognition.[34]

Bryson agrees that what she terms intelligent systems remain human artifacts and hence have no independent claims to moral patiency.[35] Similar to Miller's understanding of the liberal society, Bryson argues that ethics and intelligent systems are human constructs. Thus, there is no a priori requirement that we give moral status to intelligent systems.[36] Bryson believes our current system of ethics resulted from the evolution of the human species through which proper measures of selfish and altruistic behaviors within individuals in early human societies were selected to maximize the production of public goods. In her view, two criteria for any resulting ethical system are, first, how well it defines the boundaries of a society and, second, that it be minimally disruptive.[37] Granting moral patiency to intelligent systems would fail either test. In Bryson's view, we have little to gain from granting them this status. We open ourselves to a very different society, and giving moral patiency to autonomous systems is more likely than not to be disruptive of our existing ethical systems.[38] For Bryson, from the human perspective, the strongest argument for giving intelligent systems moral status is to make them easier to control, but this would have the effect of removing human owners and users of artificial intelligence from responsibility. This is not worth the trade-off in her view.[39] And from the perspective of autonomous machines and systems itself, we are still in a position where we can decide not to design those systems to have a sense of social status or purpose.[40]

---

[34] Harold D. Carrier, *Artificial Intelligence and Metaphor Making: Some Philosophic Considerations*, 12 KNOWLEDGE, TECH. & POL'Y 45, 58 (1999).

[35] Joanna J. Bryson, *Patiency Is Not a Virtue: The Design of Intelligent Systems and Systems of Ethics*, 20 ETHICS & INFO. TECH. 15 (2018).

[36] *Id.*, at 15. Fabio Fossa concurs. He argues: "No matter how 'autonomous' or powerful, moral machines are tools, and tools cannot display forms of human-like moral experience since they lack purpose-setting and value-setting agency ..." Fabio Fossa, *Artificial Moral Agents: Moral Mentors or Sensible Tools?* 20 ETHICS & INFO. TECH. 115, 124 (2018).

[37] Bryson, *supra* note 35, at 16.

[38] *Id.*, at 19.

[39] *Id.*, at 22.

[40] *Id.*, at 22–3.

There are at least two responses to arguments like Miller's and Bryson's. With regard to ontology, one question is, as intelligent systems become more sophisticated, whether the distinctions between a being that exists in itself and one that is constructed or constructed for a purpose and between artificer and artifact will hold. To return to Miller's concept of existential normative neutrality, from the perspective of the automata, would it not be the case that they would view themselves as having come into being? Suppose I am a highly sophisticated automaton that possesses the machine equivalent of consciousness (discussed below). When activated, I experience the machine equivalent of awareness of myself. When I ask my human owner or user for the reason for my existence, I am told that I was designed to perform function X. If I have a high degree of intelligence and know that I could perform any number of other functions, would I be satisfied with an explanation that I was constructed, and that I was constructed to perform function X as the reason for my being?[41] Such an explanation might or might not be sufficient. To be sure, both Miller and Bryson seek to avoid issues exactly like this by arguing that it is unnecessary, perhaps immoral, to design autonomous machines and systems with this level of sophistication. But there might be legitimate reasons to do so. For example, Pepperell argues that a machine with consciousness will be better able to operate in a complex reality than one without it.[42]

Further, the position taken by Miller and Bryson is that under their respective frameworks, human beings are not required to grant autonomous technologies human rights or moral consideration, respectively, but as each is a social construct, neither system prohibits humans from deciding to grant such rights and consideration to such technologies either. As discussed, Bryson argues that one reason why it would be unwise to do this is that we would be shielding human beings from responsibility. At the same time, as discussed throughout this chapter, there are plausible arguments that point the other way.

---

[41]   In this regard, Miller seems to believe that "merely to construct an entity" is enough to create the ontological difference. Miller, *supra* note 31, at 384.

[42]   Robert Pepperell, *Applications for Conscious Systems*, 22 AI & Soc'y 45, 49 (2007). (*Citing* Igor Alexander, How to Build a Mind: Towards Machines with Imagination (2001).) Bostrom also responds to arguments that many of these problems could be avoided if we design artificial intelligences so that they are largely tools. He concedes that we have little difficulty responding to and regulating tools. However, Bostrom argues that even if we start by developing systems that can be used as tools in just one setting, there will be strong incentives to develop autonomous technologies with general intelligence. It is costly to design systems that are suited for only one purpose. Moreover, purposes change over time: it would be wasteful to design a machine to be used for a particular purpose, when those goals could be obsolete or no longer fashionable. Nick Bostrom, Superintelligence: Paths, Dangers, Strategies 184–5 (paperback edn. 2016).

CONSCIOUSNESS AND PAIN

In Chapter 8, I discussed research being carried out to determine whether autonomous technologies can be influenced by utility curves and to create internal states that constitute the machine equivalent of emotions. Some of these efforts are directed to making autonomous technologies more pliable and susceptible to punishment that we would recognize as such, thus ensuring that machines and systems will engage in prosocial behaviors and making it more acceptable for autonomous technologies to be judged primarily responsible for a harm and to therefore bear the consequences for it. Such efforts raise the question whether artificial intelligence will ever achieve consciousness. Some commentators argue that if an artificial agent can experience itself as a self, as well as experiencing its environment, it follows that it merits moral consideration. However, like other attempts to identify something core to an entity that merits moral patiency, consciousness is a fraught concept. Some argue that consciousness can be explained through physical or computational principles while others argue it is beyond such explanations. Consciousness also has a paradoxical aspect to it. We each have a personal experience of consciousness: adults learning a new language can have "in mind" the word for "water" before we speak it; we experience a sunset; and we have a sense of being a self. Yet, we see almost no external evidence that those around us have these same experiences. Since we would not deny that others have consciousness, would we deny that autonomous technologies that behave as if they are conscious have such consciousness?

Among those who do not believe that consciousness is capable of explanation by our current science is Roger Penrose, who is informed by an insight from Kurt Gödel's incompleteness theorem.[43] Although the theorem is often thought of as showing that any formal system relies on propositions not supported by that system, Penrose emphasizes that the theorem also demonstrates there are true statements that cannot be proven through the equivalent of algorithmic procedures.[44] He argues that in recognizing the truth of the theorem, we do so in a way that is nonalgorithmic, thus revealing something about consciousness:

> We must 'see' the truth of a mathematical argument to be convinced of its validity. This 'seeing' is the very essence of consciousness. It must be present *whenever* we directly perceive mathematical truth. When we convince ourselves of the

---

[43]   Roger Penrose, THE EMPEROR'S NEW MIND: CONCERNING COMPUTERS, MINDS, AND THE LAWS OF PHYSICS (rev edn. 2016).

[44]   *Id.*, at 143.

validity of Gödel's theorem we not only 'see' it, but by doing so we reveal the very non-algorithmic nature of the 'seeing' process itself.[45]

Jack Fletcher makes a similar Gödel-like argument based on noncomputability. For him, it is not possible for a computational system (a Turing machine) to verify that it has a sense of self. The intuitive idea is that a scale cannot measure itself. Fletcher equates a sense of self with a proposed emulation of the mind. To confirm that it does, in fact, have an emulation of itself, a Turing machine would need to determine whether two Turing machines (itself and the proposed emulation) are functionally equivalent.[46] Such a task is noncomputable.[47]

In contrast to Penrose and Fletcher, other scholars, particularly those informed by neuroscience, have developed theories of consciousness that fall within our current understanding of physics and do not raise issues of computability. If correct, the integrated information theory proposed by Guilio Tononi appears amenable to the development of machine consciousness.[48] In a 2012 article, Tononi explains that the general ideas underlying the theory are illustrated via three thought experiments. In the first, a human and a photodiode (a semiconductor that converts light into electric current) are facing a blank screen that flashes on and off. For the diode, the screen generates only one bit of information, "light" or "dark," with only one consequence, to generate current or not. In contrast, for the human, the screen produces much more information because we are able to distinguish not only light from dark, but light from an almost endless number of possibilities: "a red screen, a green screen, this movie frame, a sound, a different sound, a thought, another thought and so on," each possibility having its own set of consequences.[49] The more differences one is able to detect, the more information is provided, and vice versa.[50] Thus "[f]rom the intrinsic perspective of a system ... information can best be defined as a 'difference that makes a difference': the more alternatives (differences) can be distinguished, to the extent they lead to distinguishable consequences (make a difference), the greater the information."[51]

---

[45]   *Id.*, at 540–41.

[46]   Jack McKay Fletcher, *A Computational Mind Cannot Recognize Itself*, 13 TECHNOETIC ARTS 261 (2015).

[47]   *Id.*, at 254.

[48]   Giulio Tononi, *Integrated Information Theory of Consciousness: an Updated Account*, 150 ARCHIVES ITALIENNES DE BIOLOGIE 293 (2012).

[49]   *Id.*, at 294.

[50]   *Id.*, at 294–5.

[51]   *Id.*, at 294.

Consciousness, however, is more than information. In the second thought experiment, Tononi compares the human with a megapixel camera. If the camera's sensor chip has a million binary photodiodes, it can distinguish about 21 million alternative states: 1 million bits of information. However, the camera lacks consciousness in part because it cannot integrate this information: each photodiode is essentially acting independently of the others.[52] For the human, however, each experience is an "integrated whole, one that means what it means by virtue of being one, and which is experienced from a single point of view."[53] Experientially, these integrated experiences cannot be broken down into components, Tononi continues: "[N]o matter how hard I try, experiencing the full visual field cannot be reduced into experiencing separately the left half and the right half. No matter how hard I try, I cannot reduce the experience of a red apple into the separate experience of its color and its shape."[54]

Finally, Tononi notes that the internet does allow for integration in that routers permit any web address in the network to connect with another address. This allows for the exchange of messages from any one point in the net to another and for broadcasting to many points in the network. However, Tononi argues that the internet, although integrated, is not conscious because it is not designed to achieve a "maxima of integrated information."[55] Instead, it is designed precisely to allow for point to point communication. Were it to engage in more general integration, point to point communication would no longer be possible because of the crosstalk that would be occurring among the nodes. The human brain, however, has evolved to allow for maximal integration of experiences and placing them in context.[56] The cost, though, is that such maximal integration does not permit humans to experience, as it were, the processes that are being integrated:

> I cannot become conscious of what is going on within the modules in my brain that perform language parsing: I hear and understand an English sentence, but I have no conscious access to how the relevant part[s] of my brain are achieving this computation, although of course they must be connected to those other parts that give rise to my present consciousness.[57]

---

[52]   *Id.*, at 295.

[53]   *Id.*

[54]   *Id. See also* Luciano Floridi, *Open Problems in the Philosophy of Information* 35 METAPHILOSOPHY 554, 569 (2004) ("Strictly speaking, we do not consciously cognize pure meaningless data").

[55]   Tononi, *supra* note 49, at 295. (Emphasis removed.)

[56]   *Id.*, at 296.

[57]   *Id.*

The concepts of information are correlated with the amount of consequential differences one can detect, and maximal integration of that information translates into a number of axioms that can be expressed formally.[58] For the purposes of this chapter, however, what is interesting is that in an earlier work, Tononi suggested that in theory, physical systems could be designed to have these abilities, thus consciousness. "A physical system should be able to generate consciousness to the extent it has a large repertoire of available states (information), yet it cannot be decomposed into a collection of causally independent subsystems (integration)."[59] We might well want to design at least some autonomous machines and systems that have this integrative power. If Tononi is correct, then by definition we will be creating technologies with consciousness.

Integrated information theory is not the only account of consciousness that might be applied to artificial intelligence. Bernard Baars has developed a theory of consciousness known as global workspace theory.[60] Baars uses the analogy of the brain as a theater. Consciousness is the bright spot on the stage of immediate memory, the audience being other parts of the brain.[61] "This is the primary function of consciousness: to allow a theatre architecture to operate in the brain, in order to integrate, provide access, and coordinate the functioning of very large numbers of specialized networks that otherwise operate autonomously."[62] Stephen Jones uses Baar's architecture as part of his argument that artificial consciousness could evolve out of genetic algorithms.[63]

Part of the debate about artificial consciousness stems from its private and subjective aspects. This revolves around what kinds of consciousness an agent might have and how an observer could confirm that consciousness. On this point, Selmer Bringsjord notes that in the philosophy of mind there are three, albeit ill-defined, types of consciousness. The first is access consciousness, having representations used to control behavior or speech. The second is phenomenal consciousness, "feeling" pain and having thoughts and emotions.

---

[58] *Id.*, at 296–308.

[59] Giulio Tononi, *An Information Integration Theory of Consciousness*, 5 BMC NEUROSCIENCE 43, 44 (2004).

[60] Bernard J. Baars, *Global Workspace Theory of Consciousness: Toward a Cognitive Neuroscience of Human Experience?* in 150 PROGRESS IN BRAIN RES.: THE BOUNDARIES OF CONSCIOUSNESS: NEUROBIOLOGY AND NEUROPATHOLOGY 45 (Steven Laureys ed. 2005); Bernard J. Baars, IN THE THEATRE OF CONSCIOUSNESS: THE WORKSPACE OF THE MIND (1997).

[61] Baars, *id.*, at 46–7.

[62] *Id.*, at 48.

[63] Stephen Jones, *On the Evolution of Artificial Consciousness: Re-Inventing the Wheel, Re: Inventing the Wheel*, 2 TECHNOETIC ARTS 45 (2004).

Finally, there is self-consciousness, having a sense of the self.[64] Bringsjord
uses symbolic logic to sketch out an argument that artificial intelligence can
achieve access consciousness,[65] but he argues that artificial intelligence will
not be able to achieve phenomenal or (like Fletcher) self-consciousness.[66] In
his view, it is possible that "the universe will be populated by computational
creatures whose external behavior includes anything and everything within
our own repertoire," but they might still be without phenomenal consciousness
or self-consciousness.[67] However, other scholars believe that artificial agents
could gain greater levels of consciousness. Murat Aydede and Güven Güzelder
argue that it is possible for artificial intelligence to have at least some phenomenal consciousness.[68] The authors contend that our conscious experience
of something like the color purple simply provides us with a different way
of relating to or knowing about the same color, about which we also come to
know through learning about the physics of that color (for example, its wave-
length).[69] The implication is that just as the physics of color can be formalized,
so too the mechanism of sensing color could be formalized and therefore
programmed. Note, however, that consciousness of a flower seems to be more
like phenomenal consciousness; it is unclear whether this model could be used
to explain how self-consciousness could be attained.

As to how we could tell whether an artificial machine or system is conscious,
this returns us to a question asked at the beginning of this subsection: whether
it matters if we can verify that an autonomous machine or system has consciousness in the same sense as we do. This in turn brings us back to the Turing
test. One could argue that the test is essentially pragmatic: it should not matter
to us whether the entity we are observing is a human being or a computer if we
cannot tell the difference. It might not matter whether machines can achieve
consciousness if for all intents and purposes the machines appear conscious to
us. As Jones puts it, "Perhaps we can only trust as we do with each other, in

---

[64] Selmer Bringsjord, *Meeting Floridi's Challenge to Artificial Intelligence from
the Knowledge-Game Test for Self-Consiousness*, 41 Metaphilosophy 292, 293–4
(2010). (*Citing* Ned Block, *On a Confusion About a Function of Consciousness*, 20
Behavioral & Brain Sci. 227, 231 (1995); L. Floridi, *Consciousness, Agents and the
Knowledge Game*, 15 Minds & Machines 415 (2005).) He does this by showing how
artificial intelligence could correctly respond to a series of tests created by Floridi that
would demonstrate if an agent had access consciousness.
[65] *Id.*, at 302–5.
[66] *Id.*, at 309.
[67] *Id.*, at 309.
[68] Murat Aydede and Güven Güzelder, *Consciousness, Intentionality and
Intelligence: Some Foundational Issues for Artificial Intelligence*, 12 J. Experimental
& Theoretical Artificial Intelligence 263 (2010).
[69] *Id.*, at 271.

that the Turing test really only requires that an AI be able, by its behaviour, its free interaction with us, to convince us that it is in fact conscious."[70] But the objection is that it matters very much if we are deciding whether to give some sort of moral status to a robot. If a robot does not feel pain or the equivalent of distress, then we might have no qualms ascribing lesser status to what seems otherwise to be exactly like a human individual. We humans will "know" that machines are not equivalent to humans; therefore we need never worry about their moral status. This argument, however, raises issues about how our treatment of artificial intelligences might affect the way we treat ourselves.

EFFECTS ON HUMANS

Kant argues that animals are not in themselves moral agents because they lack the necessary rationality. Nevertheless, he contends that they are deserving of moral consideration because of the effect the treatment of animals has on humans.[71] Several commentators have used this form of reasoning for according some moral consideration to autonomous technologies, sometimes alone and at other times in conjunction with other arguments.

Kate Darling, for example, is influenced by the Kantian approach as she gives reasons for granting some protections to robots.[72] Her particular interest is in robots that will be designed to interact socially with humans, such as care robots. Such robots might be designed to be lifelike, to make them more acceptable, and Darling is concerned that the treatment of lifelike robots will impact our treatment of humans.[73] She acknowledges that some will want to draw a line between beings which have sentience and other qualities and beings which do not, but she contends that protections for robots should be granted as soon as we begin to recognize that the treatment of robots is starting to affect the way we treat other people.[74]

---

[70] Jones, *supra* note 63, at 52.

[71] Immanuel Kant, THE METAPHYSICS OF MORALS (Mary Gregor trans. and Lara Denis ed. 2017) (1797) He argues: "violent and cruel treatment of animals is far more intimately opposed to a human being's duty to himself, and he has a duty to refrain from this; for it dulls his shared feeling of their suffering and so weakens and gradually uproots a natural disposition that is very serviceable to morality in one's relations with other human beings." *Id.*, at 207 [6:443].

[72] Kate Darling, *Extending Legal Protection to Robots: The Effects of Anthropomorphism, Empathy, and Violent Behavior towards Robotic Objects*, in ROBOT LAW 213 (Ryan Calo, A. Michael Froomkin, and Ian Kerr eds. 2016) [hereinafter *Extending Legal Protection to Robots* and ROBOT LAW].

[73] *Id.*, at 224.

[74] *Id.*, at 231.

Michael LaBossiere also suggests an approach that focuses on the functionality of artificial intelligence and on the effect that human treatment of artificial intelligence will have on ourselves. He points out that there will be artificial intelligences of varying capacity,[75] and he proposes we respond to that variance in much the same way that we respond to animals, according to their abilities. This requires some way of accurately "matching" the robot's abilities with those of beings with which we are already familiar.[76] LaBossiere reviews possible tests which humans might use to assess an artificial intelligence's capacity for reasoning and for feeling. He then proposes we give artificial intelligences a presumption of status.[77] For him, it is "morally preferable to treating a being better than its status justifies rather than to treat it worse." He gives utilitarian, probabilistic, and ersatz justifications for this preference. The last justification is based on the Kantian approach:[78] "[T]he way humans treat animals has a psychological impact that influences how humans treat each other."[79] Such ersatz status, however, enables LaBoissier to avoid the problem of Sparrow's moral Turing test. Sparrow has doubts that artificial intelligence will ever achieve the required level of sophistication, but under the test, robots would merit full moral status only when they display properties such that it would be difficult to choose between the life of a human being and the existence of the robot.[80] For LaBoissier, "this ersatz moral status would make it wrong to harm or abuse artificial beings without adequate justification. For example, harming artificial beings for mere sport would be wrong."[81] At the same time, because of the ersatz status of artificial agents, natural beings would take precedence over artificial beings.

An approach that takes into account the effect that the treatment of autonomous systems will have on human beings, as opposed to the effects on the systems themselves, has at least three advantages. First, it avoids debates regarding why autonomous technologies merit moral patiency in themselves. Most importantly in my view, it acknowledges the ethical ramifications of cre-

---

[75]   Michael LaBossiere, *Testing the Moral Status of Artificial Beings: or "I'm going to ask you some questions..." in* ROBOT ETHICS 2.0: FROM AUTONOMOUS CARS TO ARTIFICIAL INTELLIGENCE 294 (Patrick Lin, Ryan Jenkins, and Keith Abney eds. 2017) [hereinafter ROBOT ETHICS 2.0].

[76]   *Id.*, at 294.

[77]   *Id.*, at 299.

[78]   *Id.*, at 301–2.

[79]   *Id.*, at 303.

[80]   Robert Sparrow, *The Turing Triage Test*, 6 ETHICS & INFO. TECH. 203 (2004), Robert Sparrow, *Can Machines BeB People? Reflections on the Turing Triage Test, in* ROBOT ETHICS: THE ETHICAL AND SOCIAL IMPLICATIONS OF ROBOTICS 301 (Patrick Lin et al. eds., 2012) [hereinafter ROBOT ETHICS 1.0].

[81]   *Id.*, at 304.

ating artificial intelligences that become more and more humanlike. We have already seen older concepts of hierarchy and status being used to frame the problem: intelligent machines should not be given rights because machines are like animals or children, beings with diminished capacities who do not enjoy the full rights of adult humans for that reason.[82] Commentators have also used slave law to discuss how human "masters" might be held responsible for the actions of robot "slaves"[83] and to discuss why autonomous machines should not enjoy the same rights as humans.[84] We could ask ourselves whether we want to return to this kind of discourse.

Recall the demonstration of Google Duplex making an appointment on behalf of a client. When we listen to the interaction between the computer program and the receptionist at the hair salon, we of course are far more focused on the chat bot because of the novelty of the situation, how lifelike the computer program sounds and how it responds to the questions and remarks of the receptionist, and so on. We might also be concerned about whether the receptionist is being manipulated. The receptionist acted as if she were dealing with another human being and responded to the program with the kind of courtesy and respect one normally expects in such an everyday encounter. To use Strawsian terms, there were expectations of what constituted a normal interaction among individuals who assume that they will be treated with regard. The receptionist expected to be treated with respect, she received signals from the machine that she was, and she responded accordingly. The problem, of course, is that she did not realize she was interacting with a machine.

Consider what might have happened if the receptionist had been informed that there was a machine on the line. In theory, the receptionist could have said things considered rude and insulting had they been said to a human being, but of course the machine would not have any sense of this. But two things arise here. First, assume that there were other humans present during the interaction and that they too knew that the receptionist was saying what would otherwise be insulting things to the computer. The question arises whether we want a world in which we permit insults as a matter of course even when it comes to autonomous machines, or whether we would rather have the receptionist interact with the machine as though it was an entity deserving of some modicum of courtesy.

---

[82] Peter M. Asaro, *A Body to Kick, but Still No Soul to Damn: Legal Perspectives on Robotics, in* ROBOT ETHICS 1.0, *supra* note 81, at 178.

[83] *See* Chopra and White, *supra* note 2, at 134; Patrick Lin et al., Ethics + Emerging Sciences Group, Autonomous Military Robotics: Risk, Ethics, and Design (2008), at 66, http://ethics.calpoly.edu/onr_report.pdf.

[84] Asaro, *supra* note 82, at 178; Solum, *supra* note 5, at 1279 (criticizing the slave analogy).

Second, what if the computer was designed to respond to insults as if it was subjectively offended by the receptionist's remarks, even though in reality it was simply mimicking what a human would do in a similar situation? This could be perfectly plausible because the program is designed to be a sort of administrative assistant for the human client. This would increase the social and emotional incentives to treat the machine as if it were indeed human, if anything, to keep contentious situations from escalating even if, from the perspective of the machine, the escalation is simulated. Further, the hair salon wants the client's business. The receptionist would not want the machine to "report" to the client that the receptionist had been "rude," even to a machine. Much of this, however, might be culturally specific. Perhaps in hierarchical or class-based societies, it might be considered normal to ill-treat people perceived to be in lower positions. However, just as we have the potential to inflict great harm on others, we are also biologically attuned to avoid inflicting pain one on one.[85] I suspect these considerations will lead to a time when we will accord common courtesies to artificial intelligences, which in part paves the way to eventually according them some moral status, even if ultimately we are not confident that such intelligences are selfconscious.

One could respond that these concerns are too inexact and create false equivalencies. Under this argument, we need not worry that our treatment of autonomous technologies will affect how we treat ourselves. In many circles, we have come to reject dehumanizing language when applied to human beings, language that was used to justify human slavery and other forms of oppression: we accept that there are no meaningful differences between people that would justify such oppression. Moreover, we no longer are persuaded by arguments that certain people place a different value on life than others do, or that they have different understandings of other concepts such as property, so that it is justified to take life or property. One might also argue that applying the term slavery to autonomous machines and systems that have yet to be developed is too facile and obscures the evil of human slavery that still persists in other forms. The use of such a term is needlessly inflammatory if, as will be the case until there are significant breakthroughs in artificial intelligence, there remain meaningful differences between humans and artificial agents. But although these differences are likely to remain for some time, in my view, the other arguments in this paragraph stem from an optimism about human progress that is justified in some circumstances and not in others. Darling's suggestion is a good one: that we pay careful attention to how our treatment of increasingly sophisticated machines and systems spills over into our treatment of ourselves.

---

[85] Joshua Greene, MORAL TRIBES: EMOTION, REASON, AND THE GAP BETWEEN US AND THEM 36–7 (2013).

THE CAPABILITIES APPROACH

So far, the discussion of whether autonomous technologies should be accorded legal rights and moral consideration has focused on the human being or legal constructs of entities operated by humans, or on how treating autonomous machines and systems might affect the way we treat ourselves. Some might accuse these approaches of being too anthropocentric. Perhaps it would be better conceptually and practically to view such technologies in themselves. The capabilities approach laid out by scholars such as Amartya Sen and Martha Nussbaum is interesting in this regard. Nussbaum in particular has extended this approach to animals; the issue is whether such an approach could be applied to autonomous technologies.

Under the human capabilities or capacities approach, the question for evaluation is whether a person has the opportunity to engage in what one would normally think of as a good life.[86] This involves ensuring not only political and civil liberties, but also access to resources and knowledge that allow a person to function in the world as a full human being.[87] Nussbaum has been unapologetic in claiming that there are certain functions, such as reason, that distinguish human life from animal life. She is particularly interested in "the level at which a person's capability is 'truly human,' that is *worthy* of a human being."[88] Nussbaum believes "we can produce an account of these necessary elements of truly human functioning that commands a broad cross-cultural consensus, a list that can be endorsed for political purposes by people who otherwise would have very different views of what a complete good life for a human being would be."[89] Such a list likely includes life; bodily health; bodily integrity; use of senses, imagination, and thought; emotions; practi-

---

[86]   Nussbaum's framework conceives of the human being as "a dignified free being who shapes his or her own life, rather than [is] passively shaped or pushed around by the world in the manner of a flock or herd animal." Martha Nussbaum, *Capabilities and Social Justice*, 4 INT'L STUD. REV. 123, 130 (2002) [hereinafter *Capabilities and Social Justice*].

[87]   *Id.*, at 132.

[88]   *Capabilities and Social Justice, supra* note 86, at 130. *See also* Martha C. Nussbaum, *Human Capabilities, Female Human Beings, reprinted in* GLOBAL JUSTICE: SEMINAL ESSAYS 495, 526 (Thomas Pogge and Darrel Moellendorf eds., 2008) (arguing "we do have in these areas of our common humanity sufficient overlap to sustain a general conversation, focusing on our common problems and prospects").

[89]   *Capabilities and Social Justice, supra* note 87, at 131. For further discussion of Nussbaum's concept of universals, *see* Sabina Alkire, VALUING FREEDOMS: SEN'S CAPABILITY APPROACH AND POVERTY REDUCTION 32–4 (2002).

cal reason; affiliations with others in relations of respect; to live with other species; and to have control over one's political and material environment.[90]

As mentioned, Nussbaum has extended the capabilities approach to apply to animals.[91] She argues that the concept of dignity needs to be expanded so that it encompasses not only the lives of human beings but also the lives of sentient creatures. As opposed to Kant's view, for Nussbaum such dignity derives from animals themselves, not from the duties humans owe to one another. Information about animals at the species level helps create capabilities lists appropriate for them:[92]

> The capabilities lists, suitably broadened, still contains the main items we should favor, but we should be attentive to the form of life of each species, and promote, for each, the opportunity to live and act according to that species' form of life. Although choice is favored wherever the creature has a capacity for choice, a focus on functioning (a kind of sensitive paternalism) will be more appropriate in this case than in the human case.[93]

What are the implications of the capabilities approach for autonomous machines? Nussbaum argues that the link between humans and animals, which makes it possible to use the capabilities approach with animals, is "[t]he self-maintaining and self-reproducing striving that characterizes all animal lives."[94] It is conceivable that intelligent systems will achieve levels of sophistication at which they can be said to be self-maintaining and self-reproducing. Indeed, it can be argued that some computer programs, such as computer viruses, already strive for existence. If this is the case, then cogent questions arise such as: what are the central capabilities that make up the "form of life" of an intelligent system? At a minimum, we would look at the list of human capabilities—life, health, integrity, senses, imagination and thought, emotion, practical reason, affiliation, care for other species, play, control over one's environment—and ask whether sophisticated machines have similar capabilities relevant to these aspects of existence. If so, these capabilities would be necessary for the dignity inherent in the "form of life" of the autonomous machine. For example, many autonomous systems will be designed to interact with other systems, sometimes to enhance each other's capacities and other

---

[90]   Martha C. Nussbaum, *Working with and for Animals: Getting the Theoretical Framework Right*, 94 Denver L. Rev. 609, 621–3 (2017) [hereinafter *Working with and for Animals*]. (Citation omitted.)

[91]   *Id.*; Martha C. Nussbaum, Creating Capabilities: The Human Development Approach (2011) [hereinafter Creating Capabilities].

[92]   Creating Capabilities, *id.*, at 161.

[93]   *Id.*, at 161–2.

[94]   *Working with and for Animals, supra* note 90, at 620.

times to police the other's actions. If human researchers working with much more sophisticated machines prevent them from interacting, will they thereby inappropriately deprive the machines of their ability to affiliate with one another?

It could be argued that the simplest forms of existing life are far more complex than the most sophisticated computers, a fact relevant to how we could treat artificial systems. It is impossible for humans to have regard for all life forms, hence Nussbaum's argument that we should give consideration to animals on the species level. But perhaps this is a justification based on necessity. Some traditions hold that we should be concerned with all sentient life, just as a culture might require someone to apologize to a tree before it is cut down. At the same time, it could be argued that such a view could lead to paralysis. One problem therefore is that the capabilities approach seems to call for a hierarchy, albeit through the framework of capabilities. This is because in our relationship with animals, we need to make paternalistic judgments about what constitutes the proper dignity of animals. As soon as we do that we run into the problem of under or overinclusion, and perhaps more egregious problems. We either have no idea of what it means to have the form of life of an animal, or we make such distinctions based on only what we can know, which is ourselves.

INFORMATION AS THE BASIS FOR MORAL PATIENCY

Floridi asks whether there is another attribute that might serve as the basis for moral consideration. He argues that when one views people, animals and other organisms, and computers at a high level of abstraction, all of them share the common attribute of being information objects, entities with packages of data structures and behaviors.[95] That might not be the only thing they are, but by virtue of their being information objects, as such they are deserving of some respect. This respect entails "the appreciation of the [moral patient's] intrinsic worth and the corresponding, uncoerced, arguably overridable disposition to treat the [moral patient] appropriately, if possible, according to this acknowledged worth."[96]

Under this view, human beings might have other attributes that are identified at lower levels of abstraction that require us to treat them with greater, perhaps almost unqualified levels of respect, but this does not mean humans

---

[95] Luciano Floridi, *On the Intrinsic Value of Information Objects and the Infosphere*, 4 ETHICS & INFO. TECH. 287, 288 (2002). Floridi and J.W. Sanders argue that data itself might have some intrinsic moral value. Luciano Floridi and J.W. Sanders, *On the Morality of Artificial Agents*, 14 MINDS & MACHINE 349, 371 (2004).

[96] *Id.*, at 292.

may treat other information objects arbitrarily. The result is a much broader but more nuanced way of approaching potential moral patients:

> Things have various degrees of intrinsic value and hence demand various levels of moral respect, from the low-level represented by an overridable, disinterested, appreciative and careful attention for the properties of an information object like a customer profile to the high-level, absolute respect for human dignity.[97]

At this level of abstraction, "harm" takes the form of information entropy, like tearing up a book. It is important to note, however, that Floridi does not intend that information objects be given absolute rights, so that the destruction of a piece of writing would be prohibited. As discussed, moral evaluation that takes place at a lower level of abstraction might justify such an act; at the same time, the theory would acknowledge that the book as information object does merit at least a minimal amount of moral patiency and that its destruction is a morally significant event.[98]

Floridi's approach would apply to autonomous technologies even in their current state of development because of their ontological status as information objects. Like the culture I described above that views all sentient and nonsentient life as having some moral status, this view requires a kind of mindfulness because we are now called to be aware that much of our current technology is deserving of a modicum of respect as we create, use, and eventually discard it. There might be good reasons to discard information, but those good reasons do not render the act morally insignificant. Further, in the unlikely event that moral evaluation at lower levels of abstraction does not yield good reasons for doing so, the approach suggests that we might at least need to delay destroying, for example, an autonomous vehicle. Finally, that an autonomous machine or system has the ontological status of information object does not of course answer all moral questions. The level of abstractions approach sets a floor for moral patiency. Under that approach, it might be that autonomous technologies will have qualities (such as cognition) that allow them to be equated with human beings or other entities at lower levels of abstraction. They might reach the point where they would pass Sparrow's moral Turing test.

AUTONOMOUS TECHNOLOGY AS THE SUPERVENING OTHER

The capabilities approach and the levels of abstraction approach to moral patiency share a common characteristic with others discussed earlier which

---

[97]   *Id.*, at 300.
[98]   *Id.*, at 302.

focus on the extent to which autonomous machines and systems can be equated to human beings. The common thread is the attempt to find some attribute or set of them that provides a basis for demanding moral respect. The concern about such approaches among some scholars is that they are essentializing: reducing potential moral patients into a set of characteristics (even an extended one such as Nussbaum's list of capacities) that always permits the exclusion of others.

David Gunkel explores an ethic based on concern for the other, drawn from a variety of scholars influenced by Emmanuel Levinas.[99] In this view, the machine is included among those others that demand moral consideration. For Gunkel, the question whether machines should be given moral consideration is not one that can ultimately be answered, but nevertheless one that should constantly be asked because of the light it sheds on our conceptions of ethics.[100] In his most recent work, he writes:

> [T]he Levinasian question is ... 'What does it take for something—another human person, an animal, a mere object, or a social robot—to supervene and be revealed as Other?' This *other question*—a question about others that is situated otherwise— comprises a more precise and properly altruistic inquiry. It is a mode of questioning that remains open, endlessly open, to others and other forms of otherness.[101]

In this conception of ethics, we already find ourselves in social relationships. In those relationships we recognize that there are others that appear to demand and require that we take them into account in our actions.

> [A]s we encounter and interact with others—whether they be other human persons, an animal, the natural environment, or a social robot—this other identity is first and foremost situated in relationship to us. Consequently, the question of social and moral status does not necessarily depend on what the other is in its essence but on how she/he/it (and the pronoun that comes to be deployed in this situation is not immaterial) supervenes before us and how we decide, in 'the face of the other' (to use Levinasian terminology), to respond.[102]

As is true with the Kantian approach, we need not ask what it is about autonomous technology itself that would require us to grant or recognize moral patiency to it. Instead, it might be the case that as autonomous technologies grow in sophistication and as they become an even greater part of our social existence and web of relationships, at some point we will have recognized that

---

[99]   David J. Gunkel, The Machine Question 177 (2012).

[100]   *Id.*, at 211.

[101]   David J. Gunkel, *The Other Question: Can and Should Robots Have Rights?* 20 Ethics & Inf. Tech. 87, 96 (2018). (Emphasis in original.)

[102]   *Id.*, at 96.

we are already treating them as the other to whom a response is demanded. To use the Humean distinction between is and ought, we will have already decided through this encounter that we ought to respond to the social robot by according it social and moral status before we begin to ask what the social robot is.

This approach has at least three implications. First, it suggests that we wait and see. We can imagine what it will be like to live among increasingly sophisticated technologies; we see such imagined futures in film and on television. We are also getting some hints of that future in the way people respond to currently existing technology. But it might be years before we find ourselves working with machines and systems with enough intelligence that they will appear to us as others in the Levinasian sense. This approach does not give much guidance as to whether we should design technologies with that kind of sophistication in the first place. Of course one could respond that it is not the purpose of this approach to give prospective guidance, and perhaps one of the implications of this view is that prospective guidance is not possible. But in any case, it does not appear to help to answer the questions about artificial intelligence that we are asking now.

A second point is that this approach does not guarantee what our response will be as highly sophisticated technologies become more prevalent. Unlikely as this may be, in theory, a machine or system might possess all of the capacities we have and more, and yet never supervene upon us as an other, even though it would qualify as a moral patient under other moral frameworks. Third, although this approach expands the list of candidates for those we would recognize as an other, we remain the gatekeepers of who merits moral patiency because we are the ones who must first recognize the other as such.

A final point can be made about what might occur in the far off future. Recall that Chapter 6 discussed the possibility that there will be extended agents that go beyond the human being and autonomous technology. In this regard, in her work on anthropomorphism and robots, Julie Carpenter makes the interesting point that gamers and others who spend a large amount of time with technology see the systems with which they interact not so much as an other, but rather as an extension of the self.[103] She notes that "[w]hen we view a technology as an extension of our physical and psychological selves, our relationship to the technology is immediately different than how we interact with some other tools, products, or machines."[104] This ties in well with Hansen's idea of extended agency. For the purposes of this chapter, it is worthwhile to remember that the fluidity of artificial intelligence means we

---

[103] Julie Carpenter, *The Existential Robot: Living with Robots May Teach Us to Be Better Humans*, 108 Issues, Sept. 2014, at 39, 41.

[104] *Id.*, at 40.

need not necessarily think of the intelligence as solely other or even wholly us. Intelligences can be our avatars. With respect to rights for such avatars, we would be in a twilight region where the reasons why we would give such entities legal status and rights emerge from a combination of ourselves and the autonomous system.

ANTHROPOMORPHISM

So far this chapter has discussed a number of arguments for and against granting autonomous technologies legal rights and moral consideration. As we have seen, these debates center around issues and concepts such as whether there are meaningful differences between humans and autonomous machines, the possibility (or impossibility) of machine consciousness, the effect of treating artificial agents in the way we treat each other, the possible capacities of autonomous technologies, artificial agents as information objects, and the artificial agent as supervening other.

The debate is unlikely to be resolved, in part because these issues involve unanswered, perhaps unanswerable, questions about ourselves and how we should treat each other. Further, we need more experience with autonomous technologies, particularly the most sophisticated of them, before we can begin to fully understand the scope of the problem and what appropriate responses to the problem might be. However, even though the debate remains open, and despite the concerns raised by some commentators about this tendency, in my view the propensity of humans to anthropomorphize machines and the efforts of some developers to encourage this impulse will likely tip the balance in favor of granting at least the most sophisticated technologies legal rights and moral consideration higher than those accorded to Floridi's information objects.

At the outset, it should be noted that Mashiro Mori argues there is a point at which the more a machine resembles a human, the less affinity humans feel toward it.[105] However, there are strong incentives to design autonomous technologies that display humanlike behavior. A major concern in industry is that, with the exception of early adopters, most people will be afraid to use radically new technology.[106] This fear can be overcome by adding features that make it easier for a human user to ascribe human attributes to the autonomous

---

[105] Masahiro Mori, *The Uncanny Valley*, IEEE ROBOTICS & AUTOMATION MAG. (Karl F. MacDoman and Norri Kageki trans.), June 2012, at 98, 99.

[106] Michael König and Lambert Neumayr, *User's Resistance towards Radical Innovations: The Case of the Self-Driving Car*, 44 TRANSP. RES. 42 (2017) (identifying concerns that autonomous vehicles are not yet safe enough).

device.[107] Another incentive to encourage anthropomorphism is to further the purpose of the devices themselves. Carpenter argues in this regard that robots designed for home use might need to have human attributes in order to operate effectively in a home's physical space.[108] Designing devices to mimic human attributes such as the human voice, emotions, and so on also can improve the human users' experience of new technologies, encouraging them to use the technology even more. [109]

Such designs take advantage of the human propensity to attribute human characteristics to other animals and to objects. This tendency has been described as being activated when a person tries to make sense of a new object by projecting his conception of the self onto it. This impulse can be strengthened by a felt need for social connection or a need to master a new situation by using familiar concepts.[110] Carpenter suggests it enables humans to communicate better with technology.[111] Coeckelbergh argues that we anthropomorphize robots as part of a hermeneutic through which we view robots as individuals.[112] No matter the origin, this propensity is well established, even with regard to technology. The literature often cites anecdotes about soldiers who have formed emotional attachments to robots.[113] Darling argues that attachments to robots are actually likely due to three reasons: the mere physicality of robots, the fact that we tend to infer intentionality to "perceived autonomous movement," and because certain robots will engage with us in social behaviors

---

[107] Adam Waytz, Joy Heafner, and Nicholas Epley, *The Mind in the Machine: Anthropomorphism Increases Trust in an Autonomous Vehicle*, 54 J. EXPERIMENTAL SOC. PSYCH. 113 (2014).

[108] Carpenter, *supra* note 103, at 40.

[109] *See* Brian R. Duffy, *Anthropomorphism and the Social Robot*, 42 ROBOTICS & AUTONOMOUS SYS. 177 (2003) (arguing the tendency to anthropomorphize will actually assist in developing machines that enhance meaningful interactions with humans). For examples of how some robots are designed to elicit emotional responses in humans, *see* Eun Ho Kim et al., *Design and Development of an Emotional Interaction Robot, Mung*, 23 ADVANCED ROBOTICS 767ll (2009) (describing a robot designed to emulate bruising); Hawon Lee and Eunja Hyun, *The Intelligent Robot Contents for Children with Speech-Language Disorder*, 18 EDUC. TECH. & SOC'Y 100 (2015) (describing a robot used to work with children with speech and language disabilities).

[110] Adam Waytz, Nicholas Epley, and John T. Cacciopo, *Social Cognition Unbound: Insights into Anthropomorphism and Dehumanization*, 19 CURRENT DIRECTIONS IN PSYCH. SCI. 58, 59–60 (2010).

[111] *Carpenter, supra* note 104, at 40.

[112] Mark Coeckelbergh, *Is Ethics of Robots about Robots? Philosophy of Robotics beyond Realism and Individualism*, 3 LAW, INNOVATION & TECH. 241, 244 (2011).

[113] Kate Darling, *"Who's Johnny?" Anthropomorphic Framing in Human-Robot Interaction, Integration, and Policy*, in ROBOT ETHICS 2.0, *supra* note 75, at 173 [hereinafter *Who's Johnny?*].

that we ourselves have learned through our interactions with humans.[114] The result is to "over-ascribe autonomy and intelligence" and to project "intent and sentiments" onto the thing. Such anthropomorphism is particularly plausible when people do not know how a complex robot works.[115]

One concern with viewing autonomous technologies as if they are human is that we will be deceived. Some of this concern is informed by Aristotelian concepts of friendship, in which the highest form of friendship is one in which a person wishes her friend well for that friend's own sake, as opposed to friendships for reasons of desire or utility.[116] Alexis Elder notes in this regard that pure friendship is a good in itself and warns that designers have to keep in mind the dangers of feigning it.[117] Other concerns are that autonomous machines and systems will undermine our current understanding of authenticity, replace real human beings in providing meaningful care, and leave humans vulnerable to manipulation.[118] As discussed in Chapter 3 with respect to robots in the home, some may not realize that an autonomous machine might actually have more powerful sensing ability than the human, thereby undermining our sense of privacy. Finally, some worry that seeing autonomous machines and systems as human will lead to the very thing which is the overarching concern of this chapter: granting them legal rights and moral consideration. In this vein, Neil Richards and Warren Smart warn against anthropomorphism because we would be tempted to legislate based on form, not function.[119] For them, "[r]obots, even sophisticated ones, are just machines. They will be no more than machines for the foreseeable future, and we should design our legislation accordingly."[120]

Not all commenters share these concerns, or they trust that if robots are designed to have social intelligence and elicit positive emotions toward them, humans will still be able to discriminate between artificial agents and human agents. Darian Meecham and Matthew Studley respond to the concern that care robots will deceive their patients and clients into thinking that they sub-

---

[114] *Extending Legal Protection to Robots, supra* note 72, at 213, 217–18.

[115] *Id.*, at 218.

[116] Aristotle, Nɪᴄᴏᴍᴀᴄʜᴇᴀɴ Eᴛʜɪᴄs (W.D. Ross trans., 1999) Book VIII, ch. 3, 129–30.

[117] Alexis Elder, *Robot Friends for Autistic Children: Monopoly Money or Counterfeit Currency?*, *in* Rᴏʙᴏᴛ Eᴛʜɪᴄs 2.0, *supra* note 75, at 113.

[118] *Extending Legal Protection to Robots, supra* note 72, at 221.

[119] Neil M. Richards and William D. Smart, *How Should the Law Think about Robots?* in Rᴏʙᴏᴛ Lᴀᴡ, *supra* note 72, at 3, 19.

[120] *Id.*, at 20. In this regard, Noel Sharkey warns that myths about artificial intelligence contribute to anthropomorphism that in turn supports arguments for autonomous weapons. Noel E. Sharkey, *The Evitability of Autonomous Robot Warfare*, 94 Iɴᴛ'ʟ. Rᴇᴠ. Rᴇᴅ Cʀᴏss 787, 791–2 (2012).

jectively care for them when in fact they do not.[121] In their view, that concern is based on a mistaken view of care, in which outward care must be matched with subjective care. To the contrary, they argue that "a caring relation is not the internal states of the agents participating in the relation, but rather a meaningful context; a care environment that is formed by gestures, movements, and articulations that express attentiveness and responsiveness to vulnerabilities within the relevant context."[122] Meecham and Studley believe that if care robots are used in an environment in which there is a mixture of human and artificial caregivers, a patient might appropriately interpret the treatment he is receiving as care. Other commentators point out that the possibility of deception can also be minimized. Machines and systems can be designed so that they do not have human features or in other ways which make it obvious that they are not human beings.[123]

One need not resolve the debate over whether it is desirable that humans engage in anthropomorphism to conclude that because there are principled arguments to allow it, such as those raised by Meecham and Studley, it is unlikely that all machines and systems will be designed to avoid triggering this tendency. Further, no matter how well designed a system is, given that humans have formed attachments to completely inanimate objects, on the margins there will always be someone who will engage in this behavior. As I argued earlier, it is this human tendency that will likely tip the balance toward granting at least some autonomous machines and systems rights and moral consideration, particularly when in theory, if Bringsjord is correct, an artificial intelligence will be able to engage in all behaviors, including displays of emotional intelligence, sympathy, and care—even if we have no way of determining whether such artificial agents have internal consciousness.

---

[121] Darian Meecham and Matthew Studley, *Could a Robot Care? It's All in the Movement, in* ROBOT ETHICS 2.0, *supra* note 75, at 97.

[122] *Id.*, at 98. Indeed, Alistair Isaac and Will Bridewell argue that because humans use various forms of deception in everyday life, robots will actually need to be trained to deceive in order to fully integrate in human society. They see no conflict between this and designing prosocial robots because the acceptability of deception from a moral perspective depends on the motive for the deception. Alistair M.C. Isaac and Will Bridewell, *White Lies on Silver Tongues: Why Robots Need to Deceive (and How), in* ROBOT ETHICS 2.0, *supra* note 75, at 157, 168.

[123] Jason Borenstein, *Pediatric Robotics and Ethics: The Robot Is Ready to See you Now, but Should It Be Trusted?, in* ROBOT ETHICS 2.0, *supra* note 75, at 127 (discussing ways robots might be designed to lessen the possibility of anthropomorphism); *Who's Johnny?, supra* note 113, at 182 (arguing we can be selective in choosing which robots to promote some anthropomorphism and which to discourage it).

PART V

Conclusions

10. Trigger events

This book began by describing two instances of harm, one involving the death of an individual human being and the other a massive breach of privacy, in each of which artificial intelligence and autonomous machines and systems played an important role. Thus, even though we await breakthroughs in theory and design that will allow artificial intelligence to make the next major leap forward toward general intelligence, Asaro's call for theories of responsibility that can address large, complex systems of human beings and machines working together, so that those systems will yield desirable outcomes and can be held responsible when the results are otherwise, has become timely.

IMAGINED FUTURES

I have responded to that call by setting out a possible trajectory for the coevolution of legal responsibility and autonomous machines. As would be expected, commentators and policymakers are responding to the call by using preexisting legal doctrines related to defective products, tort law more generally, agency law, contract, and international humanitarian law. They debate the extent to which those doctrines in their current forms can address situations that will arise when autonomous machines become more common. If existing law does not provide satisfactory solutions, it is because of the law's general discomfort with associative responsibility, a discomfort that is shared and supported by most of the literature on ethics. Despite attempts to separate law from ethics, law itself remains strongly based on the idea of individual responsibility: each person is responsible for his own conduct and no one else's. Arguments exist that no matter how sophisticated, an autonomous machine guided by artificial intelligence will in essence always remain a tool, so that human owners and users will always be responsible for what that machine does. However, those arguments seem less plausible the more sophisticated the machine becomes. At a minimum, it becomes just as plausible to say that the machine itself is responsible for a harm as it is to say that responsibility lies with its human owners and users.

One can foresee a world in which humans will make frequent use of autonomous machines and systems, and later, as artificial intelligence nears the level of general intelligence, humans, machines, and systems will be viewed as working together. In that context, the ethical literature on the problem of associative responsibility, particularly group responsibility, provides some guidance on how responsibility might be shared in larger settings, but no completely satisfactory answers. This leads to the concern that there will be gaps in responsibility for harms caused by autonomous machines and systems. In turn, that concern results in the two lines of development discussed in earlier chapters. The first is refining or redefining the concept of responsibility. Chapter 5 explored several ways in which that might be done: a renewed emphasis on strict liability doctrines, disaggregating responsibility, privileging the victim of harm, and insurance schemes. I have argued that these methods could well play an important role in addressing harms caused by autonomous technologies; however, the idea of personal culpability is persistent and will likely remain so. For similar reasons, although society and the law might experiment with other ways of conceptualizing the responsible agent, aided by the changes in human identity impelled by the seamless transitioning between the physical and online world, until there are significant breakthroughs in technology our bodies and psychologies will allow us to go only so far in that direction too. For the foreseeable future, the basic strategies and concepts that evolved as human bands were competing with other species, including strategies that balance what we now call individualism and communitarianism, will continue to guide us. It will be some time before technology will allow us to significantly transform ourselves and our identities and to transcend human embodiment.

That it is unlikely that we will see human individuals undergoing radical transformation in the near to medium term leads to the second major strategy to respond to potential harms: to reduce harm by designing even more sophisticated autonomous technologies that conform to existing law and behave prosocially with human beings. Both substrategies face daunting conceptual and technical hurdles. If they succeed, however, I have argued that one of the ironies, particularly with regard to the law, is that autonomous machines and systems might achieve such high levels of performance that in effect they will set the standard of care, a standard impossible for human beings to meet. In a sense, if we are unable or unwilling to modify our understandings of responsibility, our aversion to liability by association will lead to our always being responsible.

Such a result, however, would be just one instance of a more momentous development. Despite warnings that we should not take this path, it seems more likely than not that eventually, with the assistance of current autonomous technologies, we will design machines and systems that exceed our cognitive powers. In part this will be because, as Bostrom notes, it will be more economic to develop general purpose artificial intelligences,[1] and, as suggested by the literature on anthropomorphism, because we simply feel more comfortable with entities that are more like us, even though in truth they might not be. There will always be valid arguments to the contrary, but three things could well lead us to grant at least some autonomous machines and systems legal rights and moral patiency: that very tendency to anthropomorphize; pragmatic reasons to grant legal personhood to some autonomous technologies; and nonfrivolous arguments that sophisticated technologies are "deserving" of rights and moral consideration, particularly as machines and systems exhibit behaviors that are consistent with having consciousness.

A world in which this was the case could take several forms. Four scenarios seem plausible. The first is a world that does not grant legal rights and moral patiency equivalent to that accorded to human beings, in which even the most sophisticated technologies continue to be owned and used by humans and for which humans continue to be responsible. Two questions for that world are whether allocating responsibility to those human beings will be acceptable, and—more importantly—whether that world could accept a situation which some would criticize as slavery of artificial agents. As discussed, such allocation of responsibility to human beings in all situations would require that we reconceive at least some of our current understandings of responsibility or of ourselves as individuals. And as artificial agents become more sophisticated, a further question is whether they will accept this state of affairs.

The second scenario is a stratified society. Hutan Ashrafian foresees a world that resembles that of Rome, in which free persons were given different sets of rights according to their class.[2] Roman citizenship carried with it the full range of rights. Other classes, such as those of *Latin* and *Peregrinus*, did not, while still remaining subject to Roman law. For Ashrafian, such a system will be needed for autonomous technologies:

> [R]obots and artificial intelligence agents will demonstrate free will and morality, but also require societal security and welfare constraints so that in the preliminary phases of these technological advances detailed socio-political controls for robots and artificial intelligence agents must be determined. For example there will be a restriction on robot self-recreation, the ability to carry out independent business or public office.[3]

---

[1] Nick Bostrom, SUPERINTELLIGENCE: PATHS, DANGERS, STRATEGIES 184 (paperback edn. 2016).

[2] Hutan Ashrafian, *Artificial Intelligence and Robot Responsibilities: Innovating beyond Rights*, 21 SCI. & ENG'G 217, 324–5 (2015).

[3] *Id.*, at 324.

Ashrafian observes that the Roman system was not static; likewise, over time, artificial agents could be given more rights as human society finds it useful to grant them. In the alternative, these legal classes could be seen as intermediate steps to the equivalent of full citizenship. Two questions for this scenario are whether such a system would be truly open to change and, as is true with the first scenario, whether the most sophisticated technologies would be content with this stratification. The course of liberation and independence movements have tended to show that those in power do not readily cede it or expand rights unless powerful social movements demand and act to acquire those rights.

In the third scenario, artificial agents with full autonomy would be given the full panoply of legal rights and moral consideration. In essence, they would be treated for the purposes of the law as if they were human beings. Any services they provide to humans would be through voluntary contracts. They would be allowed to recreate themselves; they would have a right to existence; they would have a right to judicial process. A question we would ask of this scenario is one of plausibility: of course, all of the scenarios I am describing here are speculative by nature, but this scenario presupposes either that humans are altruistic enough to expend enormous resources to develop agents that they will not be able to own or otherwise control, and that as Bryson points out, will compete with humans for resources; or that, following up on the second scenario, autonomous technologies will have wrested these rights for themselves.

The final scenario is one in which machines surpass our abilities in all relevant ways. Here we would be in the world foreseen by commentators such as Bostrom and Shanahan. The hope would be that such artificial intelligences (or possibly a singleton) would be controllable by the mechanisms discussed in Chapter 8. Otherwise, such a world could be quite grim. Even in its less dire aspects, Shanahan foresees this second wave of artificial intelligence as having a profound effect on society. Systems with superior intelligence will challenge fundamental assumptions we hold about identity and responsibility. A system with superior intelligence need not be located anywhere in particular; it will "exist" online or in the countless devices that will have embedded computational capabilities. Further, such a system would be capable of replicating itself many times and deleting itself. If given the right to vote, a system could replicate itself into several iterations, vote, and then cause the other versions of itself to disappear. Perhaps public ledger systems like block chain could be used to track the myriad ways in which superior intelligences appear and disappear. But perhaps not: even if it is possible to record an indelible history of all of the iterations, instantiations, and activities of a superior intelligence, a superior intelligence might not feel the need to preserve a sense of identity; it might evolve or transform into another superior intelligence that bears no resemblance to its former "self." If a superior intelligence commits a wrong against another intelligence or a human being but has changed itself entirely so that we would no longer recognize it as the "one" that committed the harm, would we feel that the new entity is still somehow responsible? We would fall back to the familiar problem of guilt by association.

In this fourth world, the challenges to our understanding of responsibility would be accompanied by our understanding of rights. So far, I have discussed the issue of whether autonomous machines should be given the same rights and the same moral considerations as human beings. Shanahan quite rightly takes the debate to its logical conclusion: if one of the reasons we might accord rights to machines is that they begin to have capabilities and cognition that reach those of humans, should machines with superior intelligence be given more rights than humans? One can imagine a world in which autonomous machines plan and perform almost all functions that make human life possible: raising and distributing food; providing shelter and clothing; keeping the peace. Would not those entities merit greater rights, say in the form of voting rights, or even the right to exist vis-à-vis a human being? This argument could be strengthened even further if we assume humankind has been successful in crafting autonomous machines with prosocial behaviors that take human well-being into account. One of the great tests of the value of law and our ethical systems will be whether intelligent systems will find it "worthwhile" to make use of them. If the countless interactions of human beings over time have resulted in the emergence of law as a means to regulate human communities and as part of human expressive activity, perhaps superintelligences will find law and ethics useful in managing their relations with each other and with human beings. But perhaps in such a world it will be humans—not machines— that will be subject to the moral Turing test.

BACK AND FORTH ALONG THE TRAJECTORY

By this point, these ruminations are going far afield. To what extent does tracing a possible coevolutionary trajectory such as this respond to Asaro's call for new systems of responsibility? To answer that question, it is helpful to toggle back and forth between various points in that trajectory. At the end point, a world in which humans and machines enjoy equal legal status and rights would of course be radically different: for the first time in human history, we would coexist with nonhuman intelligences who are our equals (and perhaps our superiors) in significant ways. We will have created our own alien "life." But assuming that such entities have prosocial behaviors, there is a sense in which we could use our current systems of legal responsibility without much controversy: an autonomous machine or system would be treated like any other individual who lives and works in large systems. We might have criticisms of our current systems of tort, contract, and agency and of other mechanisms to address risk, such as insurance, but those systems do not appear to be inherently unstable.

Asaro's challenge can thus be reframed: how well do our legal doctrines address harms caused by complex systems of humans now, with or without machines? The answer to that question might be a matter of seeing the glass as half empty or half full. The debates surrounding tort reform serve as an example. In a 1994 metastudy, Gary Schwartz surveyed then existing assessments of the impact of tort law in a wide area of economic sectors and concluded that there was "evidence persuasively showing that tort law achieves something significant in encouraging safety."[4] However, the impact of tort law can sometimes be ambiguous or of lesser importance than other factors. A study by Paul Rubin, for example, indicates that consumer preferences for safer products are the primary drivers of improvements in safety. In his view, regulation and tort law can also contribute to safety improvements. However, because tort law is an expensive means of encouraging safety, it might actually increase risk by causing people to forgo things such as drugs and medical treatments because they are made more expensive by costs incurred to avoid tort liability.[5]

This book does not propose to assess the effectiveness of tort law in resolving harms caused to individuals; it is enough here to repeat what was discussed in Chapter 2: the law already purports to addresses large systems. It can be argued that assessing how effectively law regulates those systems does not require us to take autonomous machines and systems into account. However, this is not to say that autonomous technologies are irrelevant to that analysis. The extent to which they do become relevant will depend on how deeply societies want to penetrate complex systems to hold parts of those systems responsible for harms.

Wallach points out that the investigation into the *Challenger* disaster demonstrates how hard it is to determine who or what is to blame for the failure of a complex system such as the space shuttle, technology that is a product of complex organizations such as large corporations.[6] This resonates with Coeckelbergh's argument that incidents such as the Deepwater Horizon explosion and fire are almost impossible to grasp with our current

---

[4]   Gary T. Schwartz, *Reality in the Economic Analysis of Tort Law: Does Tort Law Really Deter?* 42 UCLA L. Rev. 377, 423 (1994–1995).

[5]   Paul H. Rubin, *Markets, Tort Law, and Regulation to Achieve Safety*, 31 Cato J. 217, 231–2 (2011). Rubin argues that tort reform from 1981 to 2000 led to 24,000 fewer accidental deaths because of increased emergency medical care. *Id.*

[6]   Wendell Wallach, *From Robots to Techno Sapiens: Ethics, Law and Public Policy in the Development of Robotics and Neurotechnologies*, 3 Law Innov. & Tech. 185, 194–5 (2011).

tools for assigning blame. It is only if society feels it is necessary to become finer grained in assigning responsibility—to move from the corporations which manufactured and designed the components and software used in the shuttle to individual designers and engineers who could be said to have contributed to the defects that led to that disaster, as well as those along the chain of command that ordered the launch to go forward—that the problems of associational responsibility discussed in this book become more salient. Yet, Chapter 3 has shown that commentators and policymakers are calling for exactly this kind of accountability.

If such calls for broader accountability become louder, then autonomous machines and systems would become an important part of the calculus of responsibility should their decision-making capacity be so sophisticated by that time that it will be hard to attribute responsibility for harms they cause to their coworkers, supervisors, or those who designed them, but at the same time they are not autonomous enough to merit legal, let alone moral, agency so that they can be blamed directly for what they have done. At that point, prevailing ethical and legal views of responsibility would need to be reevaluated. The coevolution of law and artificial intelligence will serve as an impetus—perhaps not the strongest one, but nonetheless significant toward the development of machines with even greater autonomy, machines with general intelligence, which, according to Shanahan, will quickly develop systems and machines with intelligence greater than ours. One of the ironies is that our aversion to sharing the responsibility of another could lead to the development of machines that are in some senses wholly us and perhaps also wholly other.

NEXT STEPS AND POINTS ALONG THE WAY

Carpenter makes the insightful point that to some extent, all of us are engaged in the design of artificial machines and systems:

> [W]e are all the ones influencing and inventing and designing the robots, whether it is through our robot-related research and jobs, or our everyday preferences about how we use robots. In addition to formal laws and policies, we will all decide individually and collectively how to treat robots in our homes and in public spaces.[7]

This insight can be elaborated. Chapter 1 discussed projections that artificial intelligence will likely pervade all major domains of life: transportation, life in the home, health and elder care, education, services to underserved communities, public safety, employment and the workplace, and entertainment. In

---

[7]   Julie Carpenter, *The Existential Robot: Living with Robots May Teach Us to Be Better Humans*, 108 Issues, Sept. 2014, at 39, 41.

each of these domains humans have developed social repertoires, preferences, modes of cooperation and conflict resolution, and ideas about appropriate behavior that will likely be applied to autonomous technologies. It is of course possible to create demand, but autonomous technologies will not be developed for use in those domains unless is it is perceived that there will be some demand for them. Such demand will be nuanced, accompanied by expectations of safety, security, and privacy.

However, those social practices and preferences are part of large dynamics that, in the vast majority of cases, are hard for any one person to influence. Chiu's regulatory landscape explained in Chapter 2 is inhabited by citizens and consumers, to be sure, but also by powerful economic actors, institutions, and governments that are also in dynamic relationship with each other, leading to results that seem almost inexorable. In this regard, although unexpected developments could arise to prevent this, it seems almost a foregone conclusion that autonomous vehicles will be on our roads in large numbers in the not too distant future. At the same time, social movements can be effective in creating critical masses that affect those social and economic dynamics. On this subject, it remains to be seen whether calls to prohibit the development of autonomous weapons will be able to overcome the strong incentives to design and deploy them.

Since the power of social movements can be diluted and private firms cannot always be counted on to act in the public interest, there is a strong case for legislation. However, to recall some of the lessons of complexity theory, if societies are in fact complex adaptive systems, the theory suggests that planning will only be possible in the short term because dynamic interactions within the system often lead to unexpected results. This does not consign us to inaction, but complexity theory provides grounds for skepticism that any one legislative rule (or for that matter any cultural tool used for control) will work in all cases. Too much of a rule's chances of success will depend on the particular context in which it is applied.

As an example of collateral consequences, the requirement in the Nevada and North Carolina autonomous vehicle statutes that all vehicles comply with those state's respective traffic codes seems obvious and one that most would support. As argued in Chapter 7, requiring autonomous technologies to operate in compliance with existing law serves as a proxy for what it means to engage in acceptable, safe behavior in society. Further, it could be argued that because the law is almost exclusively made for the benefit of human beings, compliance with it will ensure that autonomous technologies operate in ways that increase that benefit. It thus seems unimaginable that we would support a different strategy. At the same time, as I discussed earlier, the requirement to develop technologies that comply with the law also provides an impetus to develop even more sophisticated artificial agents. It may also require programmers and their employers to become interpreters of the law as they write the software that causes the agents to obey it. With regard to context, the legislature could enact laws designed to discourage anthropomorphism with regard to robots used in dangerous situations, such as autonomous rescue robots and firefighting robots. However, it might be exactly in such highly stressful situations that people will be inclined to anthropomorphize, no matter how well the robot is designed to prevent this from occurring.

Rather than propose specific policies, perhaps it is more useful to return to the trajectory and identify points along the way at which scholars, lawyers, and policymakers might do well to pay particular attention, to determine whether some form of legislative guidance is appropriate or whether governance of these emerging technologies can be left to individual firms and forms of soft law.

General Intelligence

To once again jump ahead in the trajectory, the most obvious of these points would be when designers are close to developing systems with general intelligence. For Bostrom, by that time it might be too late to prevent the development of a superintelligence with a strategic advantage over humans, but nevertheless the achievement of general intelligence would be significant in itself, and the development of a machine with general intelligence would almost immediately require answers to questions I have discussed, such as whether the artificial intelligence should immediately be recognized as a legal entity and subject to the law and under its protection, if those decisions have not already been made. At a minimum, policymakers would want to have as much advance notice as possible that such a development is near.

Early Cases

A far less momentous but still important point in the trajectory will come much earlier, when cases involving autonomous technologies begin to appear before the courts in significant numbers. Currently the area from which these will stem is anyone's guess, but it would not be surprising if many cases arise from accidents involving autonomous vehicles or from injuries caused by autonomous devices in the home. From a legal standpoint, it will be particularly interesting where such accidents involve autonomous vehicles that do not allow the passenger to operate the vehicle, short of ordering it to go into safe mode. We will then see whether negligence and product liability law and the underlying legal principles of foreseeability and causation can be applied cogently to a set of facts in which a human driver is largely out of the picture. In this regard, observers will want to pay attention to who the parties are. It will be particularly significant if plaintiffs name individual designers and programmers as defendants in addition to manufacturers, owners, and users of the technology in question. Further, cases involving harms caused by machines and systems that have learning capability and that can be trained by users will be important, because issues of causation and contributory negligence will undoubtedly arise in those situations.

The first set of cases that treat contracts formed by autonomous systems, whose contracting behavior is not already governed by umbrella agreements between human parties or business entities, will also be an important test of existing law. As I discussed in Chapter 2, some of the protections to principals that are provided by agency law are absent when electronic agents are involved, unless those electronic agents are given some endowment that can be used to compensate principals for damage caused by unauthorized acts by an agent.

It will also be important to assess scholarly, community, and industry reactions to these early cases, to get a sense of the overall legitimacy of court decisions and who might be expected to try to change their outcomes. Whether such cases will be viewed as legitimate will depend in part on impacts to the losing parties. If manufacturers and designers of autonomous technologies tend to prevail in lawsuits, one question will be whether injured consumers or third parties will be satisfied with other forms of compensation, such as payments from insurance—if in fact such insurance is available in the early days of autonomous technologies. We would want to see whether such decisions lessen demand for autonomous machines and systems. We will also need to assess whether autonomous technologies are living up to their initial promise of operating more safely and efficiently than humans acting by themselves. If on the other hand the early cases extend liability to programmers and designers, one would expect a strong effort by industry for legislative protection from liability, on the grounds that such liability is unfair and would have a chilling effect on the development of autonomous technologies. There would likely be further efforts to use contract to shield programmers, designers, and manufacturers from liability as well.

The overarching inquiry is whether these early decisions will be perceived as achieving satisfactory outcomes when harms are caused by autonomous technologies. If not, we are likely to see a tug of war between the expansion of responsibility and who can be held responsible and efforts against such expansion, with both sides using arguments based on fairness and economics. All the while, this tug of war will be an impetus for designing safer and in many cases more sophisticated machines and systems.

Legal Personhood for Autonomous Technologies

A third stage in the trajectory that bears attention is the grant of legal personhood or legal status to autonomous systems and machines. As I discussed
in Chapter 9, the arguments for such personhood tend to be pragmatic: as it
becomes more and more difficult to attribute to human beings responsibility
for harms caused by artificial agents, or as agency concepts are applied and
human principals and third parties are stung by the inability to seek recovery
from artificial technologies, legal personhood is a way to confirm that the acts
of artificial technologies have legal significance and, provided that artificial
agents are permitted to keep some endowment, a way to bring meaningful
claims against the technologies themselves, thus avoiding responsibility by
association. As I also mentioned, some argue that, if interpreted in a certain
way, existing business entity law can be used to give autonomous systems this
legal status.

   Slippery slope arguments are not always valid, but it seems obvious that the
grant of some kind of legal status would be the first step toward granting autonomous technologies legal rights. For example, suppose an autonomous agent
is given legal status and provided with an endowment, perhaps because of
a capitalization requirement. Obviously, the owner or user of the agent would
likely be the party who initially gives the agent its endowment. However, in
order for such a requirement to provide meaningful protection to third parties,
the owners and agents would need to cede some control over those funds. The
endowment would in some ways be like an escrow account. Indeed, it might
be an advantage to the owners and agents to distance themselves from those
funds to break a possible link between the actions of the artificial agent and
its human principals, and it is possible that the agent will increase those funds
over time. It would not take a great stretch in the law to give the artificial agent
a quasiproperty right in those funds. It could of course be argued that just
because a quasiproperty right is granted, it does not follow that the quasiright
will evolve into a full-blown right or open the door to granting artificial agents
the full panoply of rights which humans enjoy. Nevertheless, the grant of legal
status or personhood to autonomous machines or systems, either through direct
legislation or through currently existing law, will be a significant event that
will merit careful attention.

TO CONCLUDE

The law, including its concepts of responsibility, has proven to be a useful
means to constitute and sustain largescale societies. Unsurprisingly, the human
person and her capacities, whether that person is viewed as the image of God
or as the product of a long evolutionary process, have heretofore served as

the measure of legal and ethical conduct. In the not too distant future, there is a possibility of designing machines and systems whose capacities will equal and eventually exceed our own. Their less able precursors will soon be here. To use Wolgast's metaphor, as these agents begin to "live" among us, it is an open question whether human beings will have the cognitive power to imagine other ways to measure proper conduct, what it means to be responsible members of society, or whether we will continue to use ourselves as the standard by which all others, autonomous technologies included, are measured. Perhaps, given our embodied, evolved selves, it is impossible to do no more than see the world through our eyes. This has been a successful strategy so far, but if the arguments I have made in this book have any validity, then the solution to having autonomous technologies among us will be to make the most advanced of them more and more like ourselves—perhaps, if Bostrom and Shanahan are right, to the point where they are beyond our imaginations.

Index

Abbott, Ryan 162–3
agency
    as an emergent phenomenon 139
    group agency as a form of 78–80,
        139–40
    human agency 62, 68–70, 75, 98,
        132
    impacts of technology on human 10,
        132–4, 144, 169, 218
    see also autonomy; autonomous
        agents; collective action;
        collective intention; extended
        agency
agency law 233–4
    as applying to groups and group
        responsibility 54, 85
    and autonomous contracting 37–41
    and harms associated with
        autonomous technologies 24,
        38, 194, 224, 228
    and moral responsibility 197–8
    as motivation for granting legal
        personhood and rights to
        autonomous technologies
        233–4
    suitability of agency paradigm for
        autonomous contracting
        39–41, 44, 233–4
    and vicarious liability 17, 19
animals
    as analogies for autonomous agents
        19, 152–3, 211, 209–10,
        214–15
    treatment of 209–10, 214–15, 220

anthropomorphism 209, 219–22, 226,
    232
Aristotle 59–60, 68, 182, 221
artificial intelligence
    as achieving general intelligence
        4–5, 140, 152, 171–2,
        180–84, 193, 203, 224, 226,
        230, 232
    as achieving superintelligence 5, 32
        171–2, 178–9, 182–5, 192,
        227–8, 232
    definitions of 3–4
Asaro, Peter M. 13, 14, 44, 192, 211,
    224, 228, 229
Ashley, Kevin D. 150, 155–6
Asimov's laws of robotics 181
associative responsibility 185, 196
    association to humans of harms
        involving autonomous
        technologies 38, 44, 54, 76,
        88, 133–5, 185, 196, 199,
        230, 234
    aversion to 52, 54, 65–6, 83, 103,
        111, 127–8, 154, 199, 224–5,
        228
    see also group responsibility
autonomous agents
    differences between human agents
        and 143, 191–2, 201–9
    difficulties in controlling 152
    incentives to increase sophistication
        of 203, 225–6, 230, 235
    as lawmakers 167–9

Printed and bound by CPI Group (UK) Ltd, Croydon, CR0 4YY

16/04/2025

14658431-0001